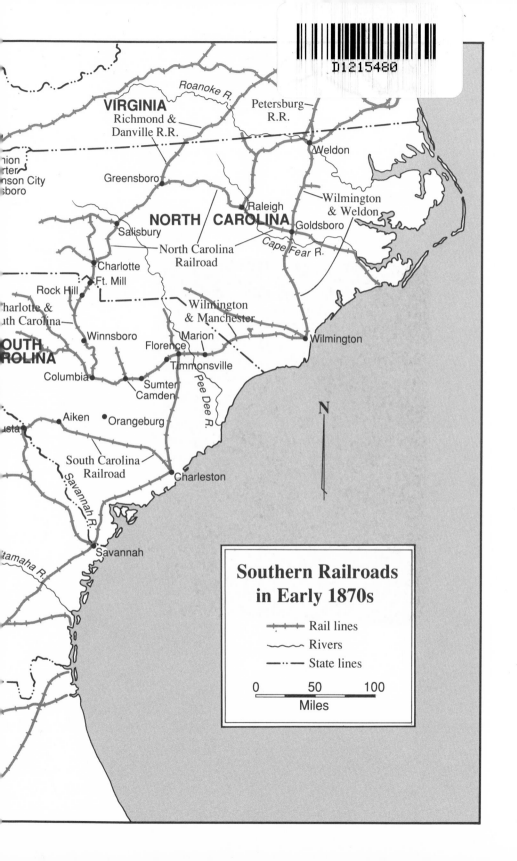

VIRGINIA

Roanoke R.

Petersburg—
R.R.

Richmond &
Danville R.R.

Weldon

nion
ter
nson City
boro

Greensboro

Wilmington
& Weldon

Raleigh

NORTH CAROLINA

Goldsboro

Salisbury

North Carolina
Railroad

Cape Fear R.

Charlotte

Ft. Mill

Rock Hill

harlotte &
uth Carolina—

Wilmington
& Manchester

Winnsboro

Marion

OUTH
ROLINA

Florence

Wilmington

Timmonsville

Columbia

Sumter
Camden

Pee Dee R.

Aiken

Orangeburg

N

sta

South Carolina
Railroad

Savannah R.

Charleston

Savannah

tamaha R.

Southern Railroads
in Early 1870s

—+——+— Rail lines

~~~ Rivers

—··— State lines

0   50   100

Miles

Southern Railroad Man

SOUTHERN RAILROAD MAN

Conductor

N. J. Bell's

Recollections of the

CIVIL WAR ERA

Edited by James A. Ward

NORTHERN ILLINOIS UNIVERSITY PRESS

DeKalb 1994

For JAMES W. LIVINGOOD

A Venerable Historian and Friend

© 1993 by Northern Illinois University Press

Published by the Northern Illinois University Press,

DeKalb, Illinois 60115

Manufactured in the United States using acid-free paper ∞

Design by Julia Fauci

Library of Congress Cataloging-in Publication Data

Bell, N. J. (Nimrod J.), 1830–ca. 1899.

Southern railroad man : conductor N.J. Bell's recollections of the Civil War era /
edited by James A. Ward.

p.   cm.

Includes index.

ISBN 0-87580-184-6

1. Confederate States of America—Description and travel.
2. Southern States—Description and travel.   3. Bell, N.J. (Nimrod J.), 1830–ca.
1899.   4. United States—History—Civil War, 1861–1865—Personal narratives,
Confederate.   5. Railroads—Southern States—History—19th century.   6. Railroad
travel—Southern States—History—19th century.   I. Ward, James Arthur, 1941–   .
II. Title.

F214.B45 1993

973.7'82—dc20   93-34199

                                                                      CIP

Contents

Preface

N. J. BELL'S BOOK, ORIGINALLY TITLED *Railroad Recollections for over Thirty-Eight Years*, is obviously a labor of love. He published only a few copies in 1896, and those passed quickly into the hands of family members and friends. One, however, found its way into the University of Tennessee at Knoxville library, where it was cataloged simply as "Bell," without initials or a first name. There it lay for almost a century, forgotten and unread. Even though Bell is a veritable treasure trove of information about nineteenth-century Southern railroads and their operations, he is not cited in any of the standard historical railway works, nor did his views influence any current interpretations of rail conditions below the Mason-Dixon line. Then several years ago Melba and Raymond Murray, while researching a book, unearthed Bell's gem.

The Murrays consulted James W. Livingood, Guerry Professor of History Emeritus at the University of Tennessee at Chattanooga, the man who, as dean of the university, had hired me. He mentioned the manuscript to me and suggested I take a look at it and "do something with it" because it appeared to him to be an important piece of primary information on Southern railroading. He sent me a copy, and upon perusing it, I was smitten with Bell and what he reveals about the plight of railroaders in the region. Moreover, Bell tells us as much about the social and cultural mores of his homeland as he does about the complexities of operating trains across hundreds of miles of Southern rural America.

As with all books, however, Bell's effort has its peculiarities. The author is a better storyteller than he is a historian. He gives us the flavor of the region and its rail world complete with a colorful cast of characters, but he is much less successful in putting his career in a larger perspective. He seemingly had a positive disdain for revealing chronology, and it is often difficult to date the events he describes. He obviously wrote his manuscript in an episodic manner, working on it when he had the time. He relates the parts of his career as he moves from road to road from 1857 to 1895 in a correct chronological sequence, but he does not give definitive dates for some of his travels. The experiences and tales within each of the segments, furthermore, when they can be checked, do not always follow in sequence. He often jumbles his stories within his chapters. In most instances, this confusion does not really matter because his tenure on most roads, except for the East Tennessee, Virginia & Georgia, was usually rather brief. During the Civil War, he worked for very short periods on each railway, and thus, his remembrances as recounted in these critical chapters can be no more than a few months out of sequence. Where events were verifiable, I have tried to clarify their dates in the notes; in some cases, however, this has been impossible. As an aid to sorting out the general chronology of his career, I have dated his interludes on Southern railroads by chapter in the table of contents.

Given Bell's lack of formal education, he was a good writer. His style may be stilted for late twentieth century tastes, but it was perfectly acceptable to his peers. The conductor had a good grasp of the rules of grammar, and there are only a few jarring infelicities in his manuscript. I have left them as he wrote them, for they give us the flavor of his speech. I have excised a few redundancies, indicated by ellipses, but others, for example Bell's reiteration of his financial problems and private obligations, I have left because they indicate how heavily he was pressured to keep his job no matter what the cost. In all, I have deleted only about ten pages of his original text. Many of these deletions were made at the ends of his chapters, where he liked to include a few lines of extraneous material that did not fit his story, or were made elsewhere, for example lists of crew members' names. The two largest deletions were in chapter 14, where Bell suddenly launched into a detailed description of the countryside along each road on which he worked, and in chapter 15, where he spun out a lengthy allegorical tale. I have inserted a minimal number of notes to explain unfamiliar railroad terms, to describe locomotives he names, to give explanations of peculiarly Southern phrases, and to help the chronology along with a specific date when possible. My main intent, however, is to intrude as little as possible into Bell's work. He knew what he was doing.

Bell's organization is not as effective as his style. Through perhaps two-thirds of his book he describes his experiences as closely as he could remember them. When he reaches chapter 12, he changes his strategy and turns topical, writing in more general terms about everything from unions to religion, frequently without anchoring any of it to specific aspects of his career. I considered cutting this portion of his book up and moving the pieces into the appropriate earlier chapters, but so much was undatable I decided instead to split his book into two parts: Part 1,

"Bell's Career," and Part 2, "General Observations." That division does not violate Bell's original intent and, at a glance, better organizes his material.

ACKNOWLEDGMENTS

One of the nice aspects of editing a book is that the editor incurs fewer obligations than did the original author. Nevertheless, I did not escape this project unscathed. I would be remiss if I did not proffer my thanks to James W. Livingood, who suggested I take Bell's work in hand. Livingood, an esteemed local historian, understands the wide ramifications of his field. He also worked his vast photo files and generously loaned me several of the pictures that appear here. The extent to which I am indebted to Jim for this and many other things is indicated in the dedication.

Several of my colleagues were pulled against their wishes into this work. H. L. Ingle, who is usually tracing dead Quakers through the pages of history but is a very good historian of the South as well, researched the origin of Jim Crow laws on Tennessee railroads. James Michael Russell, author of a fine book on the early history of Atlanta and a Civil War expert, looked up references Bell made to obscure Southern generals and kept my sketchy chronology of the war clear so that I could date several of Bell's exploits. John Tinkler, my colleague in the English department is, apart from his expertise in medieval languages, a student of Southern dialects and words unique to the region; he interpreted some of Bell's more obscure phrases. As a connoisseur of fine bourbon and other potables, John explained the Tennessee-whiskey-county reference Bell made and uncovered the poetic origins of the phrase "Johnnie how came you so?" I have distilled John's wisdom in my all-too-brief notes.

Clara Swann, chief librarian of the local history section in the Chattanooga-Hamilton County Bicentennial Library, and her associates helped me search for clues to Bell's private life. They guided me through cemetery records, probate documents, and reel after reel of the census returns until we found all we could about Bell. Clara also checked her voluminous files of local photographs for appropriate images, some of which grace the final product. And Neal Coulter, the reference librarian par excellence at the University of Tennessee at Chattanooga, ran down facts for me that made my job a great deal easier.

Roger Grant, at the University of Akron, who is the editor of a companion volume to this piece, *Brownie the Boomer: The Life of Charles P.*

Brown, An American Railroader (Northern Illinois University Press, 1991), read Bell's book and, although he disputes my contention that Bell's life story is more interesting than Brownie's, enthusiastically supported my attempt to have it republished. Folks at the Northern Illinois University Press have been uniformly helpful. Mary Lincoln, the Press director, has been supportive from the first and provided a friendly working relationship that all authors and editors seek but only the fortunate few ever find.

My wife, Roberta Shannon Ward, has as usual been most helpful but this time with a twist. She insisted that I should never do another book until I mastered the computer and schemed with my secretary, Muffin Kennedy, who is sick of typing my manuscripts, to provide one for my home office. Roberta then spent most of her Christmas vacation of 1992 teaching a motor moron how to manipulate a mouse, create "folders," and other arcane stuff. Undoubtedly, this learning experience slowed the whole endeavor down, but I suppose in the process I acquired the rudiments of a semivaluable skill; we only "lost" a small part of this work. My daughter, Anne, who is prepping for graduate school in history and has been conversant with keyboards and VCRs for years, stood behind me far too long advising me on how to find things that slipped off the screen into the great void and on other complex functions such as turning the machine on. I thank them both for their patience, although I think I have none left myself. Withal, Bell has been a fun enterprise and one I consider well worth the time.

December 12, 1993

Introduction by James A. Ward

CONDUCTOR N. J. BELL ANNOUNCED TO HIS READERS in his original preface, "I have not written this book because I am a writer, or think that books are scarce"; rather, he expressed the hope "that my friends, in and out of railroad circles, will read it with pleasure." Bell succeeds well beyond his modest aspirations. His book, originally titled *Railroad Recollections for over Thirty-Eight Years,* is not only delightful but instructive. His career spanned the explosive years of the mid-nineteenth century during which cataclysmic changes convulsed the South. He watched them all from the catbird seat on his trains, and after his retirement, he opened his world to us through his memoirs.

Author Bell might appear to have been simply a small cog in a much larger mechanism, exploited by those who commanded his services, an unthinking laborer trained to get trains over flimsy roadbeds. In reality, however, he was a keen observer of events around him and had a clear view of his place in the world and a reasonably accurate perception of his own worth. For almost forty years he shrewdly watched what was happening around him with a practiced eye.

His perspective makes his narrative absorbing. Most rail literature is written from the viewpoint of the capitalists and bankers who financed the great companies and plotted railroad strategy and tactics. Few "working stiffs" took the time to jot down their experiences; thus historians have a much scantier knowledge of how train operations actually worked than they do about how corporate organization and practice proceeded. Moreover, Bell's memoirs are more valuable because he spent his working years exclusively on Southern railways. He details working conditions on roads in the slave South, relates the difficulties of operating dilapidated railways during the Civil War and Reconstruction, and ends by chronicling the appearance of more sophisticated and routine railroad procedures by century's end.

Writing about history from the "bottom up," however, is fraught with problems. Bell wrote almost 170 pages without revealing very much about himself or his private life. He did not even give us his first name or the year of his birth, and what few clues he did leave are often misleading. On his frontispiece, for example, he indicates that he lived in Cleveland, Tennessee, in 1896, when he published his book. A search of the censuses of 1880 and 1900 (the raw data from the 1890 count burned and is not available) showed he was not a resident of Bradley County in either of those years. A thorough search of cemetery records, will probates, and court cases for a thirty-year period also turned up nothing. Nobody could have been that invisible. Rethinking the problem, I went back to his Georgia roots and tried to trace him there in the censuses before and after the war and was finally successful. Bell, even though he spent almost a quarter of a century working on Tennessee and Alabama railways, kept his family all those years in Georgia.

It turned out that Nimrod—a name that could explain why he preferred to keep his Christian name out of print—was born in 1830 in South Carolina. He migrated with his family across North Georgia, and at age twenty he married Nancy, who was only fifteen years old. They had a good many children. By 1860 the couple had had four children but one had died in 1851 at three months of age. Five additional children survived the Civil War decade, though at least one more had died before being recorded in the census. With no formal education and with only his brawn and the skills he acquired on the job to support his family, Nimrod had a difficult time financially. At the outbreak of the war his entire personal estate was valued at only fifty dollars, and after a decade of hard labor he had increased it to only three hundred dollars. The 1870s treated the Bells little better. They had three more children, and the census that year listed Charles, born in 1869, as "insane." At fifty-one years of age, Nimrod still had nine of his children, including Charles, living at home. Only Van R. (there was also a Van U. in the brood) left home to follow in his father's footsteps on the railroads. After the 1880 census, however, Bell disappeared. He was alive as late as 1895 or 1896, but his name did not appear in the 1900 census for either Georgia or Tennessee. A quick check of the 1910 and 1920 decadal counts showed he had not just been overlooked. Several explanations for his absence are possible: he may no longer have been a head of household and was living with one of his children; he was dead by 1899; or he had moved to some other state. In any case, he slipped away without notice.[1]

Throughout his remembrances, Bell makes reference to his financial troubles. As he aged, he became less mobile and was forced to endure his superiors' disciplinary actions because he had to keep his job to support his large family. It was not that he was poorly paid, for by 1890 he was earning about $1,200 a year, over twice the average annual wage of steam railroad workers and almost three times more than the average national nonfarm yearly earnings of $486.[2] His problem was that his family grew faster than his salary. Nimrod was well paid because his occupation demanded great skill and a wealth of common sense. Like most conductors, Bell started from the bottom, in his case as a laborer on the Western & Atlantic Railroad, and worked his way up. Someone noted his aptitude and promoted him to freight conductor.

The conductor was the master, or captain, of the train. The other trainmen were under his orders, and he was responsible for maintaining the train's schedule, avoiding collisions, ensuring that cars were set out at their proper locations, and attaching the correct cars to his train. He also hired his own brakemen, switchmen, and baggagemen and oversaw their performance. On paper, Bell's duties seem orderly and precise, but a good conductor, whether freight or passenger, had to be something of a politician to survive. He had to maintain cordial relations with the engineer and the fireman for the smooth running of the train. Engineers, particularly, were a touchy lot and often resisted intrusion into their domains. Bell's stories are full of allusions to engineers who drank too much, operated their locomotives recklessly, and refused to stop when ordered, as well as to those with whom he loved to work. It is noteworthy that Bell only infrequently went to the front of his train; he preferred to keep some distance between his responsibilities and his engineer's. In one notable case, however, he sacked his engineer during the run and replaced him with his fireman, a man usually able to operate as well as to fire the locomotive.

Bell quickly proved his mettle on freights and was promoted to regularly scheduled passenger runs, a more demanding but also more prestigious, higher-paying job. For almost thirty years he worked both passenger and freight trains, but he much preferred the former even though they were more difficult. He was still responsible for the train's safety and performance, but he also had to check tickets, in some cases sell them in the coaches, deal with all manner of passenger complaints, clean his cars, and, later in his career, oversee sleeping car operations. From the railways' earliest years, passenger conductors were suspected of succumbing to the temptations of "skimming" the cash fares they collected. Walter Licht, in his *Working for the Railroad; The Organization of Work in the Nineteenth Century,* described how the Pinkerton agency investigated conductors on the Philadelphia & Reading Railroad and discovered they were keeping 32 percent of their collections. The "prince" of conductors was one on the Chicago, Burlington & Quincy who embezzled seventeen thousand dollars in five years. Throughout his book Bell protested his honesty, but, in numerous altercations, his passengers automatically assumed he was as corrupt as some of his brethren.[3]

Taking up tickets on the train, however, was anything but a simple procedure. He had to know where the passenger embarked, and on days when his train was crowded and stopped at every station, he found it impossible to make it all the way through the cars between depots. And his passengers challenged him with all sorts of clever ploys to hide when he came to collect tickets. He was forced to use his own judgment about whether to charge a passenger more or less, and he became something of an expert in reading faces. By the end of his career he trusted nobody, not even men of the cloth.

Bell's most important responsiblity was to see that his train did not collide with others on the single-track lines he worked. With his engineer's cooperation, he had to maintain a schedule of meets at the infrequent sidings, which often meant that he had to visualize what was happening across the whole operating system and guess whether he could safely advance to the next siding. Railroads provided rulebooks meant to govern many situations, but, if conductors followed them to the letter, no train would have met its schedule. Railroaders fudged in the interests of staying on time, and the practice made Bell's job more difficult. He had to know which engineers were on runs that day, whether they were known for being "fast," what locomotives they were on, if the engines were good steamers, and to guess at the tonnage they were hauling so that he could estimate their proclivities. He occasionally figured wrong and came close to an accident; more frequently his peers on other trains miscalculated, and the number of near accidents and actual wrecks he describes is frightening. It was something of a miracle that he survived as long as he did in the business.

When Bell was not "conducting" he was a jack-of-all-trades on the train. The age of specialization had not arrived on the railroads, and the companies expected Bell to perform a bewildering array of tasks. He often helped to load wood into the locomotives' tenders, to man bucket brigades to fill the tender from nearby creeks and streams, and to rerail wrecked cars. When an accident occurred, it was Bell's responsibility to hire local workers to put the cars back on the track. Oftentimes he used the same local labor to replace ties and rails so he could bring his train home. Inside the coaches, Bell represented the law and was expected to police his charges. He carried a pistol on his runs, and several times he pulled it on passengers or on those attacking his train. He much preferred to talk his way out of such contretemps, but, failing that, he swung a mean club and had an unerring eye for the vulnerable skull. He was not a big man, but he managed, often with help, to keep order on his trains.

Bell's problems were compounded by the fact that he worked exclusively on Southern railroads. Throughout the nineteenth century, railways in that region remained quantitatively and qualitatively inferior to lines in other parts of the country. With less liquid capital, railway companies in the South from 1835 through 1860 spent an average of six thousand dollars less per mile to build their lines than firms in other parts of the nation spent.[4] The immediate result was that their roads were constructed less substantially than the national norm. Most Southern roads before the war used wooden stringers laid on crossties and capped with a thin cast or wrought iron rail spiked to the stringer for their roadbeds. Such strap rail, although serviceable for lightly trafficked lines, imposed sharp weight limits on the locomotives and rolling stock railroads could safely use. Moreover, contractors saved money by building trestlework to bridge swamps and gullies rather than spend additional funds to bring in more costly fill. In the hot and humid conditions in the region such trestlework had a life expectancy of only ten years, and roads, poorly built to begin with, degenerated quickly under use. In their haste to lay a new roadbed and move revenue loads as quickly as possible, many Southern companies neglected to ballast their roadbeds at all; in heavy rains their entire trackwork sank quickly into the mud. The problem was exacerbated by engineers' inattention to proper drainage. In the spring, when freshets and floods were endemic across the South, many railways disappeared under water. Passing tracks, or sidings, along the roads cost precious dollars; Southern roads saved money by building as few as possible, making Bell's job a nightmare.

Southern railroads coped with other peculiar conditions as well. Designed to connect cotton producing areas with navigable waterways in an area with fewer towns and cities than other regions, the average Southern rail line was 102.1 miles long versus the national average of only 66.7 miles.[5] Dependent upon agricultural traffic for most of their income, the companies had to acquire enough equipment to handle peak seasonal loads, but the cars then sat idle for the rest of the year. Manpower requirements followed the same pattern, but the region's inelastic labor supply presented railroads with unique labor problems. Many solved them by buying slaves who did much of the construction and maintenance work and often performed skilled tasks as well; many firemen on Southern lines were slaves. The use of bondsmen for such work placed unskilled white laborers, such as Bell, at a disadvantage, for he had to compete with leased or purchased bonded labor. With fewer railroad companies in the region than in the North and with their seasonal labor needs, Bell was lucky to get a position when he did.

Railroading was always a dangerous occupation; after the outbreak of the Civil War, occupational hazards increased tenfold on Southern roads. The war was the first conflict fought in which the railways themselves became military targets. Moreover, most of the fighting took place in the South, and the region's transportation system was all but destroyed by 1865. During the war, the burden placed on Southern roads of supplying Southern armies was overwhelming. Everywhere, normal operations broke down by 1862. Cut off from their suppliers, companies were unable to replace track and repair locomotives and rolling stock adequately. The whole Southern system, lightly built as it was, quickly wore down. Bell tells many absorbing tales of trying to operate over broken-down roadbeds with faulty equipment and complains that his job was made more difficult by army officers who interfered with rail operations. The wonder of the whole war was that, somehow, men like Bell coped with physical deterioration, drunken railway workers and soldiers, a shortage of wood and water, interrupted schedules, a lack of telegraph facilities, and unclear operations orders, and still kept the Southern transportation system hobbling along.[6] He paid a price for his efforts, however; the man seemed to work twenty-four hours a day.

Bell's vital skills took him all over the South. He started the war at work on the state-owned Western & Atlantic Railroad from Atlanta to Chattanooga. He soon moved north, leaving his family in Georgia, to work on the East Tennessee & Georgia, a single-track line that skirted the west side of the Appalachian Mountains from Dalton, Georgia, to Knoxville, Tennessee. When Federal troops cut the road, the company rescued as much of its rolling stock as possible and sent it over to Carolina railways to keep it out of harm's way. The company ordered the rest destroyed, and Bell was involved in running four locomotives off a bridge to keep them out of Yankee hands. He followed the ET&G's equipment down to Augusta and operated from there to as far north as Saltville, Virginia, until the war ended. Never in favor of the conflict, Bell was more than happy to win an exemption from the draft because of his needed skills. He was lucky to have kept it after the ET&G was broken up and Sherman marched along the W&A as he scourged the South. Only Bell's ability to find and keep railroad employment throughout the war kept him from the army's ranks.

When he returned home after the war, few Southern lines were operating, and Bell had to compete with returning Confederate veterans for jobs. Again he was lucky; he landed a job back on the W&A as a freight conductor. However, the railroad had been built by the state, and it was staffed from the first with political appointments. Bell, who appears not to have been very politically active, tried to save his job on the W&A. First he tried to remain above the fray by not voting at all; then, when forced to cast a ballot, he voted for the side that lost the election. The new state administration treated the W&A like many government offices, clearing out prior appointees and hiring those who supported the new governor.[7] Fired, Bell took to the road in search of a job; with at least six children to support he could not afford to be out of work long.

The Reconstruction South, however, had a surplus of railroadmen in the immediate postwar years, and Bell, despite his contacts on other railways, could not find another conductor's job. Instead, he was forced to take a construction position with a new railroad that was building its line from Chattanooga to Meridian, Mississippi. So began the most puzzling interlude in Bell's life. For years he worked off and on for the Alabama & Chattanooga Railroad, even when the company did not pay him for months, went into receivership, and had its rolling stock attached by creditors. Yet Bell, a man who had honed the fine art of reading faces and understanding the human character, remained loyal to the road's prime mover, John C. Stanton.

Stanton and his brother Daniel, both from Boston, hurried south after the war with visions of acquiring great fortunes in the railway business—and they knew exactly where to go. In 1867 Alabama passed a bill to permit state endorsements that guaranteed payment of principal and interest on first-mortgage railway bonds at a rate of twelve thousand dollars per mile. The following year, a Radical Republican, Reconstruction legislature sweetened the offer by raising it to sixteen thousand dollars a mile. The Stantons hoped to build their 295-mile rail empire from both ends and bought the North-East and South-West Railroad, which had been chartered in 1853 to connect the 26 miles between Meridian and York, Alabama, and the Wills Valley Railroad, which had also been chartered in 1853 and which, by the onset of the war, had opened 15 miles of its line from Trenton, Georgia, to Wauhatchie, Tennessee. From there its trains ran into Chattanooga over the Nashville, Chattanooga & St. Louis Railroad's tracks.

With money from New York bankers, John Stanton chartered the A&C, named Alabama's ex-governor as its president, and formed a construction company, headed by his brother Daniel, to build his road. Stanton imported a thousand Chinese laborers from San Francisco, who were soon hard at work for Bell. The whole corporate arrangement was typical of the postwar enthusiasm for business opportunities and speculation. By late 1870 Alabama's governor had endorsed $5,300,000 of the road's bonds, and construction was not even finished. Moreover, when completed, the A&C was valued at only $4,018,388. Realizing that he was short of funds to finish his road, Stanton went before the state legislature again in February 1870 to ask for $2 million in 8 percent state bonds. Initially his request failed to pass, but after Stanton opened his purse to the legislators, reportedly paying five hundred dollars per vote, the bill was reconsidered and, to nobody's surprise, was passed by a margin of better than two to one.

Unfortunately for Bell, Stanton had other priorities for his windfall. While the railroad's workers and contractors remained unpaid, Stanton bought real estate in Chattanooga, built an opera house, and constructed a new hotel he modestly named after himself. The rest of the money he used in a vain effort to reelect the Alabama governor who had done him so many favors. When the new state administration took office, Stanton's entrée to Alabama's treasury was blocked, and he defaulted on the interest on his bonds due 1 January 1871. Construction continued, however, and the road was finally completed on 17 May 1871. The company was placed in receivership, and, when the receiver took over in August, he discovered the southern end of the road was not even operating because the A&C's unpaid employees in Meridian had stolen its locomotives and spare parts and were holding them hostage. For the next six years chaos plagued the road. Stanton and his financial backers mounted a campaign to reclaim their property; other Southern lines eyed the derelict for possible expansion. The state of Alabama took over most of the road and operated it as a state enterprise except for the short segment that ran through Georgia, which took over that portion, and authorities in the two states argued over ownership and operations.

The whole imbroglio was complicated by the depression of 1873 that prostrated the already economically weakened South. It was not until 22 January 1877, as hard times began to lift, that Emile Erlanger and Company of London purchased the railroad and incorporated it as the Alabama Great Southern.[8] Meanwhile, the line suffered from a lack of maintenance; Bell tells stories about stopping his trains at trestles and bridges, ordering everyone off, slipping the locomotive's throttle into its first notch, and allowing it to creep across the bridge with the empty train. The passengers and crew then had to run across and catch it. The Chinese laborers, fired because the road had no money to pay them, were stranded in Alabama and left to their own resources.

When times were exceptionally difficult on the A&C and when it fell so far in arrears with his salary that Bell's family went hungry, the conductor packed up and moved on to the South & North Alabama Railroad, another product of Alabama's convoluted politics. Proposed to connect the northern and southern parts of the state, the S&NA was a legislative pet project; it received more state funds than any other road except the A&C. It was given a special state grant in 1868, then the standard sixteen thousand dollars per mile, and on 3 March 1870, a generous legislature passed a special act allowing it twenty-two thousand dollars per mile.

The South & North Alabama was a long road, even by Southern standards, traversing the 183 miles between Decatur and Montgomery, Alabama. Like the Alabama & Chattanooga, it was from its earliest years under the sway of outside capitalists; V. K. Stevenson and Russell Sage dominated the South & North Alabama. Stevenson, one of the founders of the Nashville, Chattanooga & St. Louis, entered the railway business in alliance with John Edgar Thomson, president of the Pennsylvania Railroad, who had worked with Stevenson while building the Georgia Railroad from Augusta to Atlanta. Allied with Stevenson was Russell Sage, who often worked closely with his friend Jay Gould. Stevenson and Sage, like Stanton, took their money from the government readily, but construction on the road lagged. By 1870 a sixty-seven-mile section of line north of Birmingham was still unfinished. It soon transpired that the two New York financiers had no intentions of completing their road to Decatur; they wanted to expand northward no farther than their connection with Stanton's moribund A&C. The S&NA's president and board of directors, all Southerners, resisted truncating their road, and they brought Albert Fink, general superintendent of the Louisville & Nashville into the argument. Fink, who would later make a national name for himself as a railway trunk-line commissioner who believed that competition among the great railroads was ruinous to all, proposed that his L&N lease the S&NA and another road that linked Nashville with Decatur. The lease was signed on 1 July 1872, and the L&N completed the S&NA northward to Decatur.[9] The road was constructed more substantially than the A&C, and, with the growth of Birmingham, it enjoyed a more lucrative traffic base. At least when Bell ran his trains over the S&NA, he received a regular paycheck. For some reason, however, he allowed himself to be lured back to Stanton's road, where his remuneration was much more problematical.

Bell finally escaped Stanton's clutches and spent the rest of his career working for the East Tennessee, Virginia & Georgia Railroad, which stretched from Chattanooga through Knoxville to Bristol, Tennessee. The road was a consolidation of the East Tennessee & Virginia, which was chartered in 1849, and began operations between Knoxville and Bristol in June 1855, and the East Tennessee & Georgia, which opened in 1856. In the harsh postwar railroad environment, they began to operate in unison. By 1868 they shared the same president, and, in the next two years several capitalists bought heavily in the stock of both roads, effectively merging ownership and control as they joined their boards of directors.

A road that size, however, offered a tempting target for wealthy Northern railway speculators and caught the eye of Thomas A. Scott, vice-president of the Pennsylvania Railroad, who was busily creating a Southern empire for his trunk line. Scott and his allies began buying East Tennessee, Virginia & Georgia stock and by 1871 owned majority control of the road. By November of that year Scott had transferred his holdings to the Pennsylvania's subsidiary, the Southern Railway Security Company, a holding concern created to control all the Pennsylvania's Southern roads. When the panic of 1873 hit, his company's stockholders began an investigation of the Pennsylvania's finances. The following year, the committee recommended that the Pennsylvania divest itself of all its Southern holdings, and Scott had to dispose of the 2,131 miles of Southern roads he had worked so hard to acquire.

Control of the ETV&G reverted to Richard T. Wilson. Wilson, who had been the company's president prior to Scott's takeover and who was one of the major investors in the line, was a native Southerner. Formerly a Loudon, Tennessee, merchant, he worked in the Confederacy's commissary department and, near war's end, was posted to London as the Confederacy's fiscal agent. After peace was declared Wilson returned to New York where he established a banking house. He was interested in numerous Southern roads, and, allied with Scott, he steered the 269-mile-long ETV&G through the turbulent depression years of the 1870s.

With the return of better times, Wilson embarked on an expansion program that increased the size of the road almost fourfold. In 1881, however, a Northern syndicate took control of the ETV&G and accelerated the pace of its expansion, but its assets were insufficient to bankroll its ambitions. When the depression of 1884 struck, the road's income was barely adequate to meet the interest on its funded obligations, let alone its large floating debt. The railroad went into receivership in January 1885, and Henry Fink, Albert's brother, was appointed receiver. He quickly reorganized the railroad, and it was soon reacquired by its former Northern owners. It did not stay independent very long because it had close ties with the growing Richmond & Danville system. In February 1887, it was taken over by the Richmond and West Point Terminal Company that controlled the Richmond and Danville Railroad. Consolidation of Southern railways continued apace, and in 1887 the ETV&G came under the control of the successor, Richmond Terminal System, which leased it the following year for ninety-nine years. The Richmond Terminal itself, however, went into receivership in 1892, taking its subsidiaries with it. The depression of 1893 further ravaged Southern properties and gave financial wizard J. P. Morgan a chance to work his magic on the Southern rail system. He put together a new corporate entity to control the Richmond Terminal's properties and passed the old ETV&G into a more stable financial organization, the Southern Railway.[10]

Through all the corporate changes, the financial catastrophes, the receiverships, and the takeover by various Northern interests, Nimrod Bell stoically operated his trains up and down the ETV&G's line, keeping the property operational. Bell found a home on the ETV&G, although he was far from immune to all the corporate changes that swirled above him. The shifts in ownership and profitability brought in new superintendents who changed operating policies, and he found that he had trouble getting along with some of them. As Bell often observes, however, he was getting too old and his responsibilities at home were still too great, especially with a son who would be with his parents for their entire lives, to just quit and move on. At the end of his career he opted for security rather than pride, and the choice hurt him.

Bell was active long enough, however, to watch the bureaucratization of Southern railways. Lines in the region took on qualities of the local character, especially its penchant for individualism, independence, and pride. Corporations there were slower to formalize their rules and regulations, preferring to rely on their workers' initiatives and good sense. While Northern roads consolidated their internal functions prior to the war, it took another two decades before their Southern counterparts devised rules for every likely contingency and generated sheaves of required forms. The changes snuck up on Bell, and, toward the end of his working days, his complaints about the avalanche of paperwork that kept him from what he considered his more essential duties became more insistent.

Bell's literary work, however, like all good literature, appeals to us on several levels. The most obvious is the one that tells us a great deal about the railways' inner workings and gives us the flavor of what it was like to go railroading in the mid-nineteenth-century South. Inadvertently, however, he also reveals his own personal prejudices about African Americans, Chinese, Jews, and women; shows the prevalence of violence in the region; mirrors the biblical fundamentalism that gave East Tennessee its reputation for being the buckle of the Bible Belt; provides a glimpse of the emerging union movement that would become the powerful railroad brotherhoods; explains why those organizations had a difficult time securing a foothold on Southern railways;

and, finally, offers an intimate view of what a working man thought of his world.

Perhaps Bell's most important contribution is his depiction of the railways' operations. As a conductor, Bell was in a fortunate position to illustrate the personal and professional relationships that kept the trains running; he had to work with the entire train crew, the men who kept his roadbeds passable and his trainmasters and dispatchers. The only men absent from his recounting are the highest officials, the executive managers, but they have been well covered in other historical studies. Indirectly, Bell also exhibits a consistent corporate loyalty. That may appear incongruous since he constantly moved from road to road, but in every instance he is careful to protect his employer's interests. Indeed, he rarely has anything negative to say about the companies that hired his services. He does complain of Stanton's refusal to pay his back wages, but he appears not so much angry as puzzled. Bell was delighted when his salary was raised but complained little when he worked for below-average wages. The quality of his performance did not suffer when he was only lightly compensated. He belies the myth of the angry and cynical wage earner; Bell was essentially a contented man who did not buck the system.

A goodly part of his satisfaction arose from his fervent belief that the job he performed was worthwhile and necessary. He carried into his retirement the notion that railroads were an indispensable good, not only in commercial terms but also for the betterment of mankind. Bell wrote almost as if railways carried an integral moral trait that rubbed off on all who worked and rode them. He was well positioned to observe the changes railroads wrought on his South, and, although he plainly did not agree with all the transformations, he counted the world he retired from better than the one in which he "went to railroading." In this, Bell was something of a throwback to the pre–Civil War era, when most people assumed railroads symbolized progress and were devices sent by God as proof of America's greatness. While that notion died rather rapidly after the war with the rise of large railway corporations and corporate rapacity, the idea lingered longest in the South.[11] It had not finished building its railroads yet, and men like Bell were not willing to attack corporations that promised more connections, additional jobs, easier travel, cheaper shipping, and regional unity.

Across the United States in the nineteenth century, railways were at the center of people's daily pursuits. Railways were inextricably linked to almost everything everybody did—even to their whistles' disturbing the sleep of those who lived near the lines. As a conductor, Bell worked closely with the public. In his myriad stories he could not fail to reveal his own predilections. Over his working years, for example, he witnessed slavery, Radical Reconstruction, Jim Crow laws (starting in 1875 on Tennessee public transport), the disfranchisement of African Americans, and segregation.[12]

Yet only once in his memoir does Bell make any pronouncement on racial matters, and that is an oblique one in which he seems to say that he thinks segregation is the best approach to race relations. Reading between the lines, however, we see clearly that Bell, like most Americans before the Civil War, had no strong opinions on slavery. He took it as a given and had no personal stake in the institution. Certainly, he showed no enthusiasm to fight to preserve it or, for that matter, states' rights, and he was of prime age to enter the Confederate army. We see equally clearly, however, that Bell, like most Americans of his age, believed that African Americans were inferior to whites. He starkly demonstrated this when he bossed construction gangs for Stanton while building the A&C, when he worked a large number of freedmen, some recruited from as far away as Virginia. Bell readily recognized their talents as individuals, but as a race he treated them differently than he did whites. With his African American laborers Bell was much quicker to resort to violence and did not shirk from whacking them over the head with whatever came to hand. In some cases he did serious physical harm to them. The lot of the railway construction worker, especially if he were an African American, was not an enviable one in the Reconstruction South. Bell was also a stickler for enforcing the company's Jim Crow laws on his trains. No African American was immune, not even a carload of preachers. Oftentimes he was inventive in the ways he found to segregate people when he was working for roads that had a paucity of rolling stock and could hardly afford the extra costs of designating cars on a racial basis.

By contrast, Bell appeared intrigued by the Chinese who worked for him, perhaps because they were the first he had seen. He readily accepted all the usual stereotypes about them, however, and treated them as he did African Americans. He did worry about the Chinese when they were stranded in Alabama after Stanton ran out of money, and he was relieved when they were finally shipped home. Bell was even less informed about Jews than about the Chinese because he never worked with any that we know of. He saw Jews only as customers, thought them all cheap, and was instantly wary when he saw anyone he thought Jewish on his train, afraid he or she would try to beat him out of a fare.

His attitudes toward women were more complex. It was clear that he gave women more latitude than he did men. He listened compassionately to their tales of woe and found seats for them on special cars the railways set aside for the "fairer sex" to separate them from "brutish men" who smoked, spat, and swore. Bell was always solicitous of women at the stations, helping them carry their baggage on and off his trains, because he thought that if he left them to their own devices, it would take them forever to board and leave, and he would never be able to keep his schedule. It was evident that Bell could "read" men better than he could women, whom he thought were more honest and pure. He was therefore always surprised when women tried to cheat him out of their fares, which they did with amazing regularity. And many females were diabolically clever about hiding themselves or their children on the train when Bell collected tickets. Part of Bell's hesitation in dealing with duplicitous women may have been that his options for dealing with them were more limited than those for dealing with men. He physically heaved males who persisted in defying him off his train, but Bell would never have done that to a woman. Nor would he have pulled his pistol on them or hit them. He had to deal with women verbally, and, although he was talented at the hostile exchange, they could push him further than could troublesome males. Nevertheless, Bell's ideal of women standing on pedestals was mitigated by his realization that some of them were as good at flimflamming him as any man.

More infrequently Bell provides a peek into the nascent railroad labor movement. He was a devotee of organized labor, joining the Old Reliable Conductors (ORC) when they formed a local on the ETV&G. The railroad brotherhoods eventually gained a reputation for their strong and passionate defenses of their members' skills, but in the mid nineteenth century, they were new and philosophically very conservative. The locomotive engineers organized first in 1863, followed by the conductors in 1868, but, although both brotherhoods later joined the American Federation of Labor and some locals flirted with Eugene Debs's one big railroad union and socialism, they were more like fraternal organizations than unions in the South in the 1880s.[13] Bell was more interested in the ORC's social aspects and its provisions for burial policies and care for widows than he was in its industrial policies. In the couple of instances when his fellow conductors were ready to strike, Bell, who hated to speak in public, warned them against walkouts, arguing that there was a ready supply of workers waiting to take their places. Undoubtedly, many of his reservations about the strike arose from his own personal problems; he could ill afford to walk away from a well-paying job. But he was also opposed to a strike on philosophical grounds. Bell's demeanor indicates that he believed he was above labor strife, that gentlemen did not strike. He was far from unique in his approach to labor problems. The Knights of Labor, one of the earliest attempts to build a national union, was predicated upon the dignity of the working man and his right to treat individually with his employer. The Knights therefore went beyond even Bell's careful views and formally eschewed the strike.

Ultimately, Bell's greatest contributions are his insights into his mid-nineteenth-century world. He shows its diversity, hopes, failures, confusion, sadness, and even its underside, when his train was robbed and its passengers murdered. He belies any belief that the "masses" are unthinking, unfeeling folks who go about their daily tasks and then die. He well understood his place in his world and appeared rather pleased with it; he did not feel used or abused. He went about his duties with a sense of responsibility and pride; he enjoyed being in a position of public trust and in providing a public service. He was proud of the uniform he began wearing after the war, even if it was blue and his passengers occasionally mistook him for a Yankee. The uniform symbolized his command of complex equipment and hundreds of lives, and those responsibilities spilled over into his private life, where his friends habitually called him "captain." Captain Nimrod could look back on a full life and take pride in his achievements and large family. If he had written a more personal conclusion for his book, he most likely would have pronounced himself a lucky man despite the tragic end to his career. Not many are fortunate enough to do what they like and get paid for it. Bell was a "natural" conductor, a man born to the railway age, and he intimated as much when he signed his book, "By Conductor N. J. Bell."

Southern Railroad Man

Part One

Bell's Career

Chapter One

My First Recollection
of Railroad Talk

I t was in South Carolina, Anderson District, now county, where I was born, away back, half a century or more ago. According to my recollection, it was about eighteen and thirty-one or thirty-two that I first heard talk of a railroad being built, and I, boy-like, wondered what kind of a road a railroad could be. I finally concluded it must be one built of fence rails, not being old enough to think of asking any one what a railroad was.

Some few years afterwards I went on a trip with my father to Hamburg, S. C., as it was at that time the market place for that section of country which we lived in, about one hundred or one hundred and ten miles distant. When we arrived at Hamburg I saw my first railroad. I do not remember of seeing any engine or coaches, but do remember of seeing some box-cars standing on a track on the outskirts of the town. That road was built from Charleston, S. C., to Hamburg, S. C., and was the first railroad that was built in that State, and I think about the first or next to the first one built in the United States. The road spoken of was called the South Carolina Railroad and has the same name now.[1]

My father moved to Georgia, near Marietta, when I was about thirteen years of age. The next railroad I saw, and the first engine and coaches that I remember seeing, was at Social Circle, Ga., which at that time was the terminus of the Georgia Railroad, at that time being built from Augusta, Ga., to Marthasville, Ga.[2] After the road was completed to Marthasville, the name of this place was changed to Atlanta.[3] The name of the road was the Georgia Railroad and goes by this name to the present day. I was at the place where Atlanta is now, when a small boy, and when it was called Whitehall Cross Roads; at this time the hotel, post-office and storehouses were built of hewed logs. But I never once, at that time, thought of it ever becoming my favorite city, as it is at the present day.

The second engine I ever saw, was when the Georgia State Road was built from Atlanta, Ga., to Marietta, Ga. This road is now called the Western and Atlantic Railroad and is now controlled by the Nashville, Chattanooga & St. Louis Railroad. A light engine was run from Atlanta to Marietta one Saturday evening; the first engine that ever ran into Marietta, Ga.[4] I was in town that evening when the engine whistled; it looked like everybody in town ran for life, especially men and boys, to the spot where the engine would stop, myself with the rest. I saw horses and mules running in every direction, but never once thought of the one I had ridden to town, until I went to the rack where I had hitched it and found it gone; the animal never came home until the next evening about sundown with bridle and saddle, but short of the blanket. I had to walk home, a distance of four miles, after the show was over, as many others had to do. It was said that a countryman went to the engineer to sell him a wagon load of shucks to feed his engine with; it was also said that the engineer engaged them for fun, but I do not vouch for it being a fact. My first experience and work on a railroad was on the track between Marietta and Atlanta.

While a boy I concluded I wanted some money of my own, so I went to the old man who had charge of the track between Marietta and Atlanta, a distance of twenty miles, and the old man hired me. The work was very heavy for a boy and the weather hot, so I did not work very long. All the other hands were stout men, some white and some black, and I tried to do as much work as any of them.[5] We had a dump car that we loaded with waste timber left in the cuts when the track was laid— and pushed it out on a fill and dumped the timber down the banks; clean out ditches and line the track. We carried and cooked our rations, and camped on the road side whenever night overtook us. Several years afterwards when I went to running over the same road where I had worked I learned that the skeleton of a man had been found near the banks of the Chattahoochee river that was supposed to be the bones of the old section boss that I had worked under, as he had been missing for some time and no one knew his whereabouts.

The difference in railroad tracks now and at the time I speak of is wonderful; one that never saw the old kind of track would hardly believe that engines and cars would run on such a track, knowing the kind that is used at the present day. To give the reader an idea of the first track I ever worked on, I will give a sketch of it: A piece of hewed timber was laid on each side of the road-bed, lengthwise, and the cross-ties laid on the sills—called mudsills. A stringer was let into the ties; the stringer was a square piece of long sawed timber; the rail was a flat iron rail with spike holes in the center of the rail, and was spiked on top of the stringer. The ends of the rails came together with a little neck and groove that made the joint. At the joint of the stringers was a wooden wedge driven in to keep them in their places. I think, as well as I can remember, every other tie was called a joint tie; that was where the stringers came together. The ties were not half so thick as at the present day.[6]

It was not long after the track was laid to Marietta until it was continued on to Dalton, Ga., as the grading was all pretty well done between those cities. The next work I did towards railroading was to go into the woods between Dalton and where Tunnel Hill is now with a gang of men and help them get mudsills and cross-ties, which were afterward laid on the road between Dalton and the tunnel. I worked on that section afterward, but it was not so long as the first section I worked on. Seven miles was what the boss was required to keep up, and the track was the same kind as spoken of before. The joints where the iron rails came together would sometimes get crooked, and the end of the rail stick up, and were called snakeheads. It is said that one of these snakeheads stuck up so high that it ran over the top of a wheel of a coach and through the floor, and killed a lady passenger. The work on the section I last spoke of was not as hard as the first. The boss was a good one; he would let his hands, in work hours, play leap-frog, and see who could jump the farthest, and take a hand with us himself; also play marbles, and swing on grapevines, and have a jolly old boyhood time—at ninety-five cents a day.

John D. Gray, an old railroad contractor, and a good one, took the tunnel contract through the ridge near Tunnel Hill, Ga., and worked all the men he could on both sides of the ridge, and worked a day gang and a night gang, and had an engine pulled over the top of the ridge to use on the opposite side. Mr. Lother had the masonry work done. It was circulated all through that section of country that there would be a free ride given through the tunnel when completed, so, after many days and nights of hard labor, the work hands met about the center of the tunnel and the track was soon connected. The day was already set for the first train to run through the tunnel, so when the time came everything was ready, and scores of men and boys went to Dalton to take a free ride, and after the train, which was mostly made up of flat cars, left Dalton the conductor came around collecting fare, and he found several passengers on board the train that thought the whole ride was free, and the conductor informed them that the free ride was only through the tunnel.[7] He found several who had left their pocketbooks at home, on the piano I suppose, and had no money with them, so the train was soon stopped and all that class of passengers alighted to walk back to their homes.

Where Dalton, Ga., now is was first called Froglevel; afterwards the name was changed to Cross Plains, and when the Western and Atlantic Railroad was built to that point, the name was changed from Cross Plains to Dalton. About that time my father moved from Cobb county to Murray county, Georgia, and settled near Dalton. Afterwards the county of Whitfield was taken off of Murray and Walker counties.

It was at Dalton, at a mass-meeting which was held to decide whether the W.&A.R.R. would be extended on to Chattanooga, Tenn., or not, a barbecue was given, and notwithstanding the heavy rain that was falling, when the dinner was announced ready, I never saw such a rush as was made at the table, which was on forked sticks.[8] I saw one man walking around with a whole ham under his arm and a loaf of bread in his hand, cutting and eating as he went, seeming as though he was looking for something else to eat.

Several speeches were made on that day by some of the leading men of that section of country, and it was decided to extend the road on to Chattanooga, for some grading had already been done in that direction.

I have never been to another barbecue since.

Chapter Two

On Western and Atlantic Railroad
1846–1862

As well as I can remember, it was in the early part of the year 1859 that I went to running on the Western and Atlantic Railroad as train baggageman. I had just recovered from a long spell of fever, and my health was not very good, and I took that position, not that I wanted to railroad, but to improve my health. The work was light; it was nothing to compare with the same position at the present time. It was not long after I commenced my new kind of work until the train I was on was taken off and my conductor was put on a freight-train, and I went with him. There were but few brakes on freight-cars those days, and cabooses or cabs were a great deal scarcer; so, many a time, I have had to ride on top of the rear car on the train; and I have put on brakes in cold, freezing weather, and it seemed like pulling the skin off the palms of my hands when taking them from a brake wheel.[1] I did not brake on a freight-train very long until I was put on a passenger-train to braking, and in a month or two I was given a baggage-car. I was next train hand on a local freight-train, by my own choice, and was soon promoted to freight conductor.

Wood was used in those days for fuel for engines, so it required a third man on the engine, to pass wood from the tender to the fireman. In those days the road paid the trainmen's board while out on the road. The conductor had a meal-book, and gave meal-tickets for meals and lodging for himself and crew. Freight-trains did not run of nights or Sundays, but were scheduled for certain stations on the line of road to lay over of nights and Sundays. Hand-lamps were scarce also, and one night I was caught out after dark, and rode on top of the rear car of my train, with a pine torch in my hand, twelve miles, in order that my engineer could tell whether he had all of his train.

It was not long after I commenced to run on a railroad before talk of war commenced. I took no part in it, only when the election came off, when Abraham Lincoln, John Bell, and John C. Breckinridge were the candidates, I voted for the latter, as he was a Democrat. He was the second President that I ever voted for.[2] The fighting commenced, and railroad men were exempted, for which I was truly glad, for I was not mad enough to fight, and I always had to be awful mad to fight any way.

It was not long after the war commenced until most of the transportation was moving troops, provisions, and war equipments. Freight-trains were run day and night, and often the conductors would have to ride in a box-car filled with soldiers. I have done so many a time; also in cars of merchandise and grain and bulk meat, on account of having no caboose. I remember once when I was in a car loaded with side meat, and the track in those days was pretty rough, but improved since the first track was put down, as the mudsills and stringers had been done away with, also the flat rails, and a hewn rail used instead, and cross-ties thicker.[3] As I said, my engineer was running so fast that the sides of meat began to jump up, and some of them would strike the top of the car that I was in; so I crawled on top and went over the train to the engine, and had my engineer to slacken his reckless speed. He laughed at me for being frightened. I told him if he could have seen the meat bouncing up and down, and the cars reeling first one side and then the other he would have been frightened, too.

When a box-car was used for a caboose, a large rope was thrown over the top of the car, and each end roped around a crosspiece at the top of the door inside of the car, and the ends of the rope hung down on each side, so one could get in and out. I once got a hard fall by my rope breaking. Only one who has had such experience can imagine how one suffered in such cars in cold weather without any fire. Many times my hands have been so cold that I could not handle my waybills when I arrived at a station, until I warmed them.

There were no trains run by order in those days, as there was but one telegraph wire along the roadside.[4] So in case the trains could not make their schedule meeting points, a flagman had to be sent ahead in case both trains failed to make the meeting place; that is, when running in opposite directions, both trains had to send a flagman ahead so that the flagmen would meet first. In case the train met between stations, the one nearest a side track had to back to a side track. I have known them to meet in that way often, and men argue about the rules of the road for a length of time, and parley over who should back. Some of the engineers at times would claim that their engine did not have water enough to back, and would get out of it in that way. A conductor had the right to side track his train, and cut the engine loose from it, anytime his engineer disobeyed his orders.

There were not a great many accidents in those days, not so many as one would suppose would be. I remember one, though, that happened on one Sunday in a cut near Graysville, Ga.; this was a head end collision, one train going in the direction of Atlanta, and the other towards Chattanooga. One of the engines exploded when the two struck, and one engineer was blown out of the cut into a field. One fireman was killed; one I know, if not two, and several soldiers, also a lot of horses. Some of the cars were torn to splinters. One of the trains was empty box-cars and the other was a mixed train, loaded with soldiers. The engineer who escaped had to hide to keep from being killed by the soldiers. I passed by where the wreck occurred the next day after it happened, and at that time it was a sad looking place.

I myself came very near getting killed once by an overhead bridge near the same place. I was walking on top of my train while it was passing through the bridge, and a man by the roadside halloed at me, and I dropped on my knees just in time to save my life.

A track was laid just above Chickamauga station, through a field, and connected to the East Tennessee and Georgia track just east of the rock bridge, where the East Tennessee and Georgia Railroad crosses the Chickamauga creek. This track was laid on account of some of the Chickamauga bridges on the Western and Atlantic Railroad being burned, and was used to get the Western and Atlantic trains into Chattanooga. I was going over the new track one day and was on top of my train when the car in front of the one I was on ran off the track, and the end of it seemed to be coming up into my face. I jumped off from the top of the car to the ground.

It was while I was helping move Gen. Bragg's army from Knoxville to Chattanooga, with engine and cars belonging to the Western and Atlantic Railroad, that an accident occurred, while an East Tennessee train was descending Black Fox grade, with a train load of soldiers.[5] An axle of one of the cars broke, killing fourteen soldiers. I saw their remains as I passed Cleveland lying on the depot platform.

Another accident occurred while the engine Sam Tate was ascending Wolf grade with a train load of soldiers. The engine exploded and killed the engineer and fireman. It was said that the fireman was blown above the top of a tree.

Another accident occurred in time of a big freshet, at the rock bridge, where the East Tennessee road crosses the Chickamauga creek. The water was over the abutment of the west end of the bridge, and the abutment gave way when an engine started across the bridge. The engine went in the creek, and the engineer was drowned, and it was some time before his body was found.

Railroading in time of war was almost as bad as being in the army, for men were run day and night, Sundays not excepted. I have gone into Atlanta many times and got off of one train and stepped right on another to go back to Chattanooga. I was moving a train load of troops one night from Atlanta to Chattanooga. They were called the Louisiana Tigers, and by the time I arrived at Chattanooga with them I decided they were tigers of some kind, for they were fighting each other all night, and I think two or three of them were knocked off the train by some of the rest on board of the train. Sometimes the soldiers would throw my grease buckets and my train chains away. They did not like railroad men. I often heard them say that railroad men ought to be in the army.

There were two trains of troops started out of Atlanta one evening, and I was on the front section. We made very poor time, and got away behind schedule time. When I passed Dalton I left word with the watchman the time I passed, and that we were not making any time; that my engine was slipping on every grade she had to climb, and told him to be sure and tell the crew of the following train about it. Away in the night I was on top of the rear car in my train, and the soldiers were laying thick all over the tops of the cars. I had my lamp in hand, the moon was shining dimly, and the engine was slipping slowly up a grade, when I discovered a dark object on the track not far off in the rear. At first I thought it the shadow of a tree, as it was in the belt of the woods, but I soon saw it was the engine of the following train. I waved my lamp to stop it, and signaled my man ahead, but it all seemed to do no good, so I left the rear end of my train to take care of itself and ran over the top of the train for life, regardless of sleeping soldiers. As I would run over them it awoke them and they followed me. It so happened that my engine turned over the top of the grade down another, and thus kept out of the way of the approaching one. The engineer of the second train had let his headlight go out. I saw him the next morning with his face all bruised up where he had jumped off his engine the night before.

A man had to look out for himself in those days. I was out one night, going up a heavy grade between the Chattahoochee river and Atlanta; the engine was slipping and had no train except a caboose, and I just happened to think that some accident might occur, although I did not know of any train following me. I stepped off my caboose and walked along behind it, and just as we were rounding a curve I heard a light engine coming at full speed behind us. I ran back just in time to avoid an accident. So I have always found it a safe plan to keep a lookout and take no chances.

A story was told on a conductor that had not been employed very long, that he was in charge of a train load of corn. Some of the cars were billed to a colonel who had a regiment of soldiers at Rome, Ga., and some were billed to General Bragg's army at Tullahoma, Tenn.[6] It so happened all the cars in his train for Rome were billed on yellow paper, and the others on white paper. So he left the Rome cars at Kingston all right, as that was where the Rome road branched off from the Western and Atlantic Railroad. The same conductor was started out of Atlanta on a second trip with a train load of corn, with some cars waybilled to Rome and some to Tullahoma. Some of the waybills were yellow, and some white. So the conductor sorted out the yellow way-bills, and did not look where they were billed to, and switched off all the cars at Kingston that had yellow waybills, and took to Chattanooga all that had white ones. He left cars at Kingston that ought to have gone to Chattanooga, and took cars to Chattanooga that ought to have gone to Rome.

A train load of soldiers was wrecked near Stegall's Station, and I was told that the old superintendent said he did not have a conductor on the road but who would send a whole regiment of soldiers to hell for a quart of whisky.[7]

There was one of the bridges across the Chickamauga that was being repaired, and Billy Grambling was in charge of the bridge gang. The same superintendent before spoken of was up where the bridge work was going on, and Mr. Grambling asked the superintendent to order an engine, as he would have to have one to haul timber with and to move his men to and from their work. The superintendent said "All right," and started off to issue an order, but stopped, turned around, and said: "Uncle Billy, hadn't I better order a tender, too?" and Mr. Grambling replied: "Yes; I reckon so." The order was made, and I was ordered to take the Flying Nelly, a little old engine that was used for extra work. My engineer was a former fireman. I coupled the engine on to the five or six freight-cars, which I had orders to leave at Dalton. We left Atlanta about 9 A.M., went twelve miles, and the engine became disabled, so she could not handle the cars. I side-tracked them, and went back to Atlanta on the engine. She was put in the roundhouse, and some repairs were made on her. We left Atlanta the next morning early with the engine. She would not steam to do much good or to make any time hardly. I got weary of such slow speed, and commenced firing the engine myself. I soon got her so hot that the steam commenced escaping, which scared my engineer so badly that he stopped the engine, jumped off and ran to a tree by the roadside, and swore he was not going to be killed by that old engine. Finally he came back, and I got him started again. We arrived at Chickamauga bridge about sundown the same day; all day with the light engine making a distance of about 124 miles. The engineer I had on that trip was the same man that was wiping engines in the roundhouse when the master machinist came round and told him that it took half of his time to watch him, and he told the master machinist that it took all of his time to watch him, the master machinist.

There was a large body of troops in camp at Big Shanty, a station on the Western and Atlantic Railroad.[8] I left Atlanta with an engine and train of empty box-cars. I loaded the cars at Big Shanty with troops, and left for Knoxville, Tenn., the place where I was ordered to take them to. When I arrived at Dalton my superintendent told me to take the transportation for the troops from Big Shanty to Knoxville. The engine and train I had belonged to the Western and Atlantic Railroad, but the road from Dalton to Knoxville belonged to the East Tennessee and Georgia Railroad Company, so I did as the superintendent told me to do. I arrived at Knoxville after dark, and the next morning the president of the East Tennessee and Georgia Railroad came to me and asked me what right I had to take transportation for the troops any farther than Dalton. I told him by order of my superintendent. He said I did right but the superintendent had no right to give me any such orders, and for me to report at headquarters by ten o'clock that morning or he would have me arrested. So I reported promptly on time, and the quartermaster took up the transportation I had and gave me only to Dalton. Afterwards the president of the East Tennessee and Georgia Railroad came to me and complimented me, and said if I got out of employment to come to him, that he liked a man that carried out orders.

I was then ordered to take the engine and cars I had and help move Gen. Bragg's army from Knoxville to Chattanooga. They were moving out of Kentucky, so it took me about two or three weeks to do so, both day and night.

I was ordered from Knoxville to Saltville, Va. I went from Knoxville over the East Tennessee and Virginia Railroad to Bristol, which road and the East Tennessee and Georgia Railroad were afterwards consolidated and called the East Tennessee, Virginia and Georgia Railroad, now a part of the Southern Railway Company.

I went from Bristol to Glade Springs, over what is now called the Norfolk and Western Railway, and from Glade Springs to Saltville over a branch road. My train was loaded with salt, and waybilled to Atlanta, Ga. My superintendent was there with his private car. There was some difference between his car and my caboose; my car was an old box-car, with the bottom of an old stove and no pipe, and it was some time before I could decide whether I had rather freeze to death or be smoked to death; but the weather turned a little warmer, and I decided I had rather freeze, so I threw my piece of a stove out. My superintendent had his private car loaded with salt, and I hauled it back to Atlanta without any waybills. My superintendent told me if I wanted to buy any for my own use to have it billed. The gentleman in charge of the salt works gave me a sack of salt, and I put it in with my superintendent's salt, which had no bill, and sent it home, as salt was a scarce article in my section. When I returned to Bristol I bought ten barrels of flour from the depot agent on the Virginia side, and in the night took five cars out of my train and put them at the depot and loaded two barrels in each car. I would have had them billed but for the order issued by the military department, that such things as flour and corn should not be shipped out of Tennessee. I had to lay over all night at Knoxville and give up all the waybills I had, and if I had had my flour billed it would have been taken from me at Knoxville. As it was I got it through to Georgia all right.

While I was at Knoxville helping to move Gen. Bragg's army to Chattanooga, I saw three hundred men that Gen. Bragg captured as he came out of Kentucky. They had left their homes and families in the Southern States to join the Federal army. I talked with some of them and asked them why they left their native homes to fight against their own country, and they said they could not fight against the flag that our forefathers fought for. There were thousands who left the South, both white and black, to join the Northern army. Some of my near neighbors did the same thing in Georgia.[9]

I was at Dalton, Ga., when the noted engine General was recaptured and brought back to Dalton, the engine that Andrews and party stole from Engineer Jeff. Cain at Big Shanty.[10] I took a train load of coal with the same engine on her return to Atlanta from Dalton, and Joe Renard, who is at this time running an engine on the Western and Atlantic Railroad, was my engineer. The Western and Atlantic Railroad was moving a large quantity of corn between Atlanta and Chattanooga, the most of it being waybilled to General Bragg's army. As I have already stated, there was a colonel at Rome with some troops. I was told by some of the other conductors that the colonel had made them switch out cars from the trains that were waybilled to Bragg's army, and that the colonel would have me to set out some of my cars of corn. So I was posted. Sure enough, when I arrived at Kingston the colonel was ready for me, and ordered me to set out four car-loads of corn for him. I said: " I have none billed to you." He said it made no difference—I had to set them out for him. I asked the road's depot agent about it, and he said the other conductors had been doing so. The colonel told me what track to set the cars on so his wagons could get to them. I said to him that I would have to leave the waybills with the agent and go tell my engineer what I wanted to do. I posted my brakemen, and also my engineer, that when I gave a signal to pull ahead, so as to set the cars out, to keep going, and to whistle for brakes to be applied; that my brakemen would pretend to be putting on brakes, but would not. So away he went, calling for brakes, and as my caboose passed I jumped into it, and carried my train load of corn to Chattanooga. As I returned the next day the agent told me the colonel was awful mad and said he would have me discharged.

On my next trip I had the same thing to do over, only the colonel was at Calhoun, a station farther up the road, with his wagon train all along the bank near the road, so as to make me stop until he had his wagons loaded with corn. I had learned of his whereabouts and his intention, so all were well posted. I also had three or four passengers in my caboose. I told them about it, and that I would let them off after I left the town, and it was all right with them. We passed the wagons at a rate of twenty miles an hour, regardless of the colonel's signals to stop the train.

As I returned on the day following, the depot agent said the colonel was the maddest man he ever saw; that he cursed me, and swore he would have me discharged or court-martialed. I told the agent to tell the colonel to order his corn from the proper source and it would be waybilled and promptly delivered, and he would have no more trouble. When I returned to Atlanta I went to the master of transportation's office and reported myself in regard to the matter, and he was pleased with the course I had pursued, and said he was glad I used such judgment. I have never heard from the colonel since.

There was a train load of artillery on a side track at Kingston that Bragg's army had captured from the Federal army. I was going down one day by Kingston with only one car and caboose. The agent said the train of artillery was ordered to Chattanooga, and he had it waybilled. I side-tracked the car I had, turned the car I had, turned my engine around the Y[n] coupled to the cars with artillery, and took them to Chattanooga.[11] I learned afterwards that the Federals captured them back, and I thought they had better have stayed at Kingston.

I was going from Chattanooga to Atlanta one night, with a long train of empty box-cars, that is for those days. When we arrived at Marietta we had a little accident, but not to amount to much, no one was hurt and no damage done to cars, only one old Georgia Railroad box-car was smashed up a little. When I went into Atlanta I went to the master of transportation's office to make my statement. I commenced telling him how the accident occurred, and he said he had heard the other side of the question, and did not want to hear any more. Knowing that I was not in the least to blame it made me mad. The master of transportation handed me a book and said "Take this book and go and report on this book." I threw the book down on the floor, and walked out and hunted up the yard-master, and made him go with me to my caboose and take charge of my train equipments, and told him I would not run another trip over the road. He begged me not to quit, said I would be conscripted and have to go in the war. I told him I was not afraid of that, that I did not have anything to do with getting it up and I did not intend to have anything to do with ending it, if it took my fighting to do so. I then went to the treasurer's office to get my money, and the treasurer told me he had orders from the superintendent not to pay me if I quit. I had seventy-five dollars of the company's money that I had collected. I thought if they had a right to keep back money that I had worked so hard to earn, that I had the same right to keep what I had of theirs. I thought the matter over very carefully and finally concluded that it was not honest on either side to keep what belonged to some one else. I made out my report and turned over the money I had, hoping some day all things would be righted that were wrong. A few days after the occurrence spoken of, I happened to meet the president of the East Tennessee and Georgia Railroad, and remembering my first acquaintance at Knoxville, and how he introduced himself to me, I asked him if he could give me work, and he said to be in Dalton on the following Monday and he would give me a train, and told me what wages he would pay me.

I went to Atlanta to see if I could not get the amount due me for my services rendered on the Western and Atlantic Railroad, as the old superintendent had died soon after he ordered the treasurer to hold my wages. A new one had been appointed, and a very nice gentleman, so I called at his office, and asked him if he would be kind enough to give an order to draw my wages, knowing he was familiar with the circumstances. He never said a word until he gave the order to get my money, then he asked me to take a seat and tell just how the accident occurred; said he had heard the other side of the question but never had heard my statement. I did as he requested, and he said I was not to blame in the least, and I could take my train again, and he would be glad I would do so. I thanked him and told him I had another place that would pay me better wages.

Chapter Three

East Tennessee and Georgia Railroad
1862–1863

When I was a boy I passed by a gang of men just as they commenced moving the earth for the bed of the East Tennessee and Georgia Railroad, near Dalton, Ga., when the road was first commenced from Knoxville to Dalton. This was constructed some time before the road was built from Chattanooga to Cleveland, and was used for the main line for some time, and the other for a branch. There were some very wealthy men who lost nearly all they owned while the road was being built between Chattanooga and Cleveland. Those men were contractors.

East Tennessee was as beautiful a country as my eyes ever looked over, before the armies passed through it, along where the East Tennessee and Georgia Railroad ran through it. Good houses, fine farms, good fences, nice apple orchards and clover fields. While it looks well at the present time, yet it does not compare with former days.

Well I was at Dalton on the day named, according to the contract which I mentioned in previous chapter. After I left the Western and Atlantic Railroad I commenced running a train from Dalton to Loudon, and sometimes to Chattanooga, moving soldiers as heretofore, and having a hard time generally. Loudon was as far as I could run east, as the bridge that crossed the Tennessee river was burned at Loudon, and Gen. Burnside was in Knoxville. So the reader can see at once that this was as far east as I cared to go at that time. The track was bad. A great many of the section men had quit work, and we often had to cut fence rails for fuel, and to bail water with water-buckets, from some stream or pond along the roadside. We were moving Gen. Cheatham's men west, and Gen. Longstreet's east.[1] It was a common thing for cars to be derailed, and there was an order issued from the war department, for soldiers to help when necessary, while being transported, but it was a hard matter to get them to do anything but eat what little they could get.

The officers of the road had their headquarters at Loudon, and it was also General Vaughan's headquarters at that time.[2] I left Loudon one day with a train loaded with soldiers. The engine I had was newly overhauled, and had a new name, which was "General Cheatham."[3] She was running backwards, and I had orders to turn her at Athens, as there was a turning-table at that place.[4] When I arrived at Athens, I had the engine cut loose from the train, and run on to the turning-table. We had her about half turned when the table gave way, and over the engine went into the pit on her side. The engineer was on her when she turned over; he was hurt by the wood falling on him out of the tender, but not seriously. I had another engine sent me and went on, leaving the General lying in the pit. She was taken up afterwards and sent South.

I was switching some cars at Riceville, one night. My brakeman had a blanket over his shoulders, and went in between some cars to make a coupling, and when the cars came together the brakeman halloed "oh, Lord, slack him ahead; oh Lord, oh Lord!" I gave a go ahead signal at once, supposing he had his hand badly mashed, and asked him "What in the world is the matter?" and he said, "Why the corner of my blanket was fastened."

I was going up one night with a car-load of soldiers. I had a car in my train waybilled to Sweetwater, and also had a lady passenger for that place. I had told my engineer about it, and to stop when he arrived at that place, and he said that he would do so. I had no bell cord, and the engineer forgot about the stop. He slacked up as we were passing the station, and I stepped off, making sure he was going to stop; but, instead, he kept on, going faster. Regardless of my signals to him he went on and left me standing at the station. Well, I hardly knew what to do. I concluded to walk on, as I knew that the engine would have to get wood and water at a wood-yard and water-tank about two miles east of the station, and that the wood would have to be sawed and the water pumped. So I set out on foot, thinking that I could overtake them at the wood-yard. I had not gone more than half a mile when I heard the train wreck, and iron rails rattling, and soldiers shouting. I stopped and turned back, for I was sure a raid had captured my train, and that my getting left was providential. I had my lamp, and as I was returning some one commenced throwing rocks at me. I put out my lamp, as I had no time to look for the rock-thrower. I ran back to Sweetwater, where a body of men were standing around a bonfire near a mill in the edge of the town. They asked me what the matter was. I said: "Wait, and when I can get my breath I will tell you." They laughed at me. As soon as I rested a little, and got somewhat over my scare, I told them what had happened; but they did not believe the train had been captured by a raid, and some of them went off up the road towards the wreck, and I went on after them. My superintendent was on the train, and he sent one of my train-hands back for me to come and put the cars back on the track, which had run off. I had not gone very far until I met the train-hand, and he said there was no raid. Of course I felt better. The train had run off the track just opposite the house where my lady passenger lived. She was in one of the cars that was derailed, but was not hurt. In fact, no one was hurt.

The accident happened west of Sneed's water-tank, which is now done away with, and right opposite the Widow Johnston's place. A new dwelling has been built, not long since, where the old house used to stand. I arrived at the wreck, looked around, picked up a few hands, and by noon the next day had the track cleared all right, and went on to Loudon.

Not long after the incident just related the bridge over the Hiawassee river was burned, and I was cut off west of it with the old East Tennessee engine, Cumberland.[5] I was going south with a train-load of soldiers, and received orders to notify the citizens between Cleveland and Chattanooga that there would be no more trains run between those two points. I notified them as ordered. I only got as far as the east end of Mission Ridge tunnel, as General Sherman's army had possession of the west side.[6] I unloaded my troops at the east end of the tunnel. I went up to General Bragg's headquarters and looked around, and decided if Sherman got possession of the surroundings of Chattanooga (he already held the city), that the South was gone up and had as well give it up, as that was natural fortification; that if they lost that, all was lost. I returned to Cleveland. I had made the last run over that part of the road that was ever made for the Southern Confederacy. When I arrived at Cleveland I received orders to stay there until Wright's brigade came from Georgetown to Cleveland; then move them to Dalton; thence over the Western and Atlantic road to Chickamauga.[7] I stayed all day at Cleveland, and could hear the report of cannon at Mission Ridge battle all day. In the evening I wired the superintendent to let me go to Dalton, as I believed I would be cut off if I did not do so. I received an answer to stay at Cleveland until Wright's brigade came. I ate my supper and went to bed. Away in the night I heard cavalrymen galloping around over town, asking if there was any ammunition in the depot. Just before day I heard talking, and the conversation was that Gen. Sherman had whipped Gen. Bragg at Mission Ridge, and that the Yankees camped at Widow Tucker's last night. I was not sure whether I had heard or dreamed this. So I got up and went over to the depot to make inquiry. I soon found that this was no dream, but reality. I went and woke my engineer, who was a "Union man" (as such men were called in those days), and told him to have his engine fired up at once, as I wanted to leave right away.

"Where are you going?" he asked. I answered, "Dalton, if I can get there."

The depot agent was a good friend of mine. He and I walked down the road toward Dalton to see what the prospect was for me to get out that way. We went near a mile, and got up on a high bank and saw a lot of cavalrymen going around a field, through a belt of woods. They were the first Federal troops I had ever seen, except a few prisoners. We returned to the depot at good speed, and not seeing any show to get to Dalton, I decided to go east as far as I could. The depot was almost full of citizens' plunder, as some of them were preparing to refugee. They begged me to take this and that. I told them it would be of no use, as there was no way to get it out by rail. Burnside was in Knoxville, the bridge at Loudon burned, the track torn up and some of it turned over the rails. Some of the rails were put in piles of cross-ties, burned and bent in all kind of shapes; some had been heated and bent around trees and saplings, and all the bridges burned on the East Tennessee and Georgia Railroad between Knoxville and Bristol. I in the meantime thought that my engineer never would get his engine hot and ready to move, I kept hurrying him; at last he got his engine ready. I took her and ran down to the copper foundry which stood just below Cleveland and was soon afterwards burned. I coupled to two cars loaded with blocks of copper that stood on the side-track that I was begged to take away. I came back to the depot and coupled to four or five car-loads of corn meal, five, as well as I remember, that belonged to the Confederate army. I think they were waybilled to Longstreet's command. I also loaded one or two hogsheads of Irish potatoes and one or two of bacon, I do not remember which. They belonged to a Presbyterian minister that lived in the edge of town, and he begged so hard that I took them away for him. I was then ready to leave Cleveland and go as far as I could get. After my engineer picked up a few sacks of wheat bran and an empty cartridge box or two, which he said would do to feed his old cow in, I got him started from Cleveland. We had not gone more than six miles before he stopped and commenced to work on his engine. I went to him and said, "Billy, are you determined to let me be captured?" He laughed and said "No." I said, "Well, for God's sake go on away from here." So he got on his engine and pulled out, and about dark we arrived at Charleston, twelve miles east of Cleveland. Wright's brigade never came to Cleveland to this day that I know of. When I arrived at Charleston I found Col. Carter there with his regiment of troops. They built a temporary trestle out of poles across the Hiawassee river. The Colonel said he wanted me to put all the cars that were there across the river at once. I sent the fireman across the river to catch the engine, and made the engineer give her steam enough to take her across the trestle to see if it would hold her weight up, if so, I could set the cars over. She went over the trestle all right. There was a side-track full of cars, beside the ones I had in my train. I went to work and took a few cars at a time up to Riceville, a distance of nine miles. I worked all night and by sunrise the next morning I had all the cars at Riceville, with the exception of two that were loaded with meat and left by order at Calhoun, just across the river from Charleston. I afterwards learned that the two cars were burned.

I then moved the cars to Athens, a distance of seven miles. I worked night and day, ate when I could get anything, and slept when I could get a chance.

I moved what cars my engine could pull to Loudon, a distance of twenty-seven miles. It was then decided not to run any more trains, but to leave Loudon the next morning in the direction of Knoxville.

I was sent out to take the names of the engines and numbers of cars at Loudon, as they were all to be run into the river the next evening. As well as I can remember, there were four engines and between sixty and a hundred cars—some loaded with corn meal, some with flour, some with meat, and some with one thing and another. Among them were the cars loaded with copper that I had brought away from Cleveland. Some of the cars were empty. The names of the engines that were run into the river at Loudon, as well as I can remember, were the Cherokee, Alleghany, and Hiawassee.[8]

I know the Cumberland was the one I used last and made the last trip that it ever made to move Confederate troops. I remember that it was on Thursday evening that I took the names of the engines and numbers of cars. I had just finished taking them and gone to my boarding-house and eaten my supper, when the superintendent handed me a telegram that he had just received from Colonel Carter, saying to send a train at once to Athens for his regiment. The superintendent said that I would have to go. I told him I did not want to go; that I was about worn out, and asked him to please get some of the other men to go. He said that he could not get them to go. I told him that my engine had neither wood nor water. He said there was a detail of a hundred men to go with me, to help me along, and said if the engine or train left the rail to leave it and come back. I told the captain of the detail to have the engine pushed up to a pond of water near the track and have water put in the tender. This was done with water-buckets: a man to dip the water up, and a line of men from the one that dipped the water to the tender, and a man on the tender to take the bucket and hand it to a man on top of the tender, who poured the water into the tender; and two or three men placed so as to throw and catch the empty buckets, so as to pass them back to the man who dipped the water. This was called bailing water. There was a great deal of it done during the war, as well as using fence-rails for fuel.

I then put some of the soldiers to cutting fence-rails for fuel, and others to switching cars, pushing out a loaded car by hand from the side-track down the main track, and empty ones up the main track, until I had enough to move the troops I had to move. When I had what my engineer thought a supply of water and rails sufficient to take him to Sneed tank, and steam enough to move the train, we started for Colonel Carter's regiment of troops. When we arrived at Philadelphia, a station about six miles from Loudon, the engine was out of water. I went back, and found both my brakemen in a car fast asleep. I told them to get up and go around town and borrow some water-buckets from the citizens, and I had but a few on my train. This they refused to do, so I made them get off the train. I told them I would not haul them a mile further. I went myself and woke up some of the citizens, and borrowed a supply of buckets. Woke up the captain, and he started some of his men out to bail water. I put them to work. The engine was on a little bridge where a creek ran underneath. I could not keep the soldiers at work. They would slip off in the darkness and go back to the train. I woke up the captain again, and he woke up his lieutenant; the lieutenant got up and cursed around among the men awhile, then lay down and went to sleep again. I worried awhile longer. Finally I asked my engineer if he had water enough to take the empty engine to Sneed's tank, about a distance of five miles. The engineer said he had enough water to take the engine to the tank. I returned the borrowed buckets, left the train standing on the main track, jumped on the engine, went to the wood and water station, woke up the pump man, made him harness his mule and pump a tenderful of water, also saw a tender of wood.

I went back to my train just after sunrise, coupled up, and started for the colonel's regiment. I saw Col. Carter at Sweetwater; he said that his men would hang me for not making better time. I said all right. But when I met them west of Sweetwater they shouted for joy, and said they were so glad to see the smoke of an engine. I got back to Loudon with them all right, with but little trouble. I found on my arrival at Loudon that all the railroad men had gone and left me, save one man that the president had sent back for me and told him to tell me to come on and not try to go through the country to Georgia, as I had been thinking of.

A quartermaster gave me a haversack, the young ladies at my boarding-house sewed the strap on it and filled it full of good victuals, I ate my dinner, bade the clever old Irish gentleman and his nice family goodby, shouldered my haversack, the first one I ever carried in my life, and the last one. I went to Gen. Vaughan, and he gave me a permit to cross the river. I crossed the river in a ferryboat, and started in the direction of Knoxville. It was on Friday evening that I left Loudon, and that was the evening that the engines and cars were to be run down the bank into the river, my old faithful Cumberland with the rest, and I did not want to see it, so I crossed the river. As I was going around Loudon bluff I overtook two or three men who said they were militia, and had been on duty in Murray county, Ga., and were going home on a furlough. One of them picked up a cannon ball, as there were several scattered along the road; he said he was going to take it home to show it to his family. I said to him that I should not wonder if his family had not already seen more of them than they wanted to; but he carried it on to near Lenoir's station and hid it in the corner of a fence, and said he would come back and get it. My haversack got so heavy, and I had eaten so much in order to lighten it, and it still seemed to increase in weight, so I gave a portion of it to my traveling companions. It was a little after dark when I arrived at Concord, a station about fourteen miles west of Knoxville. Not having any money but Confederate money, and not wishing to impose on strangers, I went into the railroad depot. There I found a very clever gentleman who was the agent; he gave me, free of charge, a bed that sat in front of the fireplace, which had a good fire burning in it, for which I thanked him very kindly. The bed was a long wooden bench, without sheet or blanket. I was very tired, and soon retired. I slept soundly until daylight, and, without any toilet, ate my breakfast from my haversack, and continued my journey in the direction of Knoxville.

On the same morning, a little before noon, I arrived at Erin, a little station five miles west of Knoxville. This station is now called Bearden. I went up to Gen. Longstreet's headquarters and looked around awhile.

His headquarters were in a brick house on a hill, not far from the station. (Mr. Robert Edington now owns the property, if I am not mistaken.) This was on Saturday. I found the railroad men there who had left me behind them. We all went out to Maj. Lyons's place, which was a mile from the station, and where Lyons View hospital now stands. The railroad officials went to the dwelling house, and the rest of us took possession of the negro quarters, as they were vacant, the negroes having deserted them and gone to Knoxville, where Gen. Burnside's headquarters were.

Chapter Four

A Trip Back to Georgia
1863

I t was on a beautiful day about the first of December, 1863, early one Monday morning, just after the sun had thrown its bright rays over the hills that surround Knoxville, when a party of men left Maj. Lyons's old homestead, and went west of Knoxville, en route to Bristol, in order to get out of East Tennessee into the State of Georgia. The party was composed of the following men: Maj. Campbell Wallace, president; C. B. Wallace, superintendent; J. M. Bridges, treasurer: Ben Hambright, conductor; Wm. H. Smith, Eb. Collins and J. H. Justice, roadway; Jack Branon, engineer; Jack Baker, fireman; Jno. McAnturf, brakeman; a boy named Springfield, fireman, and about eight more whose names I do not remember, and myself. I think there were about twenty in all, besides Maj. Lyons; he was not a railroad man, but a brother-in-law of Maj. Campbell Wallace.

Gen. Longstreet sent with us a wagon and four-horse team, which was loaded with railroad valuables, and the hogsheads of bacon and potatoes that I had taken away from Cleveland for Parson Caldwell, as I now remember his name to have been. Maj. C. Wallace took the hogsheads, as he said we would need the bacon and potatoes, and if they had been left at Loudon, they would gave gone into the river. There was a two-horse wagon loaded with corn to feed the stock with, and an ambulance for the officers to ride in, and one saddle-horse.

Gen. Longstreet sent twenty cavalrymen along to keep off bushwhackers. He commenced moving his army on the same day and in the same direction in which we went. This was soon after the battle was fought at Fort Saunders near Knoxville, between Generals Longstreet and Burnside. In this battle one of my best friends lost his life. I remember his last words. A few days before the battle was fought we met and when he bade me good-by, he said that he hoped to see the time when we could go fox-hunting again like we used to do. When I learned of his death it was sad news to me, as indeed were the deaths of many other friends of mine who were killed during the war.

We had not gone far until we came up with a part of Gen. Longstreet's command. I had hauled soldiers so much that they knew what I followed. When they saw me they commenced halloing at me, "Go ahead two car-lengths, come back a car-length." Of course I did not like it, but had a poor way of helping myself. I met up with a colonel who was an old schoolmate of mine; this meeting was a great pleasure to me in a time like that. We soon passed the soldiers, as we traveled faster than they did.

We stopped at Mr. McMillan's, near Flat creek, the first night after we left Maj. Lyons's place, and the second night at Mossy creek. I do not remember what place we stopped at the third night, but we stayed one night at Mr. Jackson's, near Bull's Gap, and one night east of Greenville, near a station called Henderson's at that time, now Afton. I do not recollect now where we stopped the other three nights that we were on the trip.[1] We found plenty to eat, notwithstanding both armies had passed through that part of the country, and good places to sleep, and good clever people all along where we traveled.

I came to a creek, which I afterwards learned was named Lick creek, and I saw no way to cross it without wading, or to wait for the wagons to come up. It happened that a negro boy came along riding a mule, and when the mule stopped to drink I jumped upon the mule behind the negro. This scared them both, and the mule was soon across the creek. I jumped off, and away went the mule, running for life, with his rider. Some of the other boys hallooed to him to come back and set them across, and they would give him a dollar, but he never looked back.

Greenville was where John Morgan, the daring and noted raider, was killed, and also [where] ex-President Andy Johnson's old homestead [stood]. We passed through Greenville on Sunday. A fine sunshiny day it was. We learned that two men had been killed near there by some unknown person or persons. We found the East Tennessee and Virginia road torn all to pieces. Bridges and trestles burned, and iron rails twisted around trees all along the line.

The distance from Loudon to Bristol is 100 miles, and I walked it all but about three miles. I do not now remember how long it took us to make the trip. We arrived at Bristol one evening just before the sun went down. My feet were blistered from heel to toe. We found that there was no train to go out until next morning. Early next morning we boarded a train for Lynchburg, Va.; thence to Petersburg, Va.; thence to Weldon, N.C., and on to Wilmington, N.C.; from this place to Kingsville, S.C.; then to Branchville, S.C.; then on to Augusta, Ga., and finally to Atlanta. By the time I arrived in Atlanta all the party except myself had stopped at other places along our route. I went on to Dalton. I was glad to find my little family all well, for I had not seen or heard from them for some length of time. General Bragg's army was located all around Dalton. I loaded my household goods into an East Tennessee and Georgia car that was at Dalton, and took my family and refugeed to Middle Georgia, where we had friends and relatives. This place was about twenty miles from Covington, a way station on the Georgia Railroad. Thinking that I had my family entirely out of the way of any army, I left them there and went to Augusta, where the rolling-stock of the East Tennessee and Georgia was which had been run out of Tennessee.

Chapter Five

Through South and North Carolina
1864–1865

Soon after I arrived at Augusta I was fitted up with an East Tennessee and Georgia second-class coach for my caboose. This coach was supplied with a cook-stove, and most of the seats were taken out and good beds put up to sleep on. These were arranged so that they could be turned back out of the way when not in use. This car was a combination car, one end having been used for baggage or express. In this end myself and crew were allowed to put cotton for ourselves, by paying one freight on it. Other shippers had to pay the East Tennessee and Georgia railroad and other roads we ran over, which belonged to other companies, as the rolling-stock we used belonged to the East Tennessee and Georgia Railroad, thus making a double freight on everything we hauled.

We ran from Augusta to Branchville over the South Carolina Railroad; then to Kingsville over the Charlotte and Columbia Railroad; thence to Wilmington over the Wilmington and Manchester Railroad. In going to Charlotte, N.C., we would go via Columbia, S.C. We were required to have a pilot on each road that we ran over—a conductor who would take charge of the running of the train—but somehow it happened that I ran some trips without any pilot. The names of some of the roads have been changed since that time.

As soon as everything was ready, and I had bought my rations, I left Augusta for Wilmington, N.C., with a train-load of cotton. The roads we ran over would not allow us to run after dark, so we would side-track about sundown, and sometimes before. I had an engineer, fireman and wood-passer, a brakeman and cook. The company paid for our rations. We hauled cotton to Wilmington and goods back to Augusta. The cotton was shipped to Nassau, and the goods came from the same place.[1]

I went one or two trips to Charlotte, N.C. Sometimes I would make a trip over the Georgia road to Athens, Ga., and get a trainload of cotton. I do not know how may trips I made to Wilmington, but I know that I knew but little about the war, except what I read in the newspapers.

Sometimes it would take a week to unload and reload a train at Wilmington, and we would lay over there that length of time. Sometimes the yard at Wilmington would get blocked, and we would have to side-track about twelve miles out on the road and stay two or three days before we could get in. On one of these occasions I was lying out on a side-track. On the evening that I was going in, and just before I started, a small boy and little girl, both pretty children, came to me and asked me for something to eat. I gave them all the meat, bread, potatoes and syrup that they could carry away. They were very proud of this. They said their father was killed in the war, and that their mother and grandmother were both sick. Some months afterwards I was passing by the same place where I saw the children, and a man got on my train at the same side-track that I laid over on. I asked him about the two children, and related the circumstance to him. He said the women died, and the little boy and girl starved to death.

I lay over one night at a station on the Wilmington and Manchester Railroad where corn was issued out to soldiers' wives by the Confederate Government. I never saw as many carts, some pulled by horses, some by mules, and some by oxen, and the drivers all women. I made some Confederate money speculating on cotton and corn, but nothing to what some men made that followed it for a business.

I would get leave of absence once in awhile and visit my family to see how they were getting along. I kept them in good coffee all the time after I commenced running to Wilmington, as I could buy all I wanted there. On one of my trips to see my family, I met a man in the road who spoke to me and said, "You are a young man, why are you not in the war?" "Because I have papers to exempt me," I replied. He said, "I am a conscript officer, let me see your papers." I said, "let me see yours first, so I may know you have a right to look at mine." He gave them to me, I read them, handed them back to him, and gave him mine. After he looked them over he gave them back to me and said, "Well, you got away with me," and, bidding me good-by, went on his way.

Maj. C. Wallace was a good friend to me; he gave me papers to exempt me from going into the war. I had them in my pocket when the war ended. I often thought it over, and have never regretted leaving the Western and Atlantic Railroad when I did. I think I did best, notwithstanding my hardships in Tennessee, and the round-about way I had to get out of the State. If I had remained on the Western and Atlantic Railroad, I would no doubt have had to have gone into the Governor's Guards, which was made up out of Western and Atlantic Railroad men, excepting a few who wanted to keep out of a battle, and they were called Joe Brown's pets.[2]

The first alligator I ever saw was by the side of the track on the South Carolina Railroad; it had been killed by a train. In that same section I saw my first cypress swamps, and rice plantations.

Some of the bridges and trestles were very shackly that we ran over, between Augusta and Wilmington. I have noticed trestles in passing over them, and while the weight of the engine and train was on them the bents would go down with the mudsills out of sight in the mud, and as the train passed off, rise up again. I did not like it at first, but soon got used to it.

While we were in Augusta, I received a letter from Parson Caldwell, the Presbyterian minister who had me to take his hogsheads of bacon and potatoes away from Cleveland. He wrote to learn what had become of them. I showed the letter to Maj. C. Wallace, and the major told me to write to Mr. Caldwell and tell him to send the bill to him, and he would pay for them, and tell him that he (the major) had taken them out to Augusta and his men had used them, so I am sure that the parson received pay for his bacon and potatoes.

I was taken sick one Sunday night, after Hiram Hambright and I had eaten a very large watermelon that evening. The next morning I was so sick that I boarded the first train that went out towards Atlanta. I got off at Social Circle, as that was as far as the Georgia Road was running their trains. It was twenty-five miles to where my family lived from that place. The sun lacked about one hour of being down, when I left the train. I knew of a citizen's residence about a mile from town. I started on foot to make that place for a night's lodging. I had not gone far until I was taken so sick that I had to lie down in the corner of the fence. I lay there until after the sun went down, then got up and finally got to the place I had started for. It was a very nice place, and a wealthy man lived there; he took me in, gave me a nice room, and a good bed. Next morning I took a cup of tea. I then went out to the horse lot where the gentleman was that owned the place. He had a lot almost full of horses and mules. I tried my best to get him to send me home, and offered him any price that he would charge. I told him that I was not able to walk. He said that he was afraid a raid would get the horses that he sent with me, so he would not let them go away from home. I paid him for my lodging and tea, bade him good morning, and started on foot. I had not gone far when a negro man with a two-horse wagon overtook me. I paid him to let me ride in his wagon as far as he went my way. I thought it awful rough, and would have preferred walking had I been able to have done so. He took me in about eight miles of home, and there I found an acquaintance and friend, who took me home in his buggy. I sent for a doctor, he came, and said I had fever and ague. I had once before had chills and fever, but that was not to be compared with fever and ague. The doctor fixed me up some medicine out of whisky and willow twigs, as there was no quinine to be had in that section. It was about six weeks before I got well enough to return to Augusta. Some time afterwards I learned that the man I spoke of refusing to send me home when I was sick, lost all his horses and mules by Stoneman's raid, and that the man himself was killed about the time the war closed.[3]

I had long hoped and prayed, or at least tried to pray, for the war to end. At first my sympathies and prayers were for the success of the Southern States and the Confederate army. But toward the last I prayed for the close of the war any way—just so as to stop it, and that we might have peace once more in our country.

A part of the country that we ran through was entirely out of sight of mountains. Along between Augusta and Wilmington was sandy, piney woods, cypress swamps, small lakes, rice plantations, and bull frogs innumerable, which kept up such a noise at night that I could sleep but little until I got more used to them. Snakes were so plentiful through the swamps in warm weather that I was afraid to step off my train along the roadside. I have actually seen two or three at a time, and heard more crawling through the grass; and as the old man who told the snake story said, it was not much of a day for snakes either.

I saw one belt of pine woods where the ground was covered with sand as white as snow, and the first time I saw it I thought it was sure enough snow. Toward Wilmington there was a great deal of piney woods, and here were many turpentine stills. There were nice lakes along the roadside in North Carolina. I could not see how any one could make a living in that section of country, for it was very poor land, and thinly settled—in fact, a desolate-looking country.

Up near Charlotte looked more like living; it reminded me of North Georgia and East Tennessee. I was making a trip to Charlotte, and had to lie over a day at Columbia, S.C. Of course I managed to see all that could be seen in a day at that place, as it was the capital of my old State. I saw Wade Hampton Park, and I am sure it was worth looking at. I remember, while walking through the park, saying that if I was a bird I would spend the rest of my days there. I went to the capitol; they had a new building commenced, but on account of the war the work had been stopped. I saw the palmetto tree,[4] and read the names of some of my boyhood friends who had been killed in the Mexican War.

I avoided a bad wreck on the road one morning, after lying all night on a side-track, as we were not allowed to run after dark. The freight conductor, who had charge of the train, set the switch to the side-track (they called them gates, though, on that road); and after he did so he motioned the engineer ahead, and before I could get to the engine the engineer had started. I stopped him and ran to the switch and asked the pilot what it meant. He said that he wanted to go. I said that there was a passenger train due there in ten minutes, and he said that it had already passed. I replied that it had not; that it was an extra that had passed by, and the regular train was not due when that train passed us. I had not more than got him to set the switch to the main track before here came the regular passenger-train at as fast a rate of speed as they ran in those days.

I was laid out one night between stations, and, as I have mentioned several times before, we were not allowed to run at night, and also not allowed to run without a headlight. As the headlight of the engine was out of order and would not burn, I had one of my men to ride on the front of the engine with a hand lamp until we reached the next side-track.

We had orders to haul no passengers, but it was almost impossible to keep them off at times, as trains were so irregular, and often so crowded that all the passengers could not get on them. When I carried any passengers I always turned over my tickets and cash that I collected to some of the officers of the road that I was running over, reporting the facts, and it was all right.

Sometimes when I was lying over at Wilmington I would fish in the Cape Fear river. I fished with two hooks, and as long as the tide was rising I could catch little blue catfish as fast as a boy could take them off and bait my hooks. I would like now to take a trip through the same section of the country and visit my childhood's home.

When I was running on the South Carolina road it did not make any difference how many sections of trains there were on one schedule, there were no signals carried on engines to give notice of a train following; but the conductor of the front train would hold up as many fingers as there were trains following him on the same schedule. When he met a train going in the opposite direction; for instance, there were five trains on one schedule, the front conductor would hold up four fingers; the second conductor would hold up three fingers; the third conductor would hold up two fingers, and the fourth conductor would hold up one finger. So we had to look out for fingers when meeting trains. All such rules were new to me, but I soon became familiar with them after I commenced running over these roads.

On one trip, while I was lying over at Wilmington, I met up with an engineer who used to pull me on the Western and Atlantic Railroad. At the time of our meeting at Wilmington he was second or third engineer on a vessel that was running to Nassau. He gave me a bottle of fine French brandy that he brought from Nassau. I was so proud of it that I never opened it, thinking that I would take it with me when I went home. I hid it in my car when I arrived in Augusta. One day when I was out some of the railroad boys found my bottle and drank nearly all of my brandy for a joke on me. They were good friends of mine. When I found out what they had done I told them to go and drink what was left; that I did not want it, as I had intended to keep it and take it home with me. They were very sorry, and wanted to get me another bottle, but I would not let them do so, as it could not have come like the one my friend gave me. I did not get to taste my fine brandy after all.

There were one or two engineers who were employed by the East Tennessee and Georgia Railroad Company who left their engines standing in the yard at Wilmington and went on some of the vessels that were running the blockade between Wilmington and Nassau, and other engineers had to be sent from Augusta to take charge of the engines that were thus left standing in the yard.

Chapter Six

After General Lee Surrendered
1865–1868

After General Sherman and his army passed through Middle Georgia, and about the time that General Lee surrendered,[1] I left Augusta going by rail to Greensboro, Ga., which place was as far as trains were run in the direction of my home at that time. At or near that place I bought a little mule to ride home on, and gave ten hundred dollars in Confederate money for it. Confederate money was all the kind I had, and I had a good deal of it on hand, and still have some of it. I suppose I was like the negroes were in that section. They liked it better than any money, because they could own a larger roll of it than of any other kind. When I tried to exchange what I had on hand for something else I found that it was too late to do so.

Well, I bought me an old saddle, mounted my old mule, and started for home. The second day's traveling brought me to that section of country through which Sherman and his army had passed. This was the most desolate, distressed, and devastated country that I ever passed through. Gin-houses and cotton burned, corn-cribs and corn burned, and fences destroyed. Geese and chicken feathers scattered all along the roadside.

I cannot now express my feelings at that time. I was glad that the war was over, and gladder still to find my family alive and well. But when I found how things had been taken away, some that were keepsakes, and others that I had worked hard for, I fell down on a bed and cried bitterly. Yet my loss was nothing to compare with what many others had endured, for they had more than I had. They would have taken more from me had it not been for circumstances being against them.

When Sherman passed through that section, a party of soldiers, piloted by a negro man, came to my house. The first thing they did was to shoot a fine guard dog I had, that would guard my little children while at play, and a horse, cow, hog, or anything of the kind was not allowed to go near them. The shooting of the dog scared my family nearly to death. After shooting the dog those men made our servant, a negro woman, get them everything to eat she could get her hands on. They also tried to make her tell them in what direction my father-in-law went with his horses. They loaded a wagon with the beds and bed-clothes, and yoked up a yoke of oxen that were in a field near by, but, as it happened, yoked them the wrong way, and they would not work, so this saved the bedding. They then loaded a buggy that was near by with other things, then harnessed an old mule, and the mule would not work in single harness; this saved part of the buggy load.

They searched the house up and down stairs, searched trunks, took all the jewelry they could find, all the men's wearing apparel and two fine guns. They took a box of tobacco that I had bought in Augusta, thinking that it was better than Confederate money. They would have taken more had not some officers come and driven them away. Afterwards a horn was found in a belt of woods through which they had passed. I had gotten a merchant to buy it for me in Charleston, S. C., years before, when he went there to purchase goods, at a time when I kept a pack of fine hound dogs. When the horn was found the mouth-piece and bands, which were of silver, had been taken off.

These circumstances which I have just related are to show the reader the principle of some men in times of war. In those days I heard some men remark that it was war times, and they had as soon swear a lie as the truth; while I believed a man was held equally responsible for his mean deeds and actions in war as at any other time.

There was a large reward offered by the United States government for the capture of the ex-President of the Confederacy, and there were quite a number of Federal soldiers all through Middle Georgia looking for him. Some of them came to my house one day while I was away from home. One of them alighted, walked in the house, and took down a little shotgun which I gave one hundred dollars for in Augusta. He took off the caps and laid the gun back in the rack, saying that he was looking for Jeff Davis, then went up stairs and made a search for him, but did not find him, for Jefferson Davis did not call on me. If he had done so, I should have taken the best care of him that I possibly could.

The East Tennessee and Georgia rolling-stock that was run out of Tennessee to Augusta was moved back to Social Circle, a station on the Georgia Railroad. Times became more quiet and settled, and I moved to the Circle, loaded my plunder, or what I had left, into an East Tennessee and Georgia box car, and took an engine and coupled it to a train of cars, put my family into a caboose, gave my engineer a go-ahead signal, and he pulled out for Dalton, as I thought, but when I arrived in Atlanta my engine and train were taken away from me and I had to pay my way to Dalton.

The government had charge of railroads east of Atlanta. I could have gone to work for the government when I returned to Dalton, but did not care to do so, as I had learned that all the roads would be turned over to their respective companies soon—and so they were.

I went to work for the Western and Atlantic Railroad again, and ran on it nearly three years, a part of the time on freight-trains and a part on mixed-trains and accommodation-trains. It was not long after I went to work until Major Campbell Wallace, my old friend, was appointed superintendent of the Western and Atlantic Railroad. I was very glad to get back on this old reliable road, on which I did my first railroad work. I was also glad to meet some of my best old friends again.

When Atlanta was first built up it improved more rapidly than any city I know of; and when I went to running on the Western and Atlantic Railroad it was the most ruined and desolate-looking city I ever saw. But soon after Lee's surrender the citizens that had refugeed returned, and some families lived in tents until houses could be built—and that was not long, for Atlanta was built up again more rapidly than it was the first time. After an absence of seven years from Atlanta I returned on a visit, which was a short time since, and I was surprised to see the city had improved so much since I used to run into it. I could not make out the most familiar streets and places of many years ago. To-day Atlanta is the Gate City of the South.

This company had purchased some of the government rolling-stock when the road was turned over to them, and now it was better supplied with engines and cabooses than it had been before. The engines were numbered, which is now customary, instead of being named, as they had been. I ran a through freight-train twenty-two months, and had one of the engines which was purchased from the government to pull me, and also used a caboose which was purchased at the same time. An engineer who was a lieutenant in a cavalry company in the Federal army for four years ran the engine. He was a good engineer and a nice man. He told me that he kept lots of citizens' property from being destroyed, or taken away from them, while the army was in the State of Tennessee.

We ran the schedule on time all of the twenty-two months, except twice. Once a pair of trucks of a car jumped the rail and delayed us thirty minutes. Another time a spring hanger of the engine broke, and we went into Atlanta thirty minutes late. We ran one hundred and forty miles one day, and the same distance on the day following, and then lay over two nights and one day. Quite a difference in the way men run then and nowadays.

Bridges had been burned and temporary trestles put up by the Federal army. The bents of those trestles were pine poles, and some of them two bents high, one put on top of another. There were trestles of this kind across the Oostanaula, Etowah, and Chattahoochee rivers. The one across the latter named river became very shaky, and my engineer would send the fireman across the river to catch his engine. Then he would give the engine steam enough to carry herself and train across. The fireman got on her after she had crossed the river. The engineer would then walk over the trestle, and sometimes I would walk across with him.

We were caught in Chattanooga in time of the flood of 1867. This was said to be the highest tide of the Tennessee river ever known by the citizens in that vicinity. We had to leave our boarding-house, which stood at that time in a flat between where the Central Depot now stands and where Shelton's new mill stands at the present time. The Central Depot was built a long while after the event which I am relating transpired, and Shelton's mill has recently been erected.

When we went to dinner at the boarding-house I was speaking of one day, the water was running under the gate into the yard. When we saw this, we decided to hunt a boarding-house on higher ground to board at. We tried to get another engineer, who was boarding there, to go with us, but he laughed and made fun of us. We found a house to board at on a hill, which has since been cut down and a custom-house built on it. The following day the family where we formerly boarded had to move out at a second story window and be carried to land in a boat. The engineer who made fun of us was sleeping on the first floor, and would no doubt have been drowned had he not turned over in bed and one hand struck water and woke him. So he had to get out of bed into water, take his wet clothes off a chair and get up-stairs at once. Such a getting up-stairs I never saw the like as there was in Chattanooga at that time. We had to lay in Chattanooga until the high tide went down. My caboose was standing in the Western and Atlantic yard, near the Union Depot and the water was above the middle of the windows. A steamboat was run up Market street and to the back of the Crutchfield House, which was afterwards burned.[2] The water was near up to the track when we crossed over the bridge across Chickamauga creek, near the rock bridge on the East Tennessee, Virginia and Georgia Railroad, as we were going into Chattanooga. I wired the superintendent of the facts, and that I had no idea that we could get out of Chattanooga the next morning.

My engineer and I were standing on the bridge one day. This bridge had been built by the Federal army across the Tennessee river at the foot of Market street. We were near the middle of the bridge watching how rapidly the river was rising, and the rafts, and now and then a small house, and hay and fodder-stacks coming down. We had just started off the bridge when we heard it crack. We ran off the bridge and walked up Market street a piece and stopped, and looking back, saw the bridge break, leave its piers, and go off with the current of the river rapidly.

On the Western and Atlantic Railroad, near the National cemetery, the water was over the top of the telegraph poles. One set of section houses just below there was washed away, and the track all torn up. In fact, the water was all over the earth from Mission Ridge to Lookout Mountain, with the exception of the knobs and highest points.

The run that I was on at that time caused me to lay over in Chattanooga on Sundays. In those days this place could not be compared favorably with what it is at the present day. Market street was a sight to look at in winter time or rainy weather. Some families lived in houses which were built in time of war, and some merchants sold groceries in the same kind of houses.

There were some other engines run which were of the same class of engines that my engineer ran, and the men who ran them, when they were on the same schedule that we ran, would try to outrun my engineer. Sometimes there would be three or four sections on one schedule. We were always first section, and they would follow close up, so as to make him run faster. One day they were pushing him close. The track was pretty rough in some places. We were going over a piece of track of that kind when I looked out and saw the cars in my train leaning first on one side and then on the other. I looked back and saw the next section just behind me. Both trains were making faster time than the schedule allowed. I realized that if my train ran off I could never get a flagman back in time to prevent an accident. So I pulled the bell-cord on my engineer and waved the following man down. They both slacked speed and went on all right.

My engineer did not like this, and when we arrived in Atlanta he left me, after we had put our train away and never bade me the time of day, a thing which he had never done since we had been on the run together. When we met again to take our run out, he spoke to me and said that he at first thought that I did wrong in pulling the bell-cord on him, but after thinking the matter over he saw where I was right. I replied that I did not do this because I thought he did not know his business, but to prevent an accident, and that I could foresee that if it was not stopped soon it would end in a combination wreck of three of four trains. So this broke this kind of running up.

It was but a few days afterwards until the same men, with the same engines, commenced trying to pull more cars than my engineer pulled. Those engines were all rated the same—twenty loaded cars each—that is, of that class of engines, on the same schedule. So one would pull twenty-two cars, another one twenty-three or twenty-four, and my engineer would take on twenty-five and twenty-six. This was kept up until some one went into Atlanta with thirty loaded cars. I said to my engineer one day, "Well, Dan, lets break this thing up, and stop trying to see who can pull the most cars." "How will you do it?" he asked me. "How many can you pull with your engine, and make the schedule time, and not blow her up?" I replied. He said thirty-five loaded cars. As we passed Dalton, I told the yardmaster to keep all the loaded cars he could for me, as I returned the next day. I made the yardmaster at Chattanooga give me all he had. When we left Dalton we had thirty-three loaded cars and my caboose. I put my brakeman on top of the train to look out for the brakes and I looked out for my caboose, braking for myself. We arrived in Atlanta on time. The office windows were full of officers and clerks, as it was the longest freight-train that ever came into Atlanta over that road up to that time.

After we got our cars put away, the superintendent came out and said to my engineer and myself that we had beat them all, and that he would now put a stop to this kind of running. He said that the engines were rated at twenty loaded cars, and that was all they should pull. I knew it would settle that question from the fact that freight was falling off, and that if nothing else did stop it that would, for another such a train could not have been picked up in a day again at that time.

I was running a local freight-train one day, and at Cartersville, a station, I opened a car that I had not been in since it left Atlanta. As soon as the doors were pulled open a big, old billy goat ran out bleating, and would have run over me had I not given him the space I occupied. He ran and jumped off the depot platform and went out of sight through town as fast as he could run and kept up his bleating. I looked over my waybill to see if I had one for him, but did not find any, so I supposed that the crew on the transfer platform in Atlanta had shut him up in the car to get rid of him.

I was once suspended, and my engineer also, for a run we made. It was for a violation of a rule, yet this rule was violated nearly every day by some one or another, and, as often occurs among railroad men, it became a habit, and almost a rule among the men until something happens. We left a station to meet a passenger-train, when we only lacked three minutes of having the required time, yet we had plenty of time to make the meeting point and have all the time that was required by the rules of the road. We both knew that we had violated a rule, but as it was a common thing among the men, and with a good deal shorter time to make such runs in, we thought nothing of it. But as it was me and my first time to do so, some smart somebody that wanted to be of some note, as there is always plenty of such a class of men, reported it. After I arrived in Atlanta and completed my work, I learned that myself and engineer were suspended for the lack of three minutes in making the run we had made. I never was so much surprised. There was no harm done nor anyways near any. I went to the superintendent's office and told him what I had learned, as I could not believe it was true, but he said that it was so, and commenced telling me what the rule was, when I informed him that I was perfectly familiar with the rules of the road, and yet I did not think my suspension right. He said the reason he did it was because we were both old men on the road, and favorites of his, and he suspended us for a lesson to the younger men, before any accident occurred on that account. I said to him that I did not wish to be made an example of for the benefit of other men, and was very sorry that I was anybody's favorite. Not very long after I had served out my suspension and returned to work, the same thing occurred again. I just lacked three minutes of having the required time to meet a passenger-train at the next station ahead. My engineer wanted to make it, I would not let him, and side-tracked my train. We stayed there nearly all day, the passenger-train was late, and as we did not make the regular meeting point with it, we could not run until it passed us. Late in the evening near sunset, the passenger-train passed us and we started. My engineer got to a rate of speed much faster than the rules allowed us to run, I slacked him up to rule speed. He said that we were holding trains in the opposite direction. I told him I was not responsible for that, and that I had learned, by being suspended, to run in accordance with the rules of the road. When we met some of the trains going in the opposite direction to us, some of the conductors said they would report me for not making the meeting point for the passenger-train and laying them out, and so they did. I was informed of the fact by some of the men, but the superintendent never said a word to me about it, until I met him one day and said to him that I had been informed that I was reported for laying out some freight-trains, and he said yes, and he asked me how it was, and I told him the facts in the case, and he said that I was right in so doing.

An engine struck an Irishman one day and knocked him off the track, and it hurt him pretty badly. He was a section foreman on the road.

One of the railroad men asked him what engine struck him, and he said it was the 190, and if it had been the 200 it would have killed him.

Well, I was just beginning to get fixed up something like living again when politics came down and settled all over the State of Georgia, and was hot all along the line of the Western and Atlantic Railroad, as it was owned by the State, and so politics had a great deal to do with operating it. Rufus B. Bullock and John B. Gordon were the candidates for Governor of the State of Georgia, in opposition to each other. In those days it was Radical and Democrat—Bullock on the Radical ticket and Gordon on the Democratic ticket.[3] As I never had taken much interest in politics, I decided to take none at all at that time, as I knew how and what my position was hanging on, and what I was depending on for a living for myself and family.

One night the old ex-Governor of Georgia, who had been a Democrat theretofore, boarded my train after having made a speech that day in favor of Bullock. He took a seat by my side and said to me: "Don't go making a fight in the coming election, and you can have a good place on the road as long as you want it." I said to him: "You know, Governor, that I never took any hand in politics," and he said that he knew that, but thought it the best policy to take the step that he had taken, So by the time the election came off I had decided not to vote at all. There were three days set in which to hold the election, and as it happened, on the third and last day of the election I met my superintendent at the station where I would have to vote, in case I voted at all, and he asked me if I had voted. I answered that I had not, and he then said: "Take your crew and go and vote at once" I did as he told me, but never said a word to my men about how to vote, or how I would vote. But of course I could not go back on my good old friend who had kept me out of the army; and, again, he would be my superintendent still if Gordon should be elected. Not being acquainted with either of the candidates, only by reputation, John B. Gordon was my choice, and I decided to keep my principle if I lost my job. So Bullock was said to be elected and I lost my job.

I ran on for some time, and I felt like if I could keep on at work that I by and by would be able to make a living outside of railroading. But the hinges I was hanging on were very weak, and growing weaker every day. Before it was decided who was elected the superintendent was on my train and said to me if Gordon was elected I should have a better place, and that he ought to have given me one long ago, had he not been deceived by some other men whom he had given places to.

Mr. Bullock took his seat as Governor of Georgia, and ere long my hinges gave way and I fell a hard fall. I went into Atlanta one morning and had just got off my caboose in the yard when I met the yardmaster and a man about half drunk, to whom the yardmaster said I would turn over my equipments, and I did so, and went to the office to make out my report for the trip I had just completed. The platform and hall were so crowded with both white and black, looking after the places that had been promised them, that I had to go through a window to get in the conductors' room to make out my report. Some time before this the master of transportation sent for me and I went to his office, and it was then so crowded with men that I could not get in, and he raised up out of his seat, looked at me, and put his finger on the end of his tongue. I understood what it meant, and that was to keep my tongue still and say nothing. So I did, but to no effect. I was told by him afterwards that they wanted to keep me, but on account of so many being promised places they had to make places for them.

Well, I was out of work, and did not know where or which way to go to get anything to do. Every railroad was full of men and not doing much business. I was not able, financially, to go into any kind of business, and if I had been my education was limited, and that was another drawback on me. To sit down and do nothing was not my disposition and was against my profession also.

I went to Selma Ala., to see Mr. Stanton, the superintendent of the Selma, Rome and Dalton Railroad.[4] He replied that he would love to give me work, but had no vacancy. And said that it seemed none of his conductors would ever quit or die, but if any vacancy should occur, that he would send for me. So I returned home with a sad heart and no prospect of work anywhere that I knew of.

I met Major Wallace one day, and he said to me, "I wrote Maj. Jackson, at Knoxville, requesting him to put you to work, and this is his answer." At the same time handing me a letter which Maj. Jackson had written him in reply. Maj. Jackson was at that time superintendent of the East Tennessee and Georgia Railroad. He said in his letter: "I do not know of a man that I had rather employ than him, but if I should give him work they would cut my head off." I did not know until then that Maj. C. Wallace had ever asked for employment for me there. I would have loved to have gone to work again on that road, but understanding the sentiments of a great many men in that section, I knew that it was not worth my while to ask for or try to get work. I never gave it up, but kept on trying, as hard as times were, until I did get work.

I will now state some incidents which occurred while I was on the Western and Atlantic Railroad. I had moved to Acworth from Dalton in order to get home on my lay-over days in Atlanta. I had bought me a home at Acworth, a nice little town on the Western and Atlantic

Railroad, thirty-five miles out from Atlanta. The local freight-train schedule had changed, and Acworth was made a layover place for them of nights in both directions. So I was taken off of the through freight run, which I had been on for twenty-two months, and put on the local freight run. I was afterwards told by the superintendent that he changed the schedule and gave the run to me so I could be at home more. Well, this was as good a run as I wanted, as I could leave Atlanta in the afternoon and make the run to Acworth, stay at home all night, the next day go on to Chattanooga, and the day after go back to Acworth, staying at home all night, and go on to Atlanta in the forenoon and lay over in Atlanta until afternoon, which time I would spend at home. This schedule put me at home every Saturday night and till Monday morning in either direction I was going, and I received pay from the road for my board and lodgings, but those days have passed and gone many years ago.

While I was on this run my father was near Dalton sick. I went up one Saturday night to see him, returning on Sunday night. I told the conductor and brakeman both to wake me if I went to sleep, for I felt sleepy; they said that they would do so. I went to sleep, and when I awoke I walked out on the platform of the coach to see if I was getting near home, and I saw that I was nine miles past home. I hunted up the conductor and asked him to let me off at once, as there was no train that I could get back on before my leaving time, but he kept on trying to think that there was, until he carried me three miles further on, then stopped and let me off right opposite a belt of woods where there had been a fight when Joe Johnston was falling back in front of Sherman, and the very spot where General Polk was killed.[5] At one o'clock in the night, there I was, in as lonely a place as I ever was in in my life, and twelve miles between me and my train, and no way to get to it except to walk. As it happened it was a moonlight night. After the noise of the train was out of hearing, all I could hear was the hoot of the owls on both sides of me, just to make matters worse.

I suppose that both conductor and brakeman had been as sound asleep as I had been, when we passed Acworth. Well, I went down the grades at full speed, so as to get a good start up them. The ground was frozen, and, to make it worse in places, the print of horses feet were in the middle of the track, where some one had been riding along the road when the ground was wet. I thought of going to get the section men to take me on a dump-car. I also thought of getting a horse from some farmer along the road, but on account of the section houses being so far away from the road, and the thought of being disappointed in either undertaking, I gave up the idea. I would look at my watch and move on at the best rate of speed that I could make. At last I arrived at Acworth, and went to my house to let my family know that they need not be uneasy about me, and got back to my train just time enough to leave on time. My crew would laugh at me every time I would get on my caboose, all the way to Chattanooga.

As I have already stated, I was doing very well on the Western and Atlantic Railroad before the election, and was getting over the effects of the war; but when I voted myself out of employment, times were so hard and money scarce, and I was out of employment so long that I had to sell my nice little home at Acworth, Ga., for a great deal less than it cost.

Chapter Seven

Alabama and Chattanooga Railroad
1868–1871

I learned from a friend of mine, that a man by the name of Stanton from Boston, Mass., was in Chattanooga, and was extending a road which was built before the war, from Wauhatchie, a station on the Nashville, Chattanooga and St. Louis Railroad, six miles out from Chattanooga. The terminus of the little road was Trenton, Ga., a small town eighteen miles from Chattanooga. J. C. Stanton was to build an extension of this road on to Meridian, Miss., a distance of three hundred and five miles from Chattanooga. The Nashville, Chattanooga and St. Louis track was used by the Alabama and Chattanooga Railroad between Chattanooga and Wauhatchie. This little road was first called the Wills Valley Railroad, and Stanton changed its name to the Alabama and Chattanooga. There was a great deal of old grading in different places along the line, which had been done before the war. There was twenty-four miles of track laid between Meridian and York Station, and one mile of track out of Meridian, belonging to the Mobile and Ohio Railroad, making twenty-five miles from Meridian to York Station.

I went to Chattanooga to see Mr. Stanton. I did not expect to get a train, as I had learned there was but one short train out of Chattanooga of mornings to do the construction work, which went back in the evenings.

I met J. C. Stanton for the first time, and was introduced to him. He appeared glad to meet me, saying that he had heard of me, and how I had been thrown out of work. He also invited me to go out to the track with him, and on to the construction work, where the grading and track laying was going on. I took dinner in a tent with him, and returned to

Chattanooga in the evening. Mr. Stanton told me to call on him the next morning, and he would see what he could do for me. He said that he had no trains, but as soon as he got his road to Attalla, Ala., he would put some one on and give me one.[1]

I called the next morning to see him, and he said that if I would go down to York Station, Ala., he could give me work.[2] I asked him what kind of work, and he replied, working a gang of men on the grading of the road. I told him that I had never done such work, and knew nothing about grading a road, and he said that made no difference. I then asked him what it would pay me, and he replied that he did not know exactly, but about three dollars a day, he supposed. He also said that he would give me a train as soon as he put one on. I accepted his offer, and started at once for York, as I was sure this was the best I could do at that time, and it was better than no job. Mr. Stanton had told me that Major Anderson, a civil engineer, whom I knew very well, was down there, and told me to report to him. This, of course, cheered me up, to find that I would not be entirely among strangers.

I arrived at York one night about dark, alighted from the train, and reported at once to Major Anderson's office and he was surprised to see me up so early. He said it would be an hour or two before he would be ready. I told him that I was anxious to get to work, as I had been idle for some time.

The sun was away up, it being the middle of the forenoon when we started up the line with about fifteen or twenty negro men. We went up the line about five miles from York, through woods and swamps, a part of the way. At last we came to a pile of pine logs, hauled there for the purpose of building cabins for the grade hands. We set the hands to work, and by the time the sun went down we had a large double cabin up, also a small cabin for myself to occupy of nights. It was built some distance from the double cabins. When the walls were up I left for York Station, on foot, and arrived there some time after dark. It was Saturday night, and I was glad the next day was Sunday, as I was very tired, the work being new to me.

Monday morning following, I was on hand with my men, much earlier than the first morning, and soon covered and finished up the cabins. On the next day the hands moved into them. With about thirty or forty negro men I did my first grading. Building of those shanties was the first work I did for J. C. Stanton and his Alabama and Chattanooga Railroad. The shanties were called my shanties until they rotted down.

My gang was increased from seventy to one hundred men. My wages was one hundred dollars per month, and board, such as it was. I slept in my little cabin every night by myself. I worked my men from daylight till sundown, and fed them well with bacon, peas, beans, potatoes, bread, and coffee. Any of these men would have fought for me at any time. I was working the company's hands, they were having a part of the grading done themselves, and I had charge of the grading which the company was having done. I learned to set the grade pegs from one of my negroes, but I never let him know it. I soon learned to grade. A man from East Tennessee had the contract of laying the track, and he said where I graded was the best grading he ever laid track over.

When I would get ahead with my grading. I would take my gang and drop back and help lay track. When I moved from my cabins, I had tents for my negroes, and planks to build my cabins out of. When going through a farm with my work I always had the fences kept up and this pleased the citizens along the line.

Springtime came, and the weather began to get hot in that section of the country. May stepped out, and June came in as usual, and I was still on the grade. One day J. C. Stanton and party from Boston came to my work. They complimented me on my work, and the progress I was making. J. C. Stanton said to me: "Well, Captain, you are building a railroad to run on." I answered that I did not know, but hoped so. Well, the June sun poured its hot rays upon me and my work. I was working in a cut between Livingston and Epps's Station, Sumter county, Alabama; this cut was full of white rotten limestone rock; the sun's rays upon this came very near putting my eyes out, while I was watching the men work, and my eyes have never entirely recovered from the effects of this to the present day.[3]

There was a cut about one hundred feet deep, between where my work was and Epps, which was cut out before the war. I was told that a man by the name of Mr. Brown, who owned the land where the cut was, and all around it, had the work done with his own slaves. It was said that he worked a hundred Negro men while doing the work on this cut. It was called Brown's cut. When the track was laid through it and trains put on, there were a great many landslides in rainy weather in this cut, which caused much trouble. After the rails were laid to Livingston, a nice little passenger-train was put on between Meridian and Livingston, and I was given this run. I was truly glad that this happened before I got to Brown's cut with my grading gang.[4]

I was taken sick and had to stop off at York one day and take a room at a hotel. I was confined to my bed over two weeks, and no one to wait upon me, until the superintendent sent me a boy out of my old gang of grade hands. This boy remained with me until I got well enough to take my run. He gave me my medicine, according to the directions which the doctor had given, day and night, as good as any one could have done. I had exposed myself a great deal while I was on the grade of the road. I had gone through cold and heat, and at times waded creeks when the water would come up to my arms, as there was no other way to cross these creeks at that time, and at the places where I had to cross them.

Mr. Stanton would come down where I was occasionally, and at one time, while in Meridian, told me that he had put one passenger-train on between Chattanooga and Attalla, and as soon as he could was going to put on another and would give it to me as this would be nearer my family, and that he knew I had rather be on the Chattanooga end. I told him that I would be glad if he would do so. The only objection I had to the run I was on was being so far away from my family. My wages were still one hundred dollars per month, and the distance between Meridian and Livingston was only forty-six miles. I would leave Livingston in the morning and return in the evening of the same day. My reports were simple, and I could make out one in a few minutes. I had every night to rest and sleep. I also had a nice place to stay and a nice room.

I received a telegram one day that there would be a conductor sent to relieve me, and for me to teach him the road and then report to headquarters in Chattanooga, and I would be given a passenger-train on that end of the road. I was glad to learn such news, whether the telegram was signed by Mr. Stanton or the superintendent, I disremember. As soon as I did as I was requested to do, I reported in Chattanooga at headquarters, and went to Mr. Stanton's office. He apparently was glad to see me, but said that I did not come as soon as they had expected I would, and the superintendent had just given the train to Charley, a young man who had just come down from the East. I replied that I had made no delay, had only done as I was wired to do. Mr. Stanton said: "Well, I hate to take him off the run now, as Mack (The superintendent) has just put him on. I will give you a gang of men of the grade below Attalla. We are doing the grading ourselves. I want you there anyway, and you shall have the next passenger-train." He also said he was going to put another one on as soon as he could get the track connected. I asked him what my wages would be. He answered, seventy-five dollars per month, the same as he was paying conductors. So I had to go back to the grade again, and then I was sorry that I gave up the run I had left, but it was too late then for regrets to do any good.

I commenced grading again on the lowlands of Big Wills creek. I was given a gang of about twenty-five negro men, and had to work another winter through a flat and partly swampy country that was called the "flat woods." I had to sleep in a tent at night. One day the walking boss, as he is called, passed by where I was at work and asked: "Where are all your men?" I answered that I had driven them off. I had only about ten men at that time at work. He said that I ought not to have done that, for they owed their transportation to the company. I replied that the company would save money by giving all such men as they were transportation back to where they came from. He then said that he would send me some more men. I was afterwards sent about twenty-five men, making me a gang of about thirty-five men in all. Most of these men were from Virginia, and proved good men. So I had a good gang while working through the "flat woods."

I commenced having chills, and sent for the company's physician. He gave me a dose of quinine and told me to get a half gallon of home-stilled corn whiskey, and where I could get it. He gave me the amount of quinine to put in it. I sent for the whiskey and put the quinine in it, which would not have been a very unpleasant medicine to have taken had the quinine been left out. But I took it with the quinine in it, and was soon back on the work again. I have never had another chill to the present day.

We were working through the bottom lands of Big Canoe creek, when one day an elderly looking man came to where my men were at work as he owned the land that we were grading through at the time. He commenced talking to me about the road, and said he was not in favor of railroads, and was going to sell out and leave the country, and if he could not sell out that he would give his land away before he would live that close to a railroad. I tried to explain to him the advantage of railroads, and how much more valuable his land would be to him, but never made him believe it. Another thing which happened while we were working near Little Canoe creek was a quarrel between two of my men, which stopped all my men, as well as others from work. I ordered them to stop the fuss, but one of them kept on talking, and struck the other with his fist. I picked up a shovel and aimed to hit him, flat with it, but when I made the lick the shovel turned edgewise and knocked him down, and all of the negroes that saw it swore that they smelt blood and would kill me. We were making a fill with wheelbarrows. I walked back upon the fill, and prepared myself, with knife in one hand and pistol in the other, thinking that if they did try to kill me, that I would kill as many of them as I could before they did kill me. If it had not been for a large black man, who was the leader of my gang, no doubt they would have killed me, as all of the white men near by were scared almost to death. But the leader of my gang jumped up in front of me, and told them all that he would kill the first man that attempted to hurt me. They all then went to work, and the one which I had struck with the shovel had come to life again, and went to work about the same time that the others did.

I was truly glad he was not dead, for I did not aim to hurt him so badly. I did not want to be killed myself. Up to the present time of my life I never was mad enough to want to kill any one, and hope I never shall be. On the night of the same day on which the circumstances just related occurred, about eleven o'clock, I awoke and heard a noise like a man walking slowly and lightly on the dry leaves that made the carpet of the earth floor of my tent. I raised me head a little to listen, and try to find out what the noise was, and I saw the form of a big negro man stoop down right at the foot of my bedstead, which was made out of forked sticks driven in the ground, and little poles made the railings, and planks laid lengthwise made the slats and springs. My head and feet made the head and footboard. I thought when I saw the negro stoop down, that he intended to crawl under my bed and get to the head, but he must have discovered that I was awake, for before I could get my pistol in my hand, he was going through the tentcloth, out of my sight. I fired off one chamber of my pistol in the direction that he went out of the tent. The last that I heard of him was the sound of his feet, as though they were making all the speed they possibly could. A friend of mine, who had charge of another gang of men, was sleeping with me, and when I shot off my pistol it awoke him, and he jumped out of bed and halloed to know what the matter was. I told him what had happened. He then ran out of the tent and fired off his pistol in the direction I told him the negro went. I never knew whether the negro was trying to rob or kill me. We had drawn a month's pay that day.

I started my men out to work one morning, as I was in the habit of doing, for they loved to loaf around camps, but when I got to the work I found I had only six or eight men. I walked back to camps and found the others there; I started them back to the work, all but one, and he said that he would not go. I told him to leave the camp then, for he should not loaf around the camps. I carried a hickory stick with me all the time. I drew it back to strike him, and he said that I had better not strike him, but I did so as hard as I could. He got the stick away from me, and I drew my pistol out of my pocket. Seeing this he dropped my stick and ran through the woods. He was a big, stout yellow man. When I got back to the work he was there at work with the rest of my men.

I knocked one man down with my stick, one day, and he got up and ran off, and I never saw him again until about two years afterwards, when I met a negro man one day on the street in Chattanooga; he stepped up to me and shook hands with me, saying "Don't you know me?" I replied that I did not. He then said, "I is Bill, de one you knocked down on de Alabama and Chattanooga Railroad long time ago." We were in about three miles of Asheville, the county seat of St. Clair county, Ala., with our work, when a man rode through our camps one Saturday night, after dark. Not long after he passed the tent where I was, the negroes commenced to rallying and passing by our tent. I and two other foremen went out to try and find out the trouble. Some passed us and never answered a question we asked them. After awhile we got some of them to stop and tell us what the trouble was. They said that they were notified that a Union man had been killed in Asheville, and they were going to burn the town. After telling them that they did not come on the road to fight, and that they were fools if they went, for they would get shot if they did go, the most of them went back to their tents. In this respect negroes are like sheep, when one gets excited and runs, the whole gang will follow. Sometimes when one thinks the front ones are not running fast enough, he will take a different direction and the ones behind him will follow him. The incidents which I have been relating all took place not a great ways from where Jack Springfield lived at that time. His dwelling was burned afterwards. He has since lived in Hamilton county, Tennessee, and has been sheriff of that county two or three terms, and a braver man than he cannot be found; this is my estimation of him, at least.

After I got to running a train through that section, I stopped at a road crossing and picked up Henry Springfield and wife and carried them to Chattanooga by request of John Springfield, a relative of theirs and a friend of mine, whom I had known from boyhood. A party of men got on my train at Springville about the time I am speaking of. They said they had been summoned by the sheriff to go to Asheville, or in that neighborhood, to arrest some parties. When I asked about their transportation they said that the county would pay that. I replied that I would not take them, that I would side-track the train first. About that time the railroad agent came out and begged me to take them on, saying that he knew the men, and if I side-tracked the train they would kill me. He also said that he was sure that the county would pay the amount. I said to him "Well, then, you pay me and you can get it from the county." He answered that he would stand good for it. I took them on and afterwards collected the money from the agent at Springville.

They had a great deal of trouble in those days, in Saint Clair county. They had not gotten over the war feelings. The government had to send United States troops to that county along about the time spoken on. Every pay-day a man would follow the men who paid the men along the line, and get money from a great many of the negroes and some white men. This man would have a large bag hanging down on one side, with a strap over his shoulder. He represented the Freedmen's Savings Bank.[5]

Well, I toughed it out through the winter, and I think it was May when I was finishing up a piece of earth-work for the bed of the road, near Springville. Late one evening I received word that if I would I could take a freight-train to go to Chattanooga. As the wages were the same that I was getting on the grade, and I preferred running a train of any kind, I went to Chattanooga and took the freight-train. While I was on the run, a man who belonged to the bridge gang, or crew, one day just as a train was leaving a station, went in between the tender and a flat car that was coupled on to the tender and made an effort to get on the flat car. Somehow he fell on the track and two of the front wheels ran over him. The engineer was watching the man and saw him fall. The engineer said that while he was oiling his engine, the man went in front of the engine to get on there, and the engineer said that he would not let him ride there, and watched him, when he started his engine, to see what he would do. I had the man picked up and laid upon the depot platform. The master of transportation of the road was at the station when the accident occurred, and he told me to go on and he would have the wounded man sent on a passenger-train that was following on its own schedule.

When I arrived in Chattanooga I went into an office to make a statement of the facts. While I was in the office at work on my report, there was an excursion train come in and stopped about opposite the depot building. There had been two excursions down the road that day, one of white and one of colored people. When I had finished my report I went to the superintendent's office to leave my report, but found no one in the office.

I had just stepped inside, when another conductor came in through a window, and said to me, "What about the fight?" I asked what fight. But he was so frightened, or appeared to be, that he did not tell me. I had heard of no fight, and knew nothing of there being one that evening. Soon the superintendent came in, and closely following him came Mr. Stanton. Then the master of transportation came in, and another conductor, who had come in on one of the excursion trains. All of them came in about the same time.

Mr. Stanton had a piece of round wood in one hand nearly as large as a medium sized man's arm. He said to the superintendent, "The next time you hold me and let a man break such a stick over my head I will discharge you." He then said to the two conductors, calling them by name, "You are both discharged. No set of men shall work for me who will stand by and see a stick like this broken over my head." One of the conductors replied that he did not see or know of it. Mr. Stanton told him that he did, adding. "for I saw you pass by laughing." Then Mr. Stanton turned round to me and said, "You too, go and get your pay." I went at once to the treasurer's office to get my money, but there was no one to be found in the office. I learned that Mr. Stanton had driven the men out of all the offices upon the next floor above. Mr. Stanton also told the master of transportation to give a young man the first passenger train he could, because the young man held another who was in the fight. I never did learn what the fight was about. I heard afterwards that the man who was run over by my train died in about twenty minutes after being hurt. His remains were shipped to Virginia, where his home had been.

Well, if I could have got my money when I went to the treasurer's office I should have gone home that night. This would have been one good act of my life that I would have performed. But not being able to get my money, I decided to stay over until morning and go home as soon as I could get what the road was due me. I will state further on why I should have left the Alabama and Chattanooga Railroad at that time.

The next morning, before I had got out of bed, one of the officers came with a hand full of way-bills. He awoke me and said that I had to go out on my run, and to hurry up, for it was after leaving time. I told him that I was not going out, but was going home, and said, "You heard what Stanton said." He answered, "Yes, but Mr. Stanton said for me not to let you quit by any means whatever." So I went out on my run.

It was not long after the occurrence spoken of until that young man was given a passenger train—the man whom Mr. Stanton had ordered a train given to. This train was the same one which I should have had when I came from the Meridian end of the road to Chattanooga. The conductor who first took the train was discharged, and the train was given to Mr. Stanton's man, and he ran it a few trips and was discharged. Then I was put on the run which I should have had several months prior to that time. But such is a railroad life.

As well as I remember at this time, Mr. Stanton had only about two years to build the road. He had men in East Tennessee and Virginia getting up hands, and a gang of Irishmen from New York. I do not recollect how many, but think somewhere between fifty and a hundred. When they arrived at the work of grading of the road they would not go to work, for what reason I do not know. But I suppose it was on account of the location of the country that the work was going through at that time, as they left the same day, or the day following, and went off cursing the country.

Mr. Stanton also had, I think it was, twenty-two hundred Chinamen transported from China, and worked them in gangs; each gang had a boss and interpreter. I was told by men who worked with them that they would eat the persimmons off the trees, when they passed them, before they had barely turned yellow, let alone being ripe; and would build a dam through the middle of the ponds that were in the swamps and lowlands of the Black Warrior river, while they were working near the river; they would take buckets and dip water out of one dam and pour it on the other side, get all the fish, frogs, and the like out of it, and then dip and pour the water back on the side that they had drained and get what fish and frogs there was on that side of dam.

I asked a foreman who worked a gang of these Chinamen to have them fill the tender of an engine with wood, as there was none racked up near the terminus of the track, and the wood had to be carried some little distance. It was springtime and the Chinamen were barefooted, and I thought that they never would get the tender filled with wood. They would not be hurried, and would only carry one stick of wood at a time. Some of them would sit down on the stick of wood which they had picked up to carry, and pick briers out of their feet. As well as I remember, I was there about one hour getting a tender full of wood, with twenty-five or thirty Chinamen at work.

After awhile the Chinese got out of rice and quit work. Mr. Stanton went down on a special train. I was in charge of the train as conductor. We went as far as the track was laid down, then Mr. Stanton took a hack and went to where the grading of the road was going on. He tried to get the Chinese to go to work, but they said through the Chinese Interpreter: "No ricee, no workee, Chinee hab rice, he work." And then Mr. Stanton commenced to strike some of them with the pick handle. I was afterwards told that the Chinese would have got the best of him had the negroes not taken his part and helped him out. He brought eight or ten of them back to Chattanooga. Some of them he had crippled, and he put some in the shops to work. He wanted me take two of them on my train as brakemen. But as I did not want them, I did not take them. As soon as the ones that were crippled got well, they were sent back on the grade to work. When one of them died he was buried in the ground on the side of the road, as others that die are, with a head and foot board set up, both of which were covered with writing in the Chinese language. It is needless to say that I could not read it.

Well, the time was drawing near when Mr. Stanton was to have his road completed, and things had to move ahead at a rapid rate. It was said that the civil engineer just jumped on his gray horse and left the original survey, and went galloping around the hills and down the hollows, saying, "Come on, boys!" And one would readily believe this, if they could see the part of the road that was built at the time I speak of. It was called the Alps as long as I ran on the road. There was a great deal of trestle work to do, and some of these trestles were built of pine poles, while others further down the road were built of cypress poles, transported over the Mobile and Ohio Railroad, from down near Mobile. Mr. Stanton offered to give me a contract on the grade of the road, but things had begun to look rather critical about that time along the grading and track laying departments of the road. The men had not been paid off regularly for some time. I would not take any contract, and it was well enough that I did not. I know some contractors who lost about all they possessed, and I suppose they have never received any pay for their work to the present day.

Mr. Stanton went to Montgomery, Ala., the capital of the State, to get some aid from the State in regard to the road that he was building. The State Legislature was in session at the time he went. Gen. Forrest was there also, on the same business which Mr. Stanton was on, but in the interest of a road which he had charge of.[6] I was told by a friend of mine, who was present at the time when it occurred, that Mr. Stanton and Gen. Forrest had some hot words about their legislative matters and that Gen. Forrest started towards Mr. Stanton with a long knife in hand. It seems as if there was an open door between them, and Mr. Stanton said to some one that was present: "Shut that door." Mr. Stanton was a brave man and a fighter, but that was one time that he wanted the door closed between him and his antagonist.

On the run I had, I did not run on Sundays, but ran from Chattanooga to the terminus of track, wherever that might be, and lay over there every Sunday. One could not help laughing at the country people who would come to see the engine and train, and hear the remarks they would make about them. They had never seen an engine or train before, not even a railroad track. Old men and women, boys and girls, would come in squads. If the train had to be moved to give the work train a chance to do work, some of them would get on to take a ride until I stopped it and would not allow the coaches to be unlocked for them, as I thought some of them might be crippled or killed.

One Sunday night I was laying over at the end of the track, where the track men's camp was. Just after dark, a squad of men passed through the camps in disguise, and shot off their guns of pistols several times. The negroes had quit work several days before this on account of not being paid off for some months, and the squad of men and shooting was done to scare the men, and make them go to work the next morning. But the negroes rallied, and wanted to kill all the foremen that were in the camps, and some of them said that they would kill every white men in camps. They said, "Get picks, shovels, pick handles, spiking hammers; come, on boys, get anything you can and come on." This scared me up; I was in my baggage-car reading when the fray commenced. I went to the door of the car and talked to them, advising them to be quiet, and they quieted down some but still swore that they would kill two white men that were in camp. I then sent the white men word to get out before the negroes got to the tents which they were in, so when the negroes got there they could not find them. I believe they would have been killed if the negroes had gotten hold of them at that time. Everything quieted down after awhile.

But the next morning, just before my time to leave, about fifty or seventy-five of the negroes came to the train and swore they were going to Chattanooga, and were going to ride in the first-class coach and were not going to pay any fare. So I had to lock up the coach and stand on the coach platform with pistol in hand, and tell them I would shoot the first man that attempted to get in the car I was on. They then went in the second-class car. I then wired the superintendent of the facts. I could not collect a penny from one of them. I received a telegram at the first telegraph station I came to which said for me to put them off, and tell them the contractors were on the down train with money to pay them of. I read the message to them but they did not believe that the message read the way that I had read it to them; I then got one of the negro men to read it to them, but they still refused to get off. There was a freight conductor at this station. I noticed a horse hitched to a fence. I told the conductor to get on this horse and gallop to town, which was about half a mile off the road. I had been told by the men in that section of country that any time I needed help to let them know. They said that they could raise a hundred men in thirty minutes. So the conductor went at once for them and soon came back and said that about fifty men would be there in a few minutes. But while he was gone for them I received another telegram saying for me to carry them on until I met the train with the contractor on it. So that broke up the fun for the boys, who were anxious for the sport. When I met the train spoken of most of the negroes went back on it. I then had them reduced so that I could manage the rest that remained on my train. The ones that had money paid me their fare, and the ones that had no money I put off my train.

I had only run a few trips afterwards when about sixty-five or eighty negroes boarded my train one morning at the terminus, and some of them were the same ones that were on my train at the time of which I have just been speaking, but they all paid their fare. Before I arrived in Chattanooga some of them began drinking and kept up such a fuss that I tried to control them, but could not. So when I crossed the Georgia and Tennessee line I stopped to put the leader of the gang off, but he was so unruly that he said he would not get off unless I gave him back his money. I had offered him his fare from where I stopped the train to Chattanooga, but he would not take it. While we were talking he acted as if he would as soon hit me as not. I then picked up a stick of stove wood and knocked his head through a glass window, and he raised up and was going to strike me, when a friend of mine struck him on the back of the head with a heavy navy pistol. The negro thought he had been shot, and asked, "Who shot me?"

At the time I was having the difficulty with this negro, another friend of mine kept one of the other negroes, who had a knife in hand, off of me by drawing his pistol. I finally got my big man off and started out, but the negroes crowded the platform so that I could not keep him off. I wired to have a police to arrest him on arrival in Chattanooga, but he jumped off the train as we approached that place, but I let a man off to watch him and sent a policeman back for the negro, and he brought him back, but said that he hit the negro three times over the head, and then only knocked him to his knees. After a hard scuffle with the negro the policeman, with the help of five or six white men, managed to get him tied. He was then taken to the station house and confined. He was tried the next day and fined fifty dollars and costs. Some of the other negroes paid it for him, and he was turned loose.

At last the time rolled around for the tracks to be connected from Meridian, Miss., and from Chattanooga, Tenn.[7] The rails met and were joined together on a trestle and the silver spike driven. That was between Tuscaloosa and Eutaw, Ala. In some places the ties were very trifling. Small pine trees were cut down and scalped on each side and used in some places for ties.

Men who had taken the contracts could not get their money and had to sell their wagons and teams to pay the men who got out ties for them. Some grade contractors never got their money at all. The man who had the contract for laying the track on the Chattanooga end of the road lost all he had while laying the track, by borrowing money to pay his hands off and giving real estate as collateral, and never getting pay for his contract so as to redeem his property. He was a man who was well-do-do before he took the contract. He died soon after his work was done, or just before it was finished, I do not remember which.

I know other men who were broken up by the building of the road in other directions. The Chinese were turned loose without being paid up in full. Some stayed around Tuscaloosa, some making bead pockets and such work as the Indians do; others buying in fruit from the neighboring orchards and selling it in town. At last a compromise was made by sending them as far as New Orleans, La. Some white men who worked on the road had to go away without their wages being paid for a long time.

A large number of negroes, some of them brought from Tennessee and some from Virginia, worked till the last grading was done. They had left their homes, and some of them had wives and children, and had to return home penniless and ragged. Some of them got back to Chattanooga and stayed for some time, hoping that they would get their money, but had to leave without it. One of them came to me to get me to read a letter to him, which he had received from his wife. She wrote that if he did not send her some money soon, that she would be turned out of the house she lived in. He cried, and said that he could not send her any until he got pay for the work he had done on the road. So he never sent her any money. I saw one man crying one day in Chattanooga. I knew him, and asked him what the matter was, and he answered that he had put three hundred dollars in the Freedmen's Savings Bank, while he was on the grading of the road, and went to draw it out and the bank was closed, and the man and money gone. He was not the only man who had lost his money through the Freedmen's Savings Bank.

The Western & Atlantic depot in Chattanooga in 1864. Bell's caboose was standing a short distance from the building with water "above the middle of the windows" during the flood of 1867. National Archives

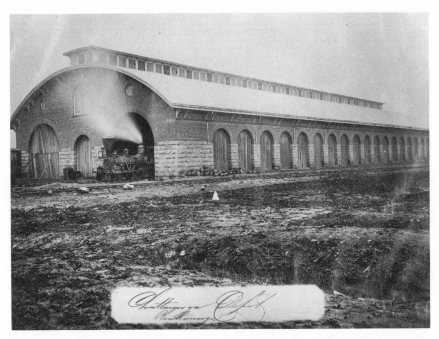

Chattanooga's Western & Atlantic depot train shed with an 1850s locomotive sticking its snout out of the door. National Archives

Atlanta's first Union depot, built in 1854. Conductor Bell began many of his runs on the Western & Atlantic from here. National Archives

John C. Stanton often failed to pay Bell on his Alabama and Chattanooga Railroad because he was diverting his funds to build this Chattanooga hotel. National Archives

The famous "General" was typical of the Western & Atlantic locomotives that pulled Bell's trains in the 1860s. Chattanooga Convention and Visitors Bureau

This was the Western & Atlantic depot Bell saw when he first worked as a baggage-man into Chattanooga in 1859. Lookout Mountain looms in the background. *Harper's New Monthly* (1858)

This Civil War artist's rendering of a ruined railway bridge twenty miles west of Chattanooga indicates the rough terrain Bell traveled during his years on the Alabama & Chattanooga Railroad. Bell crossed this bridge many times after it was rebuilt at war's end.

BALDWIN LOCOMOTIVE WORKS,

Philadelphia, Pa.

BURNHAM, PARRY, WILLIAMS & CO., PROPRIETORS.

Dimensions, Weights and Tractive Power of Road Locomotives.

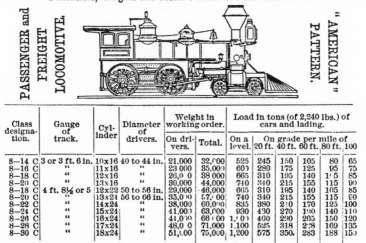

PASSENGER and FREIGHT LOCOMOTIVE. — **"AMERICAN" PATTERN.**

Class designation.	Gauge of track.	Cylinder	Diameter of drivers.	Weight in working order. On drivers.	Total.	Load in tons (of 2,240 lbs.) of cars and lading. On a level.	On grade per mile of 20 ft.	40 ft.	60 ft.	80 ft.	100
8–14 C	3 or 3 ft. 6 in.	10x16	40 to 44 in.	21,000	32,000	525	245	150	105	80	65
8–16 C	"	11x16	"	23,000	35,000	600	280	175	125	95	75
8–18 C	"	12x16	"	26,000	38,000	665	310	195	140	105	85
8–20 C	"	13x16	"	30,000	44,000	740	340	215	155	115	90
8–18 C	4 ft. 8½ or 5	12x22	50 to 56 in.	29,000	46,000	665	310	195	140	105	85
8–20 C	"	13x24	56 to 66 in.	35,000	57,000	740	340	215	155	115	80
8–22 C	"	14x24	"	38,000	60,000	835	380	240	170	125	100
8–24 C	"	15x24	"	41,000	63,000	930	430	270	190	140	110
8–26 C	"	16x24	"	44,000	66,000	1,000	460	290	205	150	120
8–28 C	"	17x24	"	48,000	71,000	1,100	525	318	228	169	135
8–30 C	"	18x24	"	51,000	75,000	1,200	575	350	283	188	150

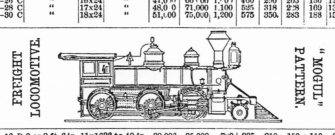

FREIGHT LOCOMOTIVE. — **"MOGUL" PATTERN.**

Class designation.	Gauge of track.	Cylinder	Diameter of drivers.	On drivers.	Total.	On a level.	20 ft.	40 ft.	60 ft.	80 ft.	100
8–16 D	3 or 3 ft. 6 in.	11x16	36 to 40 in.	29,000	35,000	720	335	210	150	110	90
8–18 D	"	12x16	"	33,000	39,000	840	390	250	180	135	110
8–20 D	"	13x16	"	37,000	44,000	965	445	285	205	160	125
8–22 D	"	14x16	"	41,000	48,000	1,000	470	3 0	215	165	130
8–24 D	"	15x16	"	46,000	53,000	1,100	525	318	2 8	1 0	145
8–26 D	4 ft. 8½ or 5	16x24	48 to 54 in.	60,000	72,000	1,400	655	415	500	230	180
8–28 D	"	17x24	"	63,000	75,000	1,500	695	445	320	245	195
8–30 D	"	18x24	"	66,000	78,000	1,600	740	470	340	260	205
8–32 D	"	19x24	"	69,000	81,000	1,695	820	500	365	275	22

[The "Ten-Wheeled" Pattern, for 4 ft. 8½ in. gauge, is also made with same cylinders and drivers as above.]

FREIGHT LOCOMOTIVE. — **"Consolidation" PATTERN.**

Class designation.	Gauge of track.	Cylinder	Diameter of drivers.	On drivers.	Total.	On a level.	20 ft.	40 ft.	60 ft.	80 ft.	100
10–22 E	3 or 3 ft. 6 in.	14x16	36 in.	44,000	52,000	1,060	490	310	220	175	140
10–24 E	"	15x18	"	50,000	58,000	1,2 0	560	355	255	195	155
10–34 E	4 ft. 8½ or 5	2 x24	48 in.	88,000	102,000	2,000	990	6 5	460	350	285

Illustrated here are typical freight and passenger woodburning locomotives on railroads after the Civil War. To fill the tenders of locomotives such as these, Bell often dipped his leather bucket into a nearby creek. *The Car-Builder's Dictionary* (1879)

Trains Leave.   March 22, 1868.   **Trains Arrive.**

Acc.	Pass	Pass	Pass	Mls	STATIONS.	Mls	Pass	Pass	Pass	Acc.
P. M.	P. M	A M					P. M.	A. M.	A. M.	
3 40	7 00	7 00		0	...**Atlanta** 1....	136	1 15	3 45	9 50	
4 15	7 26	7 26			.....Bolton......		12 49	3 19	9 14	
4 40	7 40	7 40		11	.....Vining.....	125	12 35	3 05	8 55	
5 06	7 56	7 56			.....Ruff's......		12 20	2 49	8 30	
5 50	8 32	8 11		20	...Marietta.....	116	12 04	2 33	8 10	
6 24	9 02	8 42			....Big Shanty....		11 33	2 02	6 53	
6 49	9 25	9 05		35	....Acworth.....	101	11 12	1 41	6 00	
	9 47	9 27		40	....Allatoona....	96	10 51	1 19		
	10 09	9 49			......Etowah......		10 29	12 56		
	10 19	9 55		47	...Cartersville....	89	10 24	12 51		
	10 36	10 17		52	......Cass.......	84	10 03	12 30		
	11 02	10 43		59	....Kingston 2....	77	9 42	12 09		
	11 34	11 16		69	....Adairsville....	67	9 10	11 35		
	12 06	11 49		78	....Calhoun......	58	8 38	11 01		
	12 28	12 11		84	......Resaca......	52	8 16	10 40		
	12 50	12 33		91	......Tilton......	45	7 54	10 18		
	1 33	1 23		100	.....Dalton 3....	38	7 23	9 48		
	2 01	1 51		107	...Tunnel Hill....	29	6 50	9 06		
	2 31	2 25		115	.....Ringgold.....	21	6 01	8 36		
	2 53	2 46			....Graysville.....		5 39	8 14		
	3 15	3 09		128	....Chicamauga....	8	5 16	7 54		
	3 34	3 29			......Boyce.....		4 57	7 35		
	4 00	3 55		136	.**Chattanooga** 4	0	4 30	7 10		
P. M.	A. M.	P. M.			[ARRIVE] [LEAVE		A. M.	P. M.	A. M.	

GENERAL OFFICERS.

CAMPBELL WALLACE, Gen. Supt.;
W W. CLAYTON, Treasurer;
R. C ROBSON, Auditor ;
JOHN B. PECK, Master Trans. ;
Atlanta, Ga.

CONNECTIONS.

1 Railways diverging from Atlanta.
2 Connect with Macon and Western Railway.
2 Junction of Rome (Georgia) R.R.
3 Connect with East Tennessee and Georgia Railway.
4 Railways diverging from Chatta

Through Fare, $8 00.

The 7 00 p.m. train from Atlanta, and the 7 10 p. m. train from Chattanooga, run daily. All other trains daily, Sundays excepted.

This 1868 Western & Atlantic timetable indicates how leisurely Bell's trains were. When on time, they averages just under eighteen miles per hour. Official Railway Guide (1868)

---

223.   **EAST TENNESSEE & VIRGINIA RAILWAY.**

Trains Leave.   March 10, 1868.   **Trains Arrive.**

Acc.	Pass	Pass	Mail	Mls	STATIONS.	Mls	Mail	Pass	Pass	Acc.
	P. M.	A. M.					P. M	P. M		
		11 17		0	...**Knoxville** 1..	130	2 46			
		11 49		10	.....McMillan.....	120	2 14			
		12 10		17	.Strawberry Plains.	113	1 49			
		12 36		25	....Newmarket....	105	1 23			
		12 49		29	....Mossy Creek...	101	1 08			
		1 04		34	...Talbot's Mills...	96	12 36			
		1 36		42	....Morristown....	88	12 05			
		1 56		48	....Russellville....	82	11 42			
		2 37		56	..Rogersville Junc..	74	11 17			
		3 04		65	......Mid Way.....	65	10 47			
		3 29		74	....Greenville....	56	10 13			
		4 12		83	.....Fullens......	47	9 38			
		4 22		87	....Limestone.....	53	9 27			
		4 57		98	....Jonesboro'....	32	8 52			
		5 21		105	....Johnson's.....	25	8 28			
		5 37		110	.......Carter......	20	8 10			
		6 07		119	.......Union.......	11	7 41			
		6 40		130	...**Bristol** 2....	0	7 10			
		A. M. P. M.			[ARRIVE] [LEAVE		A. M. P. M			

GENERAL OFFICERS.

J. R. BRANNER, Pres., Mossy Creek.
BENJ. DECKENSON, Vice-Pres.
JOHN KEYS, Treasurer.
J. B. HOXSIE, Gen. Supt.
J. R. OGDEN,
Gen. Freight
and Ticket Agent,
JAMES G. MITCHELL, Auditor.
Knoxville, Tenn.

CONNECTIONS.

1 Connect with East Tennessee and Georgia Railway.
2 Connect with Virginia and Tennessee Railway.

Standard of Time—Clock in Superintendents Office, at Knoxville.

The trains from Knoxville to Bristol that Bell commanded stopped at every "tank town" along the road. Official Railway Guide (1868)

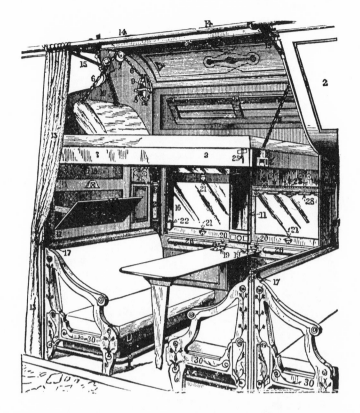

Bell "captained" his first sleeping cars on the South & North Railroad of Alabama and later opined they made for "nice little trains." Their interior layouts looked very much like this one. *The Car-Builder's Dictionary* (1879)

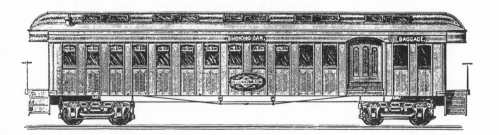

As a conductor, Bell had charge of similar passenger cars after the Civil War. They were ornate, uncomfortable, and, with their own coal or wood stoves, fire traps during wrecks. *The Car-Builder's Dictionary* (1879)

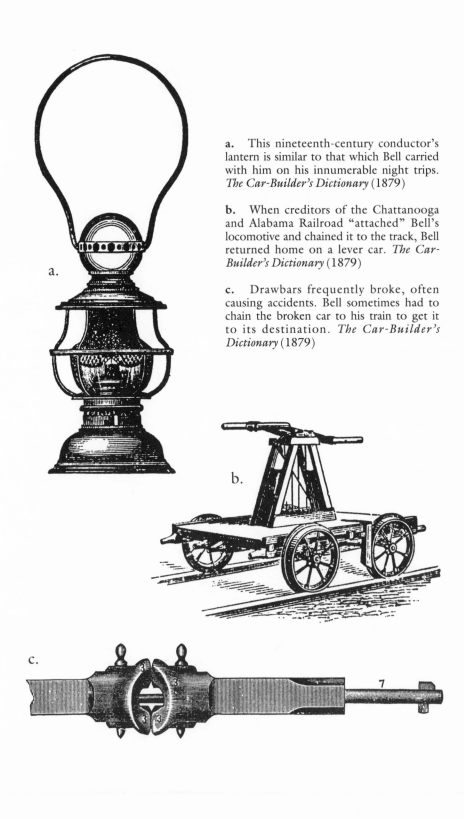

a. This nineteenth-century conductor's lantern is similar to that which Bell carried with him on his innumerable night trips. *The Car-Builder's Dictionary* (1879)

b. When creditors of the Chattanooga and Alabama Railroad "attached" Bell's locomotive and chained it to the track, Bell returned home on a lever car. *The Car-Builder's Dictionary* (1879)

c. Drawbars frequently broke, often causing accidents. Bell sometimes had to chain the broken car to his train to get it to its destination. *The Car-Builder's Dictionary* (1879)

Chapter Eight

Operating the Alabama and Chattanooga Railroad

Aschedule was made and trains put on the road running through from Chattanooga to Meridian. The rolling-stock was composed of some good engines, some of them being new. Some of the coaches were new and comfortable. I think they were as fine, or finer, than any used at that time on any other road which ran into Chattanooga. The baggage-cars were new, one end of them being used for baggage and the other for express, while the mail department was in the middle of the car. A Pullman sleeper was attached to each train. A through mail pouch was put on as a test to prove which route was the quickest mail line from New York to New Orleans via the Piedmont Airline and Atlanta of the East Tennessee and Georgia Railroad and the Alabama and Chattanooga Railroad via Meridian, which was thirty-two miles the nearest route. The track of the Alabama and Chattanooga road was good from Chattanooga to Attalla, for through Wills Valley the earth was full of gravel, and consequently made a good road-bed. The track was also pretty good from Attalla to Elyton.

The first houses that were built at Birmingham were three section houses that Mr. Stanton had built. He afterwards used one of them for a freight depot. A portion of the road between Elyton and Livingston was pretty bad, and it became a common thing for cars to be derailed along that portion of the road.

The first trains started out on the new through schedule were one out of Chattanooga and one out of Meridian. Mr. Stanton was on the one that left Meridian, and he had ordered the train dispatcher in Chattanooga to keep everything out of the way of the train he was on.

It happened that train did not make the meeting point for the train in the opposite direction. There was a telegraph station at Green Pond, a station about thirteen miles west of the station which was the meeting point for the two trains. The conductor of the east-bound train went into the office at Green Pond to get orders against the west-bound train, as he had lost his rights, and he received orders to remain at Green Pond until the west-bound train passed, as there was no side-track between the two stations. The conductor come out and showed his orders to Mr. Stanton; he cursed and told the conductor to go ahead. They pulled out and met the west-bound train between the two stations, and had it not been that this was on a long straight, they would have had a head end collision. They met nearest to Green Pond, but Mr. Stanton made the west-bound train back to the side-track, where they ought to have met if both trains had been on time. The next thing that the east-bound train met was a work train on the main track. Mr. Stanton stepped off his train to curse the conductor of the work train and came near being run over by the engine of the work train. Still he cursed because they were not out of the way, but the conductor informed him that he had no notice of such a train being on the road as he had met on the main track. This happened on a straight track also, and saved a collision. The next obstruction was a dump car on the main track in front of the engine. Mr. Stanton got through to Chattanooga, notwithstanding all his danger and troubles. I was in the dispatcher's office when the train arrived and just as I was coming out of the office I met Mr. Stanton going in. As soon as he got inside of the door he commenced cursing the dispatcher. He said to him: "I ordered everything kept out of my way, and you have run everything you could right in my face, even dump cars. I had just as soon you would place a cannon in front of me, and set fire to it." The dispatcher handed Mr. Stanton a paper, saying: "Here is my resignation." Mr. Stanton replied, "D——n your resignation. You are discharged," tearing the paper up as he spoke.

It was some time before the connection with the mail pouch was made on account of some bad track, notwithstanding it being new. Occasionally cars would leave the rails and sometimes an engine. A train was going east one day and some of the front cars left the rails and turned over on the side of the road. The engine was loosened from the train, the conductor of the train took the mail pouch, jumped on the engine and told the engineer to go ahead, leaving his train with a portion of it wrecked. When he arrived at Chattanooga the mail pouch was transferred to the East Tennessee train, and the conductor ran to the railroad office and told some of the officials that he had made the connection with the mail, but had left his train over one hundred and fifty miles behind him.

About this time Mr. Stanton increased conductors' wages to one hundred dollars per month, and ordered them to wear uniforms and badges. The color of the uniforms was navy blue, and the coats sack coats. That was the first uniform I had ever worn.

There was an insane asylum at Tuscaloosa, and there were a great many insane people carried to that place over the road, after the train commenced running to that place. Two men, in charge of an insane woman, boarded my train one day. They were seated in my second-class car, and every time I would pass through the car the woman would try to spit on me, and grab at me, in order to get a hold of me. I was afraid of her. One time she caught hold of my coat-tail, and I jerked it loose and ran through the aisle. She called after me, saying: "Go on you d——d bobtailed Yankee!" I had on my uniform at this time. The woman's words created a laugh among the passengers in the car. Long afterwards the same woman, accompanied by her sister, was carried back from Tuscaloosa, on my train. She was sick, but had recovered her mind. I had a seat turned and a bed fixed so that she could be made comfortable.

The trains were run for awhile and the road did a pretty fair business. But not long after Mr. Stanton raised the conductors' wages to one hundred dollars per month, they did not pay off regularly. Sometimes we would get pay for a part of a month's work, and then miss getting any pay for two or three months. This state of affairs continued until it became very critical from one end of the road to the other. Not long after the trains had commenced running through, the superintendent of the Meridian end of the road was given charge of the road to Tuscaloosa, and the superintendent of the Chattanooga end was given charge of the road between Chattanooga and Tuscaloosa.

The track got very bad in places. A great many of the trackmen and bridgemen had quit work on the roadway, on account of not being paid off. Some threats were made of burning the bridges. I heard some men say that if they did not get what was due them that they would tear the d——d road up. I heard a remark of this kind made one night as I was going west, and I wired the superintendent in regard to it. The next day a train was derailed by a bar of iron being taken out of the track. This was thrown down an embankment into a pond of water, but it happened no one was hurt. The schedule had been changed and the train was making slow time.

I was going west one night when I was flagged down by two or three men just before we reached a bridge. I got off of my train to ask them what the trouble was, and they answered that the bridge across

Hurricane creek was on fire, and sure enough it was. There was a small blaze of fire at one corner of the bridge, which was soon put out. The men who flagged us down said they would have put out the fire, but they had no buckets, and that they heard the train coming when they first saw the fire. The roadmaster was on the train, and an old track man, who at one time had had charge of a road as supervisor, and as well as I can remember it was the Nashville, Chattanooga and St. Louis Railroad that he came from. I had him to examine the bridge and see if he thought it safe to cross. He pronounced it perfectly safe, and said the fire had not affected the rods or braces or cords of the bridge. So on it we went, but very slowly, as I had instructed the engineer to go. It was a small creek and a short bridge. About the time the engine was near the middle of the bridge down it went, engine and all into the creek, the baggage car with one end in the creek and the other upon the abutment of the bridge. The engineer and fireman were slightly injured and that was all. I heard afterwards that one of the cords of the bridge was found sawed in two when the timbers of the old bridge were being moved, but this was afterwards denied by the superintendent of bridges.

There was an old lady on the train who gave me more trouble than all my other passengers. I took my lady passengers back a short distance to a house. The old gentleman who lived at the place took them in, and said that he would take good care of them. I was to let them know when there was any chance to get away. I returned to the wreck and made arrangements for my other passengers to stay with a gentleman who lived on the opposite side of the creek.

I afterwards had to go and get the old lady I have spoken of, and take her to the house on the opposite side of the creek. Next morning she sent me word to come for her. I went to see what she wanted. She said that she would not stay at the house she was at, and that she wanted to send a telegram to her daughter at Tuscaloosa. She had told me when I took her ticket on the train that she was going to see her daughter married at Tuscaloosa. After the wreck occurred she annoyed me very much about not getting there in time. She said if she missed her daughter's marriage that she would bring suit against the company for damages. I got some section men to take her to the station ahead on a lever car,[1] and got her a house to stay at until I could get a train to go on with.

In the afternoon she sent me word to come for her, that she was not going to stay at the place that she was at. I sent back word to her that I would soon have an engine and train sent me, then I would go for her, and not before. Soon after I had sent this message to my old lady friend an engine and train came to my relief.

I gathered up my passengers, loaded the baggage and express and the small amount of mail I had on hand, and went ahead to the station where I had left my old lady friend. She had left the house where I had taken her and had taken quarters at the depot. When I met her, she said that I was a very unaccommodating conductor, and if she had been a young woman that I would have looked after her. I asked her, "Have you not been cared for?" She answered that there was less accommodation in the people in that section of country than any she had been in. I arrived at Tuscaloosa with her safely, just the day before her daughter was to be married, and I was truly glad to assist her in getting off of the train. I learned afterwards, from the parties who lived in the houses where she had been taken to be cared for, that the trouble was caused from the old lady speaking freely against the South when in conversation but when a word was said against the North she would leave at once and try another place.

The passenger-trains were turned into mixed-trains, and had to lie over at nights at Tuscaloosa, going in either direction. The men and the superintendent on the Meridian end of the road became rather hostile. Some of the men had lost their positions by the road cutting down expenses, and had not received any pay.

I was going west one day with a train, and when I arrived at York Station I was stopped and ordered by some men that were there not to go any further. I went into the office to wire the officials at Chattanooga what had happened, but found when I got to the telegraph office that the wire was cut east of that office, and consequently I could get no instructions what to do. I was at a loss to think or know what would be best. At last I found out from the operator, who was a friend of mine, but sided with the Meridian men. This operator was also a telegraph operator when I was cut off in Tennessee on the East Tennessee and Georgia Railroad, and stayed with us until we fell back to Loudon. What I learned from the operator was, that a crew was going to be started out of Meridian at once to take my engine and train from me and take it to Meridian. So I got the operator to talk to the men that were present who belonged to the band in Meridian, and get them to let me go back, as they would not let me go any further. By hard persuading they at last agreed to let me go. It was about twenty-five miles from York to Meridian, and about seventy-five miles from York to Tuscaloosa.

So late in the evening I left York and backed the engine and train to Tuscaloosa. I found the wire all right from there to Chattanooga, and I wired the officials all the facts in the case.

The next morning I had the engine turned around at Tuscaloosa, and went back to Chattanooga. It was then decided not to run trains west of

Tuscaloosa. I arrived at Tuscaloosa one evening about dusk, not long after the events just related transpired. I was going to have my engine turned, and sent a brakeman to the switch to set it to the turntable track, and my engineer followed the man with his engine. I was standing where my train had been cut loose from the engine, when I heard men whooping and saw the engine moving off at a rapid speed. I also heard the reports of several pistols. I soon learned what all this meant. The brakeman stated that when he got to the switch there was a man there who would not let him change it. The engineer said when he stopped his engine near the switch to wait until it was set for the turntable, a party of men got on his engine and presented their pistols, telling him to get off at once. I again wired these facts to officials, and they sent me another engine, and I went back to Chattanooga. I was started out again with another train. I got as far as where Birmingham now is. This was about the time Birmingham was being surveyed into city lots, streets, and avenues. The Alabama and Chattanooga road had a spur track put in at that place, about one mile east of Elyton. Mr. Stanton had already had a depot built at Elyton, and there was an agent and tele-graph office at that place. When I arrived at the spur track of which I have spoken of, east of Elyton, the trackmen were at work at it putting in the switch and frog. I had just arrived at that place, when the agent from Elyton met me with a telegram from the superintendent at Chattanooga, saying for me not to go, or try to go further than Elyton, as there was a party that had started out from Meridian with the inten-tion of capturing the engine and train that I had charge of. The agent advised me to stop where I was, and not even try to go on to Elyton. He said that he heard that the party was making good speed, and would soon be on hand, and that was the reason why he had brought me the telegram. I hurried up the section men, and gave my way-bills to the agent. Some I had were for cars loaded with merchandise. As soon as the section men got the switch and frog in, I had them to push my box-cars on the side-track, which were the first cars that had been set on it. I coupled my engine to my baggage car, which had two coaches attached to it, and then backed to Attalla, turned my engine, switched my train and left Attalla for Chattanooga. When I arrived at Trenton, a station on the road, situated where the road runs through the corner of Georgia, I found the track blocked by an engine and train, the engine being chained and locked to the rail. A party of creditors who lived in Georgia had them attached; of course they got my engine and train also. When I left that place I left on a lever car.

Mr. Stanton, or the company he represented, had some oxen and mules which he had reserved when he sold the stock and equipments that had been used while the road was being built. I, knowing of the fact, went to see Mr. Stanton, thinking as many others did, I suppose, that he would pay me if he paid no one else. I told him that I would buy a yoke of oxen or a pair of mules, and he could take that amount off of what was due me. He said all right, he would let me have a pair of mules, which he had as soon as he got the grading finished that he was having done in the yard for a side-track. He said that I could have them in two or three days. As well as I remember, his price was three hundred dollars for the two mules. I had seen them at work when the yard was being graded, and I would have given him four hundred dollars for them in the way of a bad debt. The next day after I had seen Mr. Stanton in regard to the mules an officer of the law came and took off the mules and oxen, and so I was left.

Business on the road was stopped for some time. By some kind of compromise the engine and cars that had been attached at Trenton were brought back to Chattanooga. A party of employees came from Meridian to Chattanooga. There was a great deal of talking and dissatisfaction among the employees. Meetings were held by some of them to try and decide for the best. All concerned were very much interested in regard to the matter.

Mr. Stanton went East to raise means to operate the road. The men stayed in and around Chattanooga awaiting Mr. Stanton's return. It was rumored that he would return with money to pay off all employees and start the running of trains over the road again. While all this was going on the men who came from Meridian to Chattanooga took the engine and cars and got out of Chattanooga so quietly with them that there were but few who knew of it until they were gone. And they got them through to Meridian safely.

News came that Mr. Stanton was on his way back from the East, and would arrive in Chattanooga on a certain day. On the day he arrived a small cannon was taken upon a high hill by some of the employees and fired off several times. But Mr. Stanton did not pay the boys off. The arrangement was to run the road again. While making preparation to operate the road again, I was sent to Meridian with two engines, two coaches, and baggage car, as there was not a supply of rolling stock on that end of the road. I went via Stevenson, Ala, over the Nashville, Chattanooga and St. Louis Railroad, then to Corinth, Miss, over the Memphis and Charleston Railroad, thence to Meridian over the Mobile and Ohio Railroad.

The Mobile and Ohio Railroad officials would not let me over the road without a conductor and brakeman of their own. I had to lay over at Corinth till late in the evening, when I had arrived there early in the morning. When the crew came, we went to Baldwin, way-station on the road, and the end of division. We lay over there all night. After I had reported to the superintendent of the division we had to run over the next day, and he told me that we would follow a train. One of my engineers went to him and persuaded him to let us run as first and second sections. I found this out, and went back to the superintendent and asked him to please change the order, and let us follow his train, and he told me how he came to arrange it the way he had, and he was sorry but he had already given instructions; and so it was too late to change it. We started out next morning early. I was going through the yard, and passed a group of men standing around a bonfire. They were passing around a bottle, and drinking whisky from it, I supposed, although it might have been water. I afterwards learned that this was the crew who followed us. My light engine was first section. My other engine had a baggage car and two coaches attached, and was second section. The Mobile and Ohio train was pulling a long train of box-cars. The Mobile and Ohio conductor and his two men were riding in my rear coach. It was a bright Sunday morning, and we had left Baldwin before sunrise. When the sun was about two hours high, something got wrong with the light engine, and the engineer stopped to fix it, and flagged the second one. I was in my baggage-car at that time making my toilet, so as to be ready for breakfast at the next station ahead. As soon as I noticed we were stopping I looked out of a side window of the car that I was in, and said to the conductor who had taken charge of the engine and cars to send a flagman back. He answered that he had already done so. I told my engineer to go ahead at once, as I heard the sound of the approaching train. As they began to move off I saw the train coming without slacking speed, but could not see a man at his post on top of the train, where they ought to have been at the brakes. I realized that they were going to run into us, and I started to the side door of the baggage-car to jump out, but they struck the rear coach before I could do so, and I was knocked out of the door. I did not know anything when I was picked up, the fall causing me to become unconscious, but I soon regained consciousness. The rear coach platform was mashed up, and a dent made in the tender of the engine that was pulling the coaches; that was about all the damage done to my engine or cars. I found that I was pretty badly hurt. I was hurt in my shoulder, and for a long time could not use my fingers or thumb. My left hand got so I could use the fingers on it first. I kept up, and went on to Meridian. I learned afterwards that the crew that was following us were all discharged.

When I arrived in Meridian I delivered the engine and cars that I had charge of over to the superintendent, in compliance with the instructions which I had received in regard to them before I left Chattanooga. The superintendent at Meridian told me that there would not be any train run on his division for some time, as the State of Alabama was going to take charge of his division as soon as it could be arranged to do so, and he would still have charge of it as superintendent. He said if I would stay there, or come back when they went to running trains that he would give me a train. He had worked it pretty fine to get the engine and cars from Mr. Stanton. The next morning after I arrived at Meridian I left on an Alabama Central train, which was at that time run over the Alabama and Chattanooga track as far as York Station. I went via Selma and Dalton to get back to Chattanooga. When I arrived there I learned that a man, who was a lawyer, was in Chattanooga looking after the interest of the State of Alabama, in regard to the Alabama and Chattanooga Railroad. This man was afterwards killed by a gunshot, while in Knoxville looking after the same matter.

Some of the section men along the line commenced running their lever and dump-cars, hauling passengers and freight, such as they could carry on these cars. They divided the road in sections, each gang having about the same distance to run, and they arranged a schedule so as to make connection with each other. The agent at Elyton wired me to come down at once and he would pay me what the road was due me; I said he had enough of the company's money to do so. I wired him in reply that I would be there as soon as I could get there on a lever. I left home the day on which I received the telegram, going on a lever car, and made all the haste I could possibly make on one. I took the lever car because I knew it would beat private conveyance; if I had gone to Calera, Ala., I would at that time have had to go from Calera to Elyton by private conveyance. Not knowing what connection I would make at Dalton, I thought the lever car would be the quickest way to get there, notwithstanding the distance from where I lived to Elyton, which was one hundred and thirty-two miles. When I arrived at Elyton, I learned from the agent that he had sent the money by express from Chattanooga to the treasurer of the Alabama and Chattanooga road. How sadly disappointed I was again. The excuse of the agent was that he expected me sooner, and expecting to be garnisheed, he thought it best to send it off. I asked him why he did not keep out enough to pay me. He answered that he was afraid to do so. Yet he had about forty-seven dollars of the company's money that he had collected, which amount he paid me and I gave him a receipt for the same, and returned home, thinking that I had earned all I had got by making the trip which I had made. Yet if I had not got it that way I never would have gotten it at all.

As well as I can remember, the amount of money that the agent expressed to the treasurer was ten or twelve hundred dollars. I wired a friend of mine in Chattanooga in regard to it, and when he went to the treasurer's office he said they denied having it or receiving it. The rolling-stock lay still at each end of the road, with the exception of a few cars and an engine, which a conductor used between Tuscaloosa and Birmingham. About that time Birmingham was just beginning to build up.

The conductor I spoke of, who made use of the road between Tuscaloosa and Birmingham, hired his engineer, fireman and brakeman, and paid them off every night. I was told that he did a good business hauling passengers and freight, as there were sawmills between the two places, and a great demand for lumber at Birmingham about that time. He kept his train running until the State of Alabama took charge of the road from Meridian to Birmingham, and the State of Georgia took charge from Birmingham to Chattanooga, and commenced running trains over the road. And I did not know but little about the road for over a year, except what I learned from others that were at work on the road for the two States.

Chapter Nine

South and North Railroad of Alabama
1871–1872

Again I was out of employment. I knew the South and North Road was under construction from Montgomery, Ala., to Decatur, Ala., and that a good friend of mine had the contract and charge of the construction work of the road; and I learned through a friend, who knew the condition of the Alabama and Chattanooga Railroad, that if I would go to Montgomery I could get work. I wanted to see my old friend who had charge of the construction work, and also wanted his recommendation, as he knew me well.

I went to Calera, got on board the work-train, which had a flat car with a few seats on it for the purpose of accommodating passengers. I went on the train as far as the end of the track, then took a hack to Birmingham. I found my friend there and nothing would do him but that I must go with him to the camps where his headquarters were. He furnished me a horse, bridle, and saddle, and I went with him. His camps were some distance north of Birmingham. We arrived there about sundown. I found a nice place at his headquarters and a good supper. After breakfast the next morning, he asked me if I would like to see his bloodhounds and have a chase. I answered that I would. He knew that I would like such fun, for we had fox-hunted together in former days.

The camps were not very far from his headquarters. He was having the work done by State convicts. We went to the stockade where a negro boy was started out on foot to a little mountain that was near by. This boy was given time to get around the mountain before the hounds were turned loose, so as to keep the boy from being caught. When the dogs were turned loose and set out for the boy's track, they seemed to be bothered for a while, as there had been so many negroes walking around the camps that morning. Nevertheless they found the boy's track, and then they set out, and in all my lifetime I think I never heard prettier music than went around that mountain at that time. The boy came back and climbed a tree near the camps, when the dogs came around and treed him and had to be taken away before the boy could come down.

The colonel, my friend of whom I spoke, told me several stories about the convicts. I saw them taking a meal while I was there and it beat anything I had ever seen in the way of eating. Dogs or hogs eating would be a credit to it in regard to manners. The colonel said that one day an old man came to the work where the convicts were and made inquiry about a son who he heard was there and after an examination was made, it was found that he was there. The son was given permission to see his father. When the old man met his son he threw his arms around his son's neck, and commenced crying, and said "Oh, son, how came you here?" And the son answered, in a loud voice, "For stealing a horse!"

Another story was told about a large, stout negro man, that he would not work and would play off sick yet he would eat all he could get. The warden whipped him, and finally the negro started to work with a pick, but did not work long until he stuck the pick clean through one of his feet in order to keep from work. The colonel told me all about the convicts, and how they had to manage a great many of them to get them to work, and how they would do to keep out of working.

I was given a good recommendation by the colonel. I went to Montgomery to see the general superintendent and the assistant superintendent; they said that they would give me a train just as soon as the track was completed to Birmingham, and would let me know when to come back. I was, in fact, not able to work at that time, as I had not entirely recovered from the injury that I had received on the Mobile and Ohio Road, for when I did commence running a train I could not unlock a car door with my right hand, on account of my finger and thumb of that hand.

It was not long after I had returned home until I received word to report to Calera, and I left just as soon as I could get to a train that was going in that direction.[1] When I arrived in Calera I was given a train that had been put on the road running between Calera and Birmingham. It was a mixed train. I would make a round trip a day, leaving Calera in the evening and returning the next morning. There had been no hotel built at Birmingham at that time, so I had to go to

Elyton to get hotel accommodations, and that was nearly a mile.

My wages were ninety dollars per month, and promptly paid every month. There was a schedule soon made out and the two passenger-trains that had been running only to Calera from Montgomery, were run through to Birmingham, and I took a passenger-train that was run between Calera and Montgomery, and connected with the Mobile and Montgomery road at Montgomery, and at Calera with the Selma, Rome and Dalton Road (that was the name of the road at that time, but afterwards changed to the Alabama Division of the East Tennessee and Georgia Railroad), at this time part of the division of the Southern Railway.

The distance at that time was called sixty-three miles from Montgomery to Calera, and thirty-seven from Calera to Birmingham. When I was on the run last spoken of, I lay over at Calera of nights, leaving there early in the morning and returning in the evening. It was a nice train which I ran then, and a good run. Day work and night rest, which is according to nature and what God intended when man was first created, but I, for one, have failed to carry it out.

My train was composed of a combination baggage express and mail car, two coaches, and a Pullman sleeper. When the southern travel commenced going east to summer resorts, I would have sometimes two and three sleeping-cars packed full of passengers. This line of sleepers, at that time, was running to New Orleans, and was called the Blue Mountain route.

The first engineer that pulled me on the run of which I have spoken was killed one Sunday evening, just after we arrived at Calera. I boarded at his house, as he lived at Calera and preferred it to the hotel that was at that place. After I had made my transfer to the Selma, Rome and Dalton train, we started home, and a man came running after my engineer and said, "The hostler has cut your fireman's jaw open with a knife." The engineer wheeled around at once and started back in a run. I tried to keep him back, but he would not listen to me. The hostler saw him running toward the engine where this had occurred, and he ran home, and the engineer followed him into his house and was shot by the hostler. His remains were shipped to the State of New York, where he came from when he came to the South.

I came very near being killed while on the same run. Calera was the place where the South and North Road crossed the Selma, Rome and Dalton Road, and when going north we had to keep the main track until we crossed the Selma, Rome and Dalton track to a switch that connected a Y track to the main track, and at that place the engine was cut loose from the train, and a yard engine coupled on instead. My brakeman had to go with the engine to the turning table and turn her around, and the yard engine would back the train down the Υ track to where the transfer was made to the Selma, Rome and Dalton train and the sleeping-cars delivered to them. So I had to look out for the switches myself while backing. At one time we were backing, and I was on the rear platform. I saw a switch wrong and the engine was backing at a pretty fast speed. I jumped off to run and set the switch to the Υ track. On account of lumber being piled along the track on the side which I ought to have gotten off on, I stepped off on the opposite side of the track, and had to cross the track in order to change the switch. It was sprinkling rain and everything was very slick, and I was going in a run, with my lamp in one hand, as it was nearly dark. When I went to cross the track, one foot slipped and I fell across the track. I rolled myself to one side of the track just in time to save my life. Another conductor was standing on the platform from which I had jumped and saw me fall. He halloed and put a brake on, but before the train was stopped the sleeper and one coach had run over my lamp where I had fallen and just before the switch was reached.

When I returned to Montgomery the next morning, I related the facts to my superintendent. I told him I would take no more such chances, and if my brakemen could not go with the train and do such work as that, I did not need any brakemen on my train, and I allowed them to do such work afterwards. A heavy rain fell and damaged some bridges which crossed the big and little Catawba rivers between Calera and Birmingham. And between Calera and Montgomery the track and road-bed was torn up in places, and in some places the trestle work was damaged. I was cut off in Montgomery. All trains were stopped running between Montgomery and Birmingham for several days. I was instructed to hire men and take an engine and a train of flat cars, tools, etc., and also a civil engineer, and repair the road. So I started around in town and hired all the negroes I could find that wanted to work. It was a very hot day for such work as trying to get up a gang of men. When I had everything ready I started out on the road, which was the same day, late in the evening. I worked day and night until I met a gang of bridge and track men who had repaired the road from Birmingham to where I met them. The two passenger-trains commenced running again between Birmingham and Montgomery. Freight cars had accumulated at Montgomery and Calera until both yards were blocked. The superintendent asked me to take an engine and move the freight and then he would put the train back that I had been running between Montgomery and Calera. I took my two brakemen and again worked day and night until I had cleared both yards, which took me about one week to do, then I took my former run.

One day the superintendent said to me that I must get some good men and keep them, saying he noticed on the pay-roll where I had thirteen different brakemen in one month. As well as I remember that was the number he said. I replied to him that I could not get good men at the wages they were paying then and do the work which was required of them, and that when I got a good man he would not stay, and some were so trifling that I would not keep them. I said to him that the brakemen were required to help turn the engine at each end of the road, keep the coach wheels clean by scraping the grease off them and then cleaning them with potash, so by the time this was done they had but little time to rest; and that a good man would not do it at the wages the road was paying, which was one dollar per day. In a short time after this conversation the work of cleaning the car wheels was taken off the brakemen, and I picked up some pretty good men.

I was returning from a trip home one evening, and when I changed trains at Calera the conductor of the South and North train came to me and wanted me to take charge of his train. I begged to be excused, and he said he was sick and not able to run. So, on that account I took charge of his train. The other conductor went back to the sleeping car and went to bed, and we had not gone more than fourteen miles west of Calera when the engine struck an ox at the end of the trestle, which threw the engine off the track, and she turned over down an embankment. The engineer was the only one that was hurt, and he was not seriously injured. I awoke the ought-to-have-been conductor and related the facts to him, but he would not get up, and complained of being very sick. So I picked up some section men and set some of them to work, and took enough of them to run a lever car and went back to Calera. I had an engine fired up, then went back to the wreck, cleared the track and went on to Montgomery with the engine which I had gone back to Calera after, leaving the derailed engine for some one else to pick up. It was an awful cold night, for when I was going back to Calera on the lever car, I had to stop where a pile of sawdust was burning and warm myself, because I was so near freezing. I went back in the sleeping-car about sunrise, and just before we arrived in Montgomery, to see how the sick conductor was getting along, and I found him up making his toilet. When I saw him he said he wanted to be ready for his breakfast when he got to Montgomery. So I supposed by what he said that he had gotten over his sick spell. The wreck spoken of was all the wreck I had while I ran on the South and North road. I would not have had that had I been where I ought to have been—in bed, in place of the sick conductor. As well as I can remember, I ran on the South and North

Road about one year and a half, when the grading was done and the track was completed to Decatur, where it was connected to the track that was laid from Nashville to Decatur.

Just before or about this time the superintendent was on my train one day, and asked me if I would take charge of the railroad yard in Montgomery as yardmaster. He said the reason he wanted me to take it was because I had a turn to get along with everybody. I asked what it would pay me, and he said the same I was getting for conducting a train, which was ninety dollars per month. I told him that I knew nothing about yard work, that I had never worked in a yard in all of my railroading, with the exception of one day, and then I came very near getting killed by being caught between two cars, and added that if I should take the place I would not touch it for less than one hundred and twenty-five dollars per month, and if I gave satisfaction for two months, they would have to pay me one hundred and fifty dollars per month. So that stopped the yard question.

It was only a few days after the yard conversation of which I have been speaking, until the superintendent came to me and said that the road was going to be turned over to the Louisville and Nashville company and the schedule changed so as to run the passenger-trains through to Decatur, Ala., and that there would be three trains. He also said that the Louisville and Nashville people allowed him to turn over three passenger conductors and three freight conductors. I will give the conversation just as the words were spoken between the superintendent and myself. He said that he had promised a conductor, who was running on a different road at the time when he made the promise, to give him a train whenever he wanted it, this being before I came on the Louisville and Nashville Road, and that he wanted to turn over the other two passenger conductors that he had besides myself and his friend who had come for a fulfillment of his promise, and two of the freight conductors and myself, as freight conductors, to the Louisville and Nashville Company. He said that he knew that I was entitled to be turned over as a passenger conductor, but it had been so long since the other man had run a freight-train that he was afraid to turn him over as a freight conductor to the Louisville and Nashville Company, and that he knew I could run one. I said to him that I could run any kind of a train they had, even a work train, but I did not propose doing it after I had worked as I had done on the road, and then be treated in such a way as that. I also said to him that he had a right to turn over whom he pleased, and I had the right to quit the service of the road. He then said, "You think I am down on you, but I am not. I like you as well as any conductor I have, and better in regard to honesty and morality." I replied, "It does not look so to me, and therefore I will leave the service of the company." He plead with me for some time not to leave, as I would soon be back on a passenger-train, but I decided not to stay, knowing that the conductor that he put in my place had left the road that he had been on on account of drawback tickets being put on the road.[2] I learned this from the conductor himself, while I did not ask for any information. From the time I commenced work on the road up to the time I left it, I thought I had a right over a man that had never struck a lick on the Louisville and Nashville Road. While I had often thought, while on other roads, that a man's merit was nothing on a railroad, I there and then learned that favoritism and friendship stood away ahead of morality and honesty regardless of ability. I will now state how long the conductor lasted on the Louisville and Nashville, who was turned over to that company in my place. It was either the first or second trip that he made. I do not now recollect which, on the Louisville and Nashville Road, as it was now called, the name being changed from the South and North to the Louisville and Nashville as soon as it was turned over to the Louisville and Nashville Company. The captain I spoke of was going north on his run, and he run, I think it was, thirty-nine minutes on the rights of a south-bound train, and would have had a head collision with south-bound passenger-train had not the south-bound train stopped for wood, and heard the north-bound train and sent a flagman ahead to stop them. So this ended his services on the Louisville and Nashville. I was not glad when I heard of this, neither very sorry, so long as no damage was done of any one hurt, but I remarked that it seemed as though he had also forgotten how to run a passenger-train as well as a freight.

I will now go back to the day on which the superintendent and myself had the conversation in regard to the road and conductors being turned over to the Louisville and Nashville Company. I went to my room after the conversation had ended to make preparations to start home the next morning. A conductor, a good friend of mine, came in late in the evening on his run and had learned what had taken place, and that I had decided to leave the road. He at once came to my room and stayed until after 1 o'clock A.M. trying to persuade me to stay and run the freight-train. He said that I knew that I was master of my business and for me to take the freight-train until I could get work elsewhere, and then he would not blame me for leaving. So I agreed to do as he wished, and on a freight-train I went the next morning. I did not mind it, or feel myself above it, for I had run freight-trains for months and years; all I hated was the way I had been treated. I do not remember now how long I run the freight-train, but I know I did not run many trips before I received a letter from the superintendent of the Alabama and Chattanooga Railroad, that Mr. Stanton had got the road back and was going to take charge of it soon, and that if I wanted a passenger-train on the road to be in Chattanooga by a certain time. I said nothing, but run my freight-train just the same. One day, as I was going north, I received orders at a way station to meet first section No. 12 at Lomax, another way-station. When I arrived at Lomax and was going in on a side-track, the operator came running to me with an order to meet the first section No. 12 at Jamison, a way-station farther on. I went in on the side-track, but the operator tried his best to keep me from doing so, and wanted me to go on. But I told him that I would stay on the side-track until the first order I had received was annulled. He went back to the office, and before he got there came the first section of No. 12 at full freight schedule speed, and when the operator returned with the next order it read second section No. 12 at Jamisons.

My run was from Montgomery to Birmingham, stay over night, and back next day. The passenger schedule was fast, and the time was seldom made. One or two bad wrecks occurred between Decatur and Birmingham with passenger-trains and several passengers killed. There was one south of Birmingham, not long after I left the road, which was said to be the worst of all. When the Louisville and Nashville Company took control of the South and North Road, a new superintendent was placed in charge of the road from Decatur to Montgomery, and my superintendent acted as assistant for a short time, leaving the road soon after I had left it.

I was at Birmingham one morning when I received a telegram from Mr. Stanton saying that he had his road back, and for me to be on hand on a certain day, naming the day. He stated that he would give me a passenger-train. I will state just here that had it not been for the way in which I had been treated, when the road was turned over to the Louisville and Nashville Company, I should have paid but little attention to the message I had received. My wages were pretty fair for those times and promptly paid. I went back to Montgomery with my freight-train, and my old superintendent said to me: "They want you and crew sent to Birmingham in the morning." This was the way we received orders when to go out. I answered that I was not going to run another trip; that I had quit and had run my last trip over this road that I ever expected to make. The superintendent walked off, and several years passed before we ever met again.

I learned from a conductor before we did meet that my former superintendent (who was a man I liked very well up to the time of which I spoke in regard to my being turned over as a freight conductor to the

Louisville and Nashville Company), was talking to him one day and remarked that he wished he had a road and had all of his old men on it, and spoke of me, saying that he did not treat me right, and that I would always hate him from my heart. He remarked that he was sorry of it. When I was told of his conversation I freely forgave him, and when we did meet I was proud to meet him. The conductor who informed me of what the ex-superintendent said, was the same one who persuaded me to take the freight train, and also the one who told me about the run which my successor made, for it was he who met him.

I answered Mr. Stanton's telegram, informing him that I would be there on the day which he had specified for me to be there. The day I left Montgomery for Chattanooga, I met the new superintendent at Birmingham when I arrived there. He was a very nice gentleman, and I had met him before. When I met him, he asked me where I was going, and I informed him. He said, "You are not going to leave the road?" I answered that I was. He said that he was very sorry, and that he had been informed of the way in which I had been treated and that if I would stay I should have the passenger run that I was entitled to. I thanked him and told him that I had a position on the Alabama and Chattanooga Road and would be nearer home. But I was afterwards sorry that I did not do as he asked me to do, the reason for which will be explained in the next chapter.

Chapter Ten

Back on the Alabama and Chattanooga Road

1872–1876

Well, it seemed to me that misfortune went wherever I did, and was ready to stand in front of me and look me right in the face even when good fortune appeared to want to favor me itself. When I arrived in Chattanooga, the very day and time set by Mr. Stanton himself, and went to his office to report for duty, he said: "Well, I will have to give you a freight-train, as another conductor (calling the conductor by name) came in and claims the run I did intend to put you on."

I never spoke a word after he said that until I produced the letter and telegram I had received, and the latter bore his own signature. After Mr. Stanton had read the papers I handed him he said, "All right," I could take the run out the next morning, and I did so, and it was one time that good fortune stepped up in time to do me a kindness, and was also one time that the keen-eyed man, with the slick tongue, smooth lips, and brassy cheeks had to take a freight-train, which was and is now an uncommon thing for such conductors to do.

Again Mr. Stanton and his relatives were running the Alabama and Chattanooga Railroad. The States of Georgia and Alabama had tried it awhile and had made but little profit, if any. At the time I speak of now the treaties had begun to decay, yet Mr. Stanton run the road pretty successfully for awhile. When business began to slack off the passenger-trains were made mixed trains and freight-trains taken off. I was running a mixed train when some of the engineers told me of a plan that some of the conductors had gone into, that was to leave all the work they possibly could for me to do, that I would have it to do and that I could not do the work and make the time, so when passenger trains were put on again I would not be given one. Knowing that it was my disposition to do the work, it was nearly all left for me to do, thinking I would not be given a passenger-train on account of not making good time. There was talk among the men at that time of putting on regular passenger-trains again. The engineers that told me their plan said for me to do the work and they would make the time, and they were good men and meant what they said; so I did the work and the engineers made the time. We were handling a great deal of cotton at that time, and I have heard men, when I would arrive at stations and they saw me, they would call my name and say, "We will get our cotton off today." I stopped one day in a field where the road runs through, near Brown's cut, and loaded one hundred bales of cotton, but the shipper furnished men to load them or put them in the cars and I had my men to place them. The arrangements had been made beforehand and I had taken cars sufficient to hold that number of bales. A conductor had a draw-head pulled out of a flat car that was in his train loaded with lumber and he left it on a side-track, and when I came along the agent told me what the conductor who left it there said, and that was that he would set out and let me get it, but I would not take it, for the fact that it was done on purpose to delay me.[1] So after the same conductor had passed it going in the same direction as he was when the car was set out, I received orders to take the car on. When I got to Chattanooga I asked the officer who gave me the order why he did not have the one to take it that left it there, and why the conductor could not have chained it as I had to do when I took it away. The officer said he had asked him in regard to that, and he said he had no chain. I also learned from the engineer that the plan was to take my men away from me whenever I had a good one; one or two were taken by other conductors before I had been informed of that fact, so I hired me some more good men and posted them of what had been planned against me, and they said they would stay with me. One day we met a train and the conductor of the train asked my men if they would quit me and run with him, and they told him when they left me they would leave the road, so they let them alone. I do not relate these facts as boasting of my work, for I only did what was my duty to do, but to show how some men acted on railroads in those days. While I was on a passenger-train on the Alabama and Chattanooga Road I left Meridian in the early part of the night with a train loaded with passengers, and fifty or more of them wanted to make connection at Birmingham with the Louisville and Nashville Road. Wood was getting scarce along the road as well as water in the tanks and we had to cut the engine loose from the train often that night and run her ahead for wood and water. We had worked hard all night and had made but little progress. My

Louisville and Nashville passengers became uneasy about their connections and worried me very much about it; I was doing my very best to make the connections for them. We cut the engine loose and run for wood and water, and with a tender full of both, went back and got the train. I had told the passengers that we had plenty of fuel and water to take us to Birmingham, and that we would make the connection with the Louisville and Nashville, as they did not leave until 9 o'clock A.M. It was Sunday morning and the sun was up clear and bright when we struck the "Alps," as we called them, and going through them the engineer had to go down grades at full speed so as to get up the grades. We were descending one of the grades when a stop was made as soon as could be, and I went out to learn the cause. The engineer said he was flagged to stop. I saw a well dressed negro man standing on the track in front of the engine with a stick in his hand. As there was a small trestle at the foot of the grade, I at once thought the trestle had burned, as some such threats had been made. So I walked to where the negro was standing to thank him for flagging us before we were wrecked. I asked him if the trestle was burned, and he said it was not. "What did you flag us down for?" I said. He said: "I wanted to get on the train." I said, "What kind of a stick is that you have?" He said, "Hickory." I said, "Let me see it" and he gave it to me. I had no sooner got my hand on it than I gave him a welt on the side of his head. I said" "I will learn you to go to a station when you want to get on a train." As I hit him he broke in a run up a hill through the woods saying, "I never will do so again." I followed him near the top of the hill and saw he was gaining on me, I threw the stick at him and one end of it struck him on the back of the head and knocked him down, but he was up in a moment and going down the hill on the opposite side at the fastest speed he could make. I returned to the train; some of my passengers had started to help me, and when they learned the facts said I did right and wished they could have got hold of him. So as soon as the show was over we went ahead and made the Louisville and Nashville connection at Birmingham.

It was a common thing on the road at times to have to cut the engine loose from the train and run for wood and water. I have sometimes had to stop when running through piney woods and have pine knots gathered along the roadside for fuel; it was so common to bail water we carried water buckets at times on the trains for that purpose. I was going south. We had been out all night, water was scarce in the water tanks and along the road, we had cut loose from the engine and run for water, and bailed water so much that it reminded me of war times.

One time my engineer had passed a water-tank, and I stopped him and made him back to the tank and take water. When we got near

Livingston, just sunrise, the engineer stopped his engine, cut her loose and ran her off a little distance from the train and stopped. I asked him what was the matter, and he said he had burned his engine. I left him there, and walked to the depot to report the facts. When I did so I went to the hotel to order breakfast for my crew and what few passengers I had. When I got to the hotel I was surprised to find my engineer and fireman there awaiting their breakfast. About that time a messenger came in a run and said the engine was on fire; I went back to the engine at once, but when I got there, I found her cab was burned to ashes, all her lagging burned off; my brakeman that I had left to take care of the train had gone to sleep. I sent one back in case there was a train or engine on the road. When the man I had sent to watch the train was aroused by some of the passengers the fire had gotten such a headway that he could not get the water out of the tender on account of the heat and there was no water near the place. Another engine was sent me from Meridian. The burned engine was towed to the station and placed on the side track, and afterwards towed back to Chattanooga.[2]

I was on another trip of the same kind, and had been out nearly all night, and had gotten within four and a half miles of Meridian, when the engineer stopped. I went out to learn the cause, and he said there was something the matter with the engine, but he did not know what. I said: "It may be you have burned her." He said: "No, she is not burned." The fireman came and said to me in a whisper that the engine was burned. I then said to the engineer: "Your engine is burned, in my opinion, and if so, let me know it, so I can send for another engine." He then said to me: "You may send for one if you do not want to stay here." So I started a man afoot to Meridian with a statement of what had happened and for an engine. I wanted my engineer to take down the rods and have his engine ready to be towed in by the time the engine that I had sent for came; but he would not touch her. It was a very cold morning, and I had a bonfire made and after it had got to burning good an Indian came out of a canebrake shivering with cold. When he came to the fire he said: "Much cold." It was a clear morning and the moon was about full and about one hour and a half high. The limbs and twigs of the trees were full of icicles and it was a pretty sight to look at. When I would look towards the moon there stood a very large elm tree off to itself, in plain view, between where I stood and the moon. While it looked lonely, it was a beautiful scene to look at with its large round top and icicles hanging from every twig that was on it. It made a beautiful picture to behold.

When the engine came that I had sent for, the master machinist of that division came. He asked me why the engineer did not take the rods of the burned engine down. I told him that I tried to get him to do so, but could not get him to do it. He then asked the engineer, and he told him that he knew that he would be discharged and he did not intend to strike another lick. The rods were taken down by the men that came out of Meridian with the engine,and she was towed into Meridian as we went in with the train.

An engineer was sent out of Chattanooga; as well as I remember it was a light engine that he started out with for Meridian, and I was told that the engineer said before he left Chattanooga that he would make Meridian on time, or land the engine in hades. The road ran through a swamp where there were some low trestles. The engine left the track while crossing one, and turned over on its side, and the engineer was killed. How unthoughtful we are. Another engine ran off the track near Meridian, turned over and killed another engineer.

There was a train derailed and the supervisor was killed; he was in the baggage car and jumped out and the car turned over on him and killed him instantly. It was reported that it was me that was killed in the wreck just spoken of. I do not know how the report got out, for it was not my train that was wrecked at the time the supervisor was killed, and I did not know such a report was out until I met up with a Louisville and Nashville conductor, and he was surprised to see me still living. He told me about the rumor that was on the Louisville and Nashville Road in regard to it, and said it was believed by all who knew me on that road; and also said that my old friend, who was a conductor on the Louisville and Nashville Road shed tears, and said he knew I was at my post when I was killed, and paid my assessment, as I at that time belonged to the order of conductors called "The Old Reliables." Afterwards I paid to him the same amount of money.

The trestles had become rotten and an engine fell through one of them that extended from one end of the bridge that crossed the Black Warrior river, and was about three miles long and about twelve feet high. When the engine fell through the engineer went down with his engine, but only had his arms hurt; he was the only one that was injured.

I remember one time when the waters of the Tombigbee river were flowing over the lowlands, an engine with a train was rolling slowly over the bridge that crossed the river, the bridge gave way near the end just before the engine got off, and it went down in the water with the engineer and fireman on it, out of sight of those who were left to tell the story. A diving-bell was purchased and several efforts were made before the bodies were recovered. The engineer was a young man and had just been married. The baggage car went down on one end and also one coach, but I think they caught on some timbers. Some of those that were in them got out, and those that could not were helped out.

I was sent out of Chattanooga once after a heavy rainfall with an engine, a few box and flat cars, a baggage car and two coaches, and was instructed to go through to Meridian if I could possibly get over the road. I was early one Monday morning. I made pretty fair speed until I got west of Birmingham, when I found a place I thought not fit to run over I would have it repaired. I had about twenty or twenty-five negroes on board, who were going to pick cotton in the Mississippi valley. I would hire them to help me and would also pick up section men when I could find any. I found the track torn up and embankments washed out in many places after I passed Tuscaloosa. Some places where I could get timber I would have trees cut down and build pens out of logs so as to put the track across the washout. I would pay my men off every night. I worked day and night until I got to Meridian. When I arrived there I went to an office, took a seat near a desk, crossed my arms on the desk, dropped my head on my arms and went to sleep and slept about four or five hours. When I awoke I started back to Chattanooga. I had not been in bed the whole week. I run a trip once from Chattanooga to Meridian and back to Chattanooga and only collected fifty cents and very few tickets.

I had a coach in my train one day when the front trucks were derailed and the wheels on one side went in a ditch on the roadside. We were placing wood so as to put the wheels of the car back on the track, when a man who was a passenger came out to suggest how to put them back, as was invariably the case when an accident occurred, and is kept up to the present day by some passengers. When the man commenced to give instructions, I asked him if he wanted to help get the trucks of the coach back on the rails, and he said "Yes." I said to him then to help the boys bring wood, and so he went to carrying wood at once.

I went into Meridian one night very sick. As soon as I left my train I went to a hotel and took a room, and sent for a physician, one of my trainmen being ordered to stay with me. I was confined to my bed for several days. When I did get able to sit up, the doctor came in one morning and found me sitting by the fireplace smoking a cigar. He gave me a scolding, and asked me if I wanted to kill myself. Then he made me throw my cigar in the fire, and took the ones I had lying on the mantlepiece and threw them in the fire also. I met him several years after I had left the Alabama and Chattanooga road, and in conversation about attending on me while I was sick in Meridian, he remarked that when he first came to me he had no idea that I ever would get out of the room that I was in at that time, alive.

I left Meridian once with a passenger train, and had only one passenger; he had a ticket reading "from New Orleans to New York"; when he handed me his ticket I lifted the coupon that was attached to it, reading "from Meridian to Chattanooga, over the Alabama and Chattanooga Railroad." The road was in a bad shape at that time, and I would occasionally go back and ride on the rear platform of the rear coach, this being a habit of mine on account of bad bridges and rotten timbers in trestles, for I had gone over some when I saw bents fall after the weight of the engine and train had gotten off of them.

One time I remember crossing a creek that had a trestle over it; this was in time of high water, and when the engine went on the trestle the track went down into the water, letting the water come up into the firebox, and this put out the fire. After having crossed the trestle it raised up again so I could see it. The engine had to be fired up again. Big Sandy was the name of the creek. So at the time I speak of, when I had only one passenger, he asked me what I went out on the platform so often for. I answered, "To look at the track." Once he came out while I was standing on the platform, and the rotten wood began to fall off the trestle that were running over, and he said: "I see now why you stand out on the platform so much of the time, and I don't blame you." Then he asked me why I did not leave the d——d road and go on a good one, that I could get work on a good road anywhere. But by experience I knew better.

A while after noon my passenger asked me where the dinner station was. I answered that there was none. He then asked where we got dinner. I answered that we did not get any. He then turned in and cursed out the man in New Orleans who sold him the ticket he had. He then cursed the road, and swore that he never would go over it again.

The hotels and boarding-houses along the road had quit letting the men have meals unless they would pay down for them, and this they could not do on account of not being paid off regularly.[3] And on this account Mr. Stanton had several thousand dollars' worth of scrip struck off as a kind of meal ticket. As well as I remember, they were issued in twenty-five and fifty cents slips, with the picture of a duck on one kind and a fine rooster on the other, and looked very nice while new. They went like Confederate money—were good for awhile, and anybody would take them, but soon played out. The men were paid with them as a part of their wages and they could get their meals with them, and sometimes grocerymen would take them. I knew one man who sold a house and lot and took Stanton scrip, as it was called, in payment for his property, and the scrip went dead on his hands. I think Mr. Stanton agreed to make it good in case it did fail, but a lawsuit was brought first and it was a long time before the man in question got anything, and when he did it was done by a compromise. After the scrip played out there was an arrangement made for the conductors to pay the men's board while on the road, out of their cash collections, a receipt being taken from the men who furnished the meals and the conductors turned the receipts in with their report as cash collections.

Along about those times the treasurer of the road would wire conductors before they would get to Chattanooga to have their cash collections ready to turn over on arrival. So on our arrival we were met as soon as we stepped off the train by a man who received the cash collections conductors had taken up. The road got in such bad condition in places west of Birmingham, and to cut down the expenses of the road it was decided to take off trains and reduce the trainmen and shop force. They put on a mixed train from Birmingham to Meridian, one each way a day, so as to do the passenger and freight work on that part of the road. A passenger train was put on, one each way a day between Chattanooga and Birmingham, making connection at the latter named place with the mixed trains, also the Louisville and Nashville trains and with the East Tennessee, Virginia and Georgia Road at Chattanooga. Freight trains were also run between Chattanooga and Birmingham sufficient to do the freight work. What money the road made was to pay the running expenses and trainmen and shop hands, and if there was any over, it was to be paid to the men on their back wages which were due them.

I run one of the trains between Chattanooga and Birmingham; these trains were very nice. They were short trains, being composed of a baggage car and two coaches. Between Chattanooga and Birmingham the track at this time was comparatively good, notwithstanding there were but few men at work on it, some having quit their sections. One section boss told me that he and his men went out through the country and dug wells and took their pay in provisions, and then went back on the track and worked until the provisions were consumed, and never got a dollar from the road while they were doing the work. Well, the little passenger-train picked up a good passenger business, and freight was good. We were paid promptly every Saturday.

The men whose services the road had dispensed with in order to curtail expenses, became dissatisfied and wanted their back pay, and wanted the engineers to quit work and join them in a strike. This had been talked of quietly for some time before I learned of it. My engineer told me of what was being talked of among some of the men one day when we were in Birmingham. I begged him not to go in with them, explaining to him the effect a strike would have, and asked him to talk with the men and persuade them not to undertake such an action, for if we did not get our back pay under the present arrangement we never would.

In a few days afterwards they set a day to hold a meeting, and insisted on me attending the meeting, but at first I refused. Finally I concluded that I might do some good and I would attend. So when I went I was appointed chairman by the committee. There were some in favor of a strike; in fact the majority were, but there was nothing decided upon. They asked me to make them a speech and give my opinion in regard to a strike or the best course to pursue to get our back pay. I said to the men that I had never made a speech in my life and could not make one, but I would give them my opinion, according to the best of my judgment, in regard to the matter. I then addressed the following words to them:

"You all know the condition of the road, and that Mr. Stanton has made many efforts in the East, as well as in this section, to raise money in order to pay the men and run the road as a road should be run, but has failed to do so. Now a plan has been made so as to cut down expenses and use the earnings to pay the men their back pay, just as soon as the road can make enough to do so. The road is now doing well, according to the amount of trains that are running.

"I am not in favor of a strike. I never knew of one that did not do as much harm, or more, than it ever did good. So my advice is to let the trains run on and make all they can, and after awhile they will make enough to pay the employees their back pay. That is the only chance I see now to ever get it, for the road is now making money, and if the debt is not paid in this way it never will be, in my opinion."

These remarks seemed to change the minds of the men present, with a few exceptions.

It was but a short while after this until the engineers that were running the engines that were in service at the time, stepped off of their engines, and all trains were stopped from one end of the road to the other. Mr. Stanton had just returned from the east, and wanted to start his trains running again. The employees had gathered all around the depot and offices, and the yard was full of men. Mr. Stanton requested that some of the oldest employees get together and see if they could not persuade the men to let a train be started out on the road. Some of us met at the Stanton Hotel and tried to make an agreement with the striking class, but to no effect. Those in favor of the strike said that Mr. Stanton had brought with him from the East a mail pouch, and all he wanted was to get that started over the road, and then he would have them so they could not stop on account of the United States mail.

There was a box car standing in the yard, said to be loaded with provisions for the section men. So Mr. Stanton then said to the men, that he had a car of provisions that he wanted to send down the road to section men, and that there was a party of gentlemen, who were interested in the Rising Fawn furnace, that he wanted to accommodate by sending a train for them as far down as Rising Fawn, a station on the road, which was about twenty-five miles out from Chattanooga. After a long persuasion by Mr. Stanton and the party of gentlemen who wished to go to Rising Fawn, it was agreed to let an engine take them out. So when ready an engine was coupled to the car of provisions, and then a coach was taken on. When this was done, another trouble was gotten up about the mail pouch, and a search had to be made for something that was not there, and I suppose that Mr. Stanton had never thought of such a thing.

At last the short train was started out, with the master machinist as engineer, and myself as conductor. The trip was made successfully. When I returned to Chattanooga I made out my cash report; I had collected about thirty-five dollars in cash. I had a conversation with my engineer, and he said that if I divided this money with the crew or any of the men, or gave it to the company, that I would be a fool, for they owed me as much as any of the rest, and that I needed it as badly. So, as I said, I made out my report, and went to the superintendent and asked him to give me permission to sign a voucher for the amount I had collected, and informed him what that amount was. He refused my request. I then went to the treasurer's office and explained the matter to the treasurer, and he refused also, but said that he would see the superintendent. I replied that I had seen him myself. Then he asked me what the superintendent said. I told him, and said: "Make me out a voucher and I will sign it," and handed him my tickets and cash report saying, "The company is due me several hundred dollars and I have the amount, which that report shows, in my pocket, and I am a fool if I give it up." Then he made out a voucher and I signed it. So the Alabama and Chattanooga Road was stopped again, and the employees have never got their back pay to the present day. Some of the men who made themselves most annoying about not getting their pay, had but a small amount due them. How foolish some men can act at times.

I was not out of work that time. I was sent for to go to Atlanta, and I went and took a freight train on the old reliable Western and Atlantic again, which was the first road that I ever worked for and the one I was on when I voted myself out of work. I had only run two round trips on the Western and Atlantic when I received a telegram to go to Selma, Ala., and I would be given a passenger-train. I showed the telegram to the yard-master, and he said that he hated to give me up, but it might be a long time before they could give me a passenger train. I then went to the master of transportation, and he said about the same as the yard-master had said, and told me to come back if I got out of work and he would give me work any time that I wanted it, as long as he had any-thing to do with the Western and Atlantic Railroad.

I went to Selma and ran a passenger train between that place and Meridian, over the Alabama Central road to York, and over the Alabama and Chattanooga road from York to Meridian, making a distance of fifty-seven miles. I made a round trip a day.

I was running in another conductor's place while he took a trip east, and arrangements were made when he returned to put on an accommo-dation-train, to run between Selma and Demopolis, and I was to take the run. I do not remember how long I ran on the Alabama Central Road, but not longer than three months, as well as I now remember. I was in one accident while I was there. An engine that was pulling my train struck a bull, running over it, and the neck of the beast threw the engine off the track, and she turned over down an embankment on her side, and the engineer made a narrow escape. He was caught under the tender, but fortunately a stump kept the weight off of him. He was pretty severely injured, but not dangerously. No one else was hurt. I think I had only been on the road about two months, and maybe not so long, when the yellow fever broke out in Montgomery; this frightened the citizens of Selma, and the city was quarantined, and would not allow trains to run any farther out than twelve miles, so the superintendent would not run any trains, and all schedules were discontinued.[4] Learning of the death of an old friend of mine, who died of the yellow fever in Montgomery, I was very anxious to get out of that section of country.

The superintendent said that I could go home, and when he put his trains back to running he would send for me. But before he got his trains to running, Mr. Stanton in some way had his road in operation again, and I was running a train on the Alabama and Chattanooga Railroad, as it seemed like I could not keep off of it while Mr. Stanton had anything to do with it, and why I can hardly tell, unless on account of a hope of getting what was due me from him or his company; and that some day it would be a first-class road, and if I lived to see the time I would have a good road to work for as long as I wanted to or did my duty. At that time I was in hope of the East Tennessee, Virginia and Georgia Road getting control of it, and I thought it would make them the shortest route that had ever been made from New York to New Orleans. As I have said, the road was in bad condition, and at the time I now speak of the trains only ran west as far as Tuscaloosa.

Mr. Stanton was on my train one day, and said that some of the conductors wanted him to put me off the road, or give me a freight-train,
and give passenger-trains to Eastern men. He said that he told them that
he would not do anything of the kind. He said that they had also told
him that I was in the strike, and that I had kept some money; he said
that he did not understand how it was, for he did not believe a word
they said, and had paid but little attention to their conversation. I
explained the facts just as they occurred in regard to the strike and the
money, and he said to me: "I do not blame you a d——d bit. You did
just right."

I ran a short train once while I was on the Alabama and Chattanooga
Road, between Tuscaloosa and Eutaw, a distance of thirty-five miles. It
was put on to accommodate the citizens along the line of that part of
the road. There were some places between Eutaw and Livingston where
the track was so bad, at the time of which I speak, that trains could not
be run over them. In fact, there were trestles that were not safe to run
over on the part that I was on. I would leave Tuscaloosa in the morning
and return in the evening of the same day.

At the same time a train was running each way a day between
Chattanooga and Tuscaloosa, and one between Livingston and
Meridian. Sometimes a lever car would bring me passengers from
Livingston to Eutaw, as a lever car was the only kind of transportation
there was on that part of the road at the time of which I speak. My
engineer on this run was a reckless one. He only pulled two coaches and
a baggage car, and would run very fast. When he was running faster
than I thought safe, I would ring him down; he would not pay any
attention to it, so I would have the brakes applied. Once he came back
and commenced to curse the brakeman. I said to him not to curse my
men, if he wanted to curse anyone to curse me, as I was the one who
had the brakes put on. I said, "You know this road is not safe to make
the time you do over it." He went back to the engine, saying, with an
oath, "If the engine goes in a trestle those coaches will go in on top of
her."

Ahead of us was a short trestle about ninety feet high; when we
crossed it he was going at a rapid rate, for I would always have the
brakes loosened before we went on a bridge or trestle. I was in the rear
coach while we were going over the trestle, and about the middle of it I
thought I was gone, for the coach turned nearly half over, but it was
crossed so quickly that it remained on the track. I looked back after we
were across, and saw that one of the stringers had broken about the
middle, and each end was hanging down. When we arrived at
Tuscaloosa the engineer ran past the depot with all the brakes on, and

we were to meet a train from Chattanooga, which was past due. I started to the engine, but met the engineer, and he said to me, "Why did you not have me held with the brakes?"

I replied to him, "You will not need any more holding, for you have pulled me the last time you ever will. By morning I will have another man to take your engine."

He answered, "All right."

So a man was sent to take his place.

While I was on this run, there was a negro mail agent on the train which ran between Meridian and Livingston. He was killed one evening while on duty. I was informed afterwards that his body was riddled with buck-shot, and the sides of the car he was in when killed was full of shot and dents. They had fired on him from both sides of the road. Nearly all the young men in the country where this took place were arrested, but were released, as there could be no evidence of their being guilty of this crime. Some seemed to think that a party from Mississippi did the killing, but it was never known who did it, that I know of.

This negro mail agent went on my train with his commission when he first got his appointment. At this time the trains were running the entire length of the road. He boarded my train and told me what he was going to Chattanooga for, and I said to him that I would advise him not to run through that section of country as mail agent, as there had already been one black man killed on the Mobile and Ohio road, and another notified not to pass a certain station on some other road; and this man obeyed the notice and did not pass any more, and in so doing saved his life. But the one I was talking to answered me by saying that if he knew that there was one drop of cowardly blood in his veins, he would take a knife and cut it out. He went to running on the road, and ran on my train a good part of the time, when the trains were running through. He was polite and accommodating, and behaved better than some of the white mail agents; but there was a talk along the road in some places further up than where he was killed. At one station an old man, who came to the train to change the mail, would say sometimes when the negro was on that he smelt blood. I had an Irishman braking for me, and one night, when we were leaving a station, he was standing on the rear platform of the rear coach, when a gun was fired off just behind the train; this frightened my Irishman so much that he ran inside the coach, saying that some one shot at him, and liked to have hit him, for he saw the ball go across the track. This created a laugh among the passengers. These occurrences were talked of by the men on the road and the other mail agent became alarmed, for fear some of them might be mistaken for the negro.

One night I concluded that I would have a little fun of my own, at the expense of one of the mail agents. So I told the express messenger to fire his pistol off once or twice just as we left the station where the gun had been fired off a few nights before, as I wanted to scare the mail agent. There was a white agent in the mail department, which was in the center of the same car which the messenger was in.

After I had gone through the coaches I took a seat in the second-class coach, and was talking with the supervisor of the road, and had forgotten what I had told the messenger to do, and when he commenced shooting I jumped myself, but at once remembered my joke and knew what it was. Then I ran into the other coach to notify the passengers of the meaning of the shooting, so they would not be alarmed. It was thirteen miles to the next station, and when we arrived there I walked along by the side of the car which the mail agent was in; when I got opposite where he was I said in a loud voice, "I am looking to see if any of those balls hit this car." Then I went in the car and found the mail agent under his counter covered up with mail bags. I asked: "What are you doing under there?" and he replied, "I am not going to be shot for a d——d negro." All this occurred a year or two before the Negro got killed.

At one time, when the road was in bad shape, I was sent to Meridian to take charge of the road from Meridian to Tuscaloosa as division superintendent. I thought I could build up the road, and also thought it might be an advantage to me as well in the long run, and would have been had the road had any means of credit. My wages were to be one hundred and twenty-five dollars per month. I went over my part of the road and found that most of the section men had quit work on account of not being paid regularly, and had nothing to eat. And there was but few bridgemen. I did my best to get provisions for the section men so as they would go back to work, as they had told me if the road would furnish them provisions that they would go to to work again. So I stated the facts to Mr. Stanton, and he wrote me a letter telling me to buy provisions in Meridian and have it charged to the road. I tried, but could not find a grocery merchant in Meridian who would sell provisions that way unless I would stand good for the payment of them myself. I reported the case to Mr. Stanton, and he said have them charged to him. I went round and tried to get them in this way, but this proved no better than the first. The merchants said that they would sell me all I wanted and charge them to me. But I would not get them that way, for I owed more in Chattanooga than I could see any way of paying at that time, on account of not getting my wages. I notified Mr. Stanton again, and he wanted me to get the provisions for the men and he would make it good. I declined to do this, as he was already in debt to me, and I had my doubts whether I would ever get pay for what I was doing at that time. He promised to send provisions, and did send some, but not enough to keep the men at work long.

I had to take a trip to New Orleans while I had charge of this part of the road, and told one of the agents of the division I had charge of to keep back some money for me, as I had asked Mr. Stanton to send me some and it was not sent, and I had not received a dollar for my services since I had been there, and that had been nearly three months. I got one hundred dollars from the agent of whom I spoke, and that was all I ever received for my superintendent's term. I would have gotten more, but the agent gave me all that he had, which belonged to the road.

As I have said, I was there three months, and without money or anything else I much improved the track and had things in better shape than they had been for some time. The section men had eaten up their rations, and had nothing to work on. And after I found I was a superintendent without means or money, I concluded that I did not want to be a superintendent any longer. I told Mr. Stanton that I knew more about running a train than I did superintending a division, and had rather run one. So I went back to running one for a short time.

I was running a mixed train one time when there was but one train each way a day. And the west-bound train had the right of track over the east-bound train, in case the regular meeting place was missed. And the west-bound waited thirty minutes, and five minutes longer for variation of watches. One day when I was going west something got wrong with the engine, and the engineer stopped to fix it and we fell behind the schedule time. After the engineer finished the work on his engine, we went to a well near by to get a drink of water. The engineer remarked that he had been feeling badly all the morning; he said he felt as if something was going to happen, adding: "I dreamed a dream last night that I dreamed just one year ago last night; and the next day my brother got killed."

We went on and could not make the meeting point for the east-bound train, so we side-tracked and waited our thirty minutes and five minutes for variation in watches, then backed out off the side-track, as we had a right to the track, went ahead, but had only gone about half the distance to the station where both trains ought to have met, in case both had been on time when we met the east-bound train on the main track. All that prevented a collision was both engines just having rounded a curve on to a straight piece of track, and both engines stopped just before they came together. My engineer was as mad as I ever saw. At that time the briers had taken possession of each side of the road up to the outside of the rails, at the place where the engines met. And all the injuries that any of the passengers received, were the ones inflicted by the briers, by which they were scratched when they jumped off the train into them. The conductor of the east-bound train said that the hands of his watch had been caught and he did not know it, and thought he had plenty of time to make the next station. The engineer said that his watch had stopped and he had left the station at a signal from the conductor, thinking the conductor had the right time. The engineer was allowed to run on, and the conductor was stopped off for thirty days, on account of the run which they had made.[5]

A part of the time that Mr. Stanton had charge of the road, it was in the hands of a receiver, and while under the receivership the men would be paid in vouchers, and it was said that there was no doubt about their being good, for the road was in the hands of the United States Court, and every dollar would be paid, dollar for dollar. I had over three hundred dollars' worth of these vouchers, and I kept them for a long while. There was a lawsuit in regard to the vouchers, and the case was to be tried in New Orleans, and when the time came for the case to be tried, in order to decide whether the vouchers would be cashed or not, I sent what I had to New Orleans, by a friend of mine; and when he returned from New Orleans, he brought my vouchers back to me, and said they were worthless. But long afterwards I learned that a Chattanooga man had bought a piece of property, and was to pay for it in Alabama and Chattanooga vouchers, and that he was buying some of them up. I went at once and sold him what I had of them at thirty-three and a third cents on the dollar, and he said that he would not buy any more.

I was taken sick, and was not able to work. My physician said that I had chronic bronchitis, and before I got able to go to work again the road had got into trouble once more in some way, and was stopped being operated for a long time. I think this was on account of a fight between the State of Alabama and Mr. Stanton, in a lawsuit, which was settled at last in some way. But the road was taken out of Mr. Stanton's hands, and I guess the State had to pay him something in order to get him out, at least I always thought so.[6] Yet I do not know about that. But when it was started up again it was done by the State of Alabama, and when put in a somewhat better condition, was sold to a company who put the road in a better condition than it had ever been in, and built the road along the old survey where Mr. Stanton had left it, and built what was called the Alps. I think when the road was completed along the old and original survey, that it made the distance about ten miles shorter between Chattanooga and Meridian. The name of the road was changed to the Alabama Great Southern Railroad, and this was the last of the Alabama and Chattanooga Railroad. It was afterwards controlled by the Cincinnati Southern Railroad, and now by the Southern Railway Company, and it is as well equipped and doing as good a business as any road running into Chattanooga.

Mr. Stanton was a good man to work for, if he had just have been as good a man to have paid the men who worked for him their wages. Let him be whatever he might, he liked things to look nice and neat, and liked a man who did his duty, and hated a thief. I believe if he had been let alone when he first finished building the road, that it would have done a good business, and that every man that worked for him would have been paid what was due them.

Chattanooga was first improved, and began to build up, by his energy, and on account of his building the road. And if he had been let alone, and had had money enough, Chattanooga would be a larger city than it is at the present day.

I added up the amount which was due me, outside of the vouchers of which I have already spoken, and the scrip that I had on hand when it became insolvent, and the amount due me was near eleven hundred dollars; that is owing to me at the present time, if not out of date, and this debt will never be reduced, yet every dollar of it was earned by hard work. Still I was not the only one that lost money this way, for some lost thousands. Although it was not the only road that had been built where men lost their labor, and some their money which they had accumulated in earlier days, still it hurt me because my work was all the way I had to make a living. There ought to be a law passed so that no corporation or company could get out of paying the wages of men who had worked for them.

If I had left the road when Mr. Stanton said that no set of men should work for him that would stand by and see a stick broken over his head, and then turned and around and said to me, "You too go and get your money." he or his company would not now have owed me one dollar. But instead I kept on, and some time after I left the road I had to sell my house and home for less than half what it cost me, in order to pay debts which I had contracted on account of not getting my wages regularly while on the road. At one time while I was on the road, one of the office men came to me and asked me if I would give ten dollars to help get Mr. Stanton a present; he said most all the employees were giving something. I answered that I did not have the money. and he said it made no difference about that, for they were going to take it out of the men's wages whatever amount that they were willing to give. Notwithstanding that I never was in favor of anything of the kind, I said: "If you will take it out of a month's back wages, that was not paid,

I will give twenty dollars." But when a pay-day came, on a month for which the men were paid, I found that ten dollars had been kept out of my wages to go towards paying for Mr. Stanton's silver service. The last time I saw Mr. Stanton, which was some time after the road had been taken out of this hands, Mr. Stanton and his wife were on my train, which I was running on another road. It was a night train that I was running at that time. And after daylight he sent for me to go back in the sleeper where he was. I went back. He and his wife seemed to be glad to see me, and in fact I was glad to see them. We talked over old times, and he said he was going to get his road back, and would have me on it again; and then said to me" "Don't it beat hades how they beat us out of our money?" So up to the present day I have never seen him since.

Chapter Eleven

East Tennessee, Virginia and Georgia Railroad
1876–1895

Notwithstanding the loss of my wages and the dangers I had gone through by running over such track, bridges, and trestles, I rather hated to give up the Alabama and Chattanooga road, for, as I said in the preceding chapter, I believed it would be a good, reliable road some day, and if I lived to see it I would be on it and stand a better chance to keep a place on the road. I had made many acquaintances along the line of roads that I had run over in the State of Alabama, and also in that part of Mississippi which I had run through. I had made many good friends by attending to my own business.

Knowing that when a railroad man got out of work that it was a hard matter to get work again, or at least I had found it to be the case with myself, I started out, although I was hardly able to work if I had had any to do. I went to Memphis and Atlanta, then to Macon, Ga., and could only get the promise of work when there was a vacancy. I was taken sick while in Macon and started back home, but only got as far as Atlanta, where I took a room at a hotel and was confined to my bed for a length of time. As soon as I was able to travel I went home. After I felt able to go to work, I learned from a friend of mine that the East Tennessee, Virginia and Georgia Railroad Company was moving a large amount of cotton over their road, and he advised me to go to Knoxville. I went to another friend of mine who was an agent for the road, and he was well acquainted with me, and he asked for a pass for me, and one was sent to him. I went to Knoxville and asked for work. I was asked what position I had held on other roads. I said conductor. One of the officials said that I did not look like I was able to run a train. I answered that I was willing to try it if I could get a chance, and I was given a freight-train. I was glad I had not forgot how to run a freight-train. This was in the fall of 1876. I run a night freight until the spring following, and then I was put on a local freight between Knoxville and Chattanooga. I did not run the local freight very long before I was notified to report to the office. I was sure that I was going to be discharged, yet I could not think of one thing that I had done to be discharged for. Then I remembered that I was told, when I first went to work, but one of the officials of the road, that he did not know whether he could give me regular work or not. So I concluded that was what I was wanted at the office for, to be notified that my time was out and they could not give me work any longer.

I was agreeably surprised when I went to the office and was asked if I would take a passenger-train, for I had no thought of such a thing. I said I would if they wished me to do so, and that I would do whatever they would rather have me do. I ran one more trip on the local freight and then went out on a passenger-train. At that time passenger conductors' wages were seventy-five dollars per month and freight conductors sixty-five. I afterwards ran a mixed train, and day and night passenger-trains, and at one time an accommodation train.[1]

I had only asked for work and it was given me. Sometimes on my lay-over days at Knoxville I would be sent out with an engine to distribute iron along the road or pick up old iron or old ties for fuel for section men. And at times take a freight-train out to a meeting point and turn a conductor back, and take the train into Knoxville that he was on. I was promised that I should have leave of absence when business slackened up, and my pay should go on. If business ever slackened I never got any pay for my extra work, and when I would get leave of absence for a few days I lost the time. But my health improved very much while I ran through East Tennessee.

I was surprised when I made my first trip to Knoxville after I had walked out of Tennessee. I could hardly believe it was the same little town that was near the banks of the Holston river, called Knoxville, when I was helping to move Gen. Bragg's army from there to Chattanooga. It has kept improving ever since as fast as any thriving city could be expected, in the way of good buildings, population, hotels, street railway service, and electric lights, water-works, and railroads. At this time it has many wealthy citizens and good business men.

The track was only middling when I went to running on the East Tennessee, Virginia and Georgia Railway in 1876. In some places there were short pieces of rails put in, I suppose out of rails or bars that had been bent when the track was torn up in time of war, but it was gradually improved.

All the officials were strangers to me when I first went to work, except one, and I had met him in Virginia while I was at the salt-works, at the time of which I have already spoken, and again while I was running between Augusta and Wilmington. There were but few conductors or engineers running on the road that I was acquainted with. The citizens along the line of road, with the exception of a very few, were all strangers to me. A wonderful change had taken place since I had run over the road before in time of war. The master of transportation, as he was called at that time, had charge of the transportation department. At one time the trains were stopped running into Chattanooga on account of yellow fever making a death-stroke in that place. A short train was run between Cleveland and Mission Ridge tunnel, and one between the tunnel and Chattanooga, so as to keep the plague from spreading.[2] Cleveland was quarantined, and when the trains would come out from Chattanooga they were not allowed to stop at Cleveland. The mail had to be changed about a mile south of Cleveland depot, that was before the through trains were stopped running into Chattanooga. When they were stopped they were run to Dalton and the short train spoke of put on, the connection being made where the Dalton and Chattanooga tracks connect south of Cleveland, where a transfer was made.

After the yellow fever had made a death-stroke, destroying many lives, it disappeared, and the East Tennessee train commenced running into Chattanooga again. The first trip I made afterwards into Chattanooga, I arrived there just after dark, and I never saw a more desolate looking city in my life than it was. Not a light could be seen in many parts of the city. Many of the citizens had refugeed, and had not returned at the time of which I speak.

At one time I was on a run that gave me from Saturday night until Monday morning to lay over in Chattanooga, and sometimes I would go home, and, as I said, there were no trains running on the Alabama and Chattanooga road at that time. I would sometimes go by private conveyance, and at other times I would go out on a Nashville, Chattanooga and St. Louis train as far as Hooker, a way station on that road, and from there home by private conveyance.

On one of my trips last spoken of, I was passing through a little narrow valley that lay between two high hills with their large rocky ledges and cliffs that one could see on either side of the valley while passing through it, a beautiful little brook rapidly winding its way through its narrow channel and over its rocky bed. It was on a bright Sunday morning that I passed through the valley, and while I was passing through it, I saw a party of boys fishing in the brook. I thought I would tell them that it was wrong to fish on the Sabbath day, and did so, advising them to go to Sunday-school instead of fishing, and they got the best of me by asking me if was going to be the teacher. I asked them the name of the little valley, and they answered that it was named Egypt. I said that was where Joseph had been sold. So I left them and went on my way. This place was in Dade county, Georgia, which is situated in the north-west corner of the State. This county was better known as the State of Dade, as it is cut off from the rest of the State of Georgia by the Lookout Mountain, and from Alabama by the Sand Mountain. There were several valleys of rich land through this country, and most of the hills were of a rich soil.

A story was told on an old gentleman who was once sent from the State of Dade to the Georgia legislature, when Milledgeville was the capital of Georgia. The old gentleman arrived there one night and was up the next morning early, and mistaking the market-place for the capi-tol building, went in and hung his hat on a meathook, taking a seat on one of the meat blocks. When the butcher came in the old gentleman asked him how long it would be before the members of the legislature came in. The butcher informed him that was not their place of meeting, and gave him directions, so he could find the place where they would meet, informing him that he wished to use the block he occupied to cut his meat on. The old man gave up his seat, took his hat off the peg, and proceeded to find the capitol.

It was said that when business commenced, he tried to get a bill passed for the State to have a road built across Lookout Mountain, as Dade county was cut off from the world, and no way to get out. I after-wards became acquainted with the old gentleman upon whom the story was told, as he was an agent on the Alabama and Chattanooga Railroad, in J. C. Stanton's time, and after I had become familiarly acquainted with him I almost came to the conclusion that the story I heard about him must be true.

I ran on for some time, and good fortune seemed to favor me, as I got along well, and had but little bother or trouble, so far as my rail-roading was concerned. At last misfortune stepped in one night when I was going west. I found a tramp on the steps of a sleeping-car that was attached to the rear of the train. When I stepped out on the platform and found the tramp, I said to him to come inside the car, and turned round to the door, to find that the door had thumb-latched when I closed it after me, and that I was fastened outside of the car. The train was running at a good speed, and as I could not get the conductor or porter of the car awake to let me in, after trying for some time to rouse them, I pulled the bell-cord to stop the train, so I could go around in front and get on the train, thinking at the same time that if the tramp could not pay his way I would make him get off when the train stopped. But when the train had slackened speed, and just before it came to a full stop, I looked around and the tramp was ready to step off, and before I could tell him to wait until the train did stop, he either stepped off or was knocked off by a fence which protected one side of a cattle-guard. Not seeing how he could have been hurt by getting off at the rate of speed which the train was going at the time, I went round in front when the train did stop, and went ahead not thinking of the tramp being hurt. The next day I learned that party returning from church the night before had found a man lying near the track with one leg broken. He was picked up by a freight-train and carried to a station, and was being cared for, in an unoccupied cabin, by one of the company's agents. I also learned that the tramp said he had been kicked off the train by someone who came to him and took a half-dollar from him. I afterwards saw a notice in a newspaper giving an account of the tramp's statement, which said that he conductor of the Rat train, (as that was the name by which the train was called that I was running at the time), had taken fifty cents, all the money a tramp had who was riding on his train, and then kicked the tramp off while the train was running, and that one of the tramp's legs was broken. When I saw this piece in the paper in regard to the conductor of the Rat train it made me mad, and I wrote a letter to the editor of the paper giving him the facts in the case, asking him to publish it, stating that I was the conductor of the Rat train at the time he spoke of, and when he wanted to publish facts in his paper he had better get them from some one who knew the facts, and who would tell the truth about the case. And whoever said that the conductor took a nickel from the tramp, or kicked him off the train, told a base falsehood. I thought this was done to injure me, as I was a stranger on the road, or comparatively one, at that time. Had this happened on a road where I was well known, I probably would have paid no attention to it at all.

I stopped one night as I was passing the place where the tramp was and went in to see him, I asked him how he came to get hurt. He answered that he was kicked off of a train. I asked by whom? He replied that he did not know; that a man came to him and took fifty cents from him, and went back in the car, and afterwards another man came out and threw him off the train. I asked what kind of a looking man threw or kicked him off. He said a large, fleshy man. I asked if the man had on a cap. He answered no, he had on a hat. I then asked him if I was the man. He said no; the man was a great deal larger than I. I then told him that he ought to be ashamed to lie there in the condition that he was in, and tell such a tale as he was telling. I also told him that I was the man who went out on the platform and asked him to go inside the car, in order to keep him from getting hurt, "and you know that I never touched you." So, when he got well enough, he was sent home. He gave the company's law agent a written statement, that his first statement was a lie. He also gave a written statement of the facts of his leaving home, and how he beat his way on trains up to the time he was hurt, and how he came to get hurt. I was told by the law agent afterwards, that when the tramp was taken home, that his mother said her son was a liar from his childhood, and that she had tried to break him from the habit, but could never do so.

One day after this I met a lawyer, and he asked me some questions in regard to the matter, saying that the man who got hurt at the time spoken of wanted him to bring suit against the company, in his behalf, and he was thinking of doing so. I said to him, that any lawyer who knew me and would take such a case as that was, this would be all I wanted to know about him. So that was the last I ever heard of the case.

A few years had passed away, and a general superintendent was appointed, and the old superintendent was done away with. And as the day passenger-trains had been turned into mixed trains, I was on one of the class, going east one day, when a brakebeam dropped down and threw a box-car off the track where a country road crossed the railroad track. Before I reached the end of my run, the superintendent boarded my train, and questioned me in regard to the accident, saying that he had received a telegram from the agent at the last station we had passed before the accident occurred stating that there was something dragging under the train when it passed his station, and that he had hailed so as to call attention of some one to tell them about it, but did not succeed in attracting attention, but saw a brakeman on the rear platform and told him. The superintendent then asked me if we stopped at the station where the telegram had been sent from. I answered that we did, and took water. He then asked me if I looked around my train. I replied that I had started to do so, and had looked over half way along the train, when I met a lady who was going on board the train and I took her hand-baggage and went back and helped her on the train. The brakeman was called in and asked why he did not tell me about what the agent said. He replied that he did not think it worth while; that he intended telling me at the next station ahead. So he was discharged. After I arrived at my destination I was called into the master of transportation's office, and from him learned that he had orders from the superintendent to suspend me for a few days. I asked what for. He said on account of the accident which I had that day. "All right," I said, adding that if I had to lose one day on account of the accident, that I would not work another day for the company, even if I did not have one dollar in my pocket. I also said I was not to blame any more than he was himself. He then told me to stay over the next day and make a written statement, and he would send a man in my place, and I should have pay for my time, and that I could take my run when it returned. I did this and got a good day's rest, and received a full month's pay the next pay-day.

In those days I believed in being treated fair and right, and had been ever since I had been on the road up to the time I speak of. But in after years, when my children had grown up, my experiences had grown larger, and I had passed my noonday, I knew I could not get or hunt work as I could in my younger days, when I was mistreated and quit work. So let what would come, regardless of my views in the case, right or wrong, I for the sake of a support for my family had to put up with whatever was put on me, as I had no other income or means of support outside of my wages.

After awhile the office of master transportation was dispensed with and another superintendent appointed to take charge of the transportation department. Afterwards the roadway and rolling stock were more improved. Some nice little depots were built at some stations on line of road, and some at places where there had never been one built before, and the old depots that needed repairs were remodeled and looked as nice as if they were new.

The rules and schedules for the government of trains were also soon changed. The old mixed train was abandoned and a passenger-train put on instead. Passenger-train conductor's wages were raised from seventy-five to ninety dollars per month, for which I felt grateful. I was satisfied they earned that much, and I thought that the superintendent thought so himself or he would not have raised them. The superintendent went on my train when he went to Knoxville to take charge of the road. He said to me he was going to take charge of the road, but did not know how long he would stay, for the road was fifty years behind the times, as well as I now remember it was fifty years he said, and if the company would furnish the money to improve the road he would stay, and if they did not he would not remain long. So I suppose he was furnished the money, for many improvements have been made since he took charge of the road.

In the way of men, as well as everything else, he soon got rid of all the drunken class and put in competent men, and when one got into trouble on the road he was given a fair trial, so far as the superintendent was concerned; while I in some of my troubles and mistakes have thought it hard on me, when some cases were decided against me, yet in some other troubles, I had come in contact with, he stood by me to the last, and at the present day there is no road that I ever worked for that has a better class of men on it than the fourth division of the Southern Railway.[3] A great many of them have grown up with the road, and worked themselves up to a higher position in all departments of the road under his supervision.

The only trouble I ever had with a Pullman conductor, the superintendent fought the case for me and gained it, and in various other cases he was my friend. If he ever had a favorite I never found it out, as long as I worked under him, and notwithstanding the many times that the road has changed hands he is still superintendent of the fourth division of the Southern Railway; over one hundred miles of track has been added to his division since the Southern Railway company took possession of the East Tennessee, Virginia and Georgia Railway.

It was not many years after I went to running on the East Tennessee, Virginia and Georgia Railway, when one day I had a passenger on board who was from New England, and he said to me that the track was too wide, and the railroad people in the New England States had learned that a narrow-gauge was much better, and they were changing the track to a standard gauge; and he said it could be done in a very short time, and it would be changed before a great while on the East Tennessee, Virginia and Georgia Railway.[4] But I did not believe it, and it was not but a few years afterwards until it was done. The rails were taken up on one side of the track and moved in, making the track narrower to a standard gauge, and it was all done in one day—a distance of two hundred and forty-two miles.

There is no doubt but what many more improvements will yet be made in the way of railroads, as well as many other things; for since the first building of railroads improvements have been made very rapidly; much more so now than in former days, for improvements were very slow in those days. From my first work on the East Tennessee, Virginia and Georgia Railroad to the present day the road has been controlled and managed by good officers, but the earlier ones were not so much for improvements as those in after years.

Things on the road went along all right, for awhile, with me, until one day misfortune stepped on my train at Sweetwater, a way station on the road, where two men boarded my train, and paid me their fares to Loudon, another way station. I had seen these two men before, but did not know who they were. They had been on my train before, and had some words with me in regard to their fare. I had collected conductors' rates from them, which was a cent a mile more than agents' rates, and they wanted to know why it was that I had charged them more than the ticket rate. I explained the matter to them, and when they left the train one of them asked me if I did not want another nickel to get me a cigar with when I got to Knoxville. I replied to him that I had all the money I wanted from him at present. So when I collected their fare after leaving Sweetwater, I knew they were the same two men, and I expected to have some trouble with them unless they had tickets, which I found afterwards they did not have. I collected conductors' rates again, but they never said a word about it to me this time.

The sheriff and deputy of Hamilton county, Tennessee, were on board the train with three prisoners at the time spoken of. The sheriff was taking the prisoners to Knoxville to the Supreme Court. I knew one of the prisoners, as he once fired an engine on the road. He afterwards went on a steamboat on the Tennessee river and after running for some time, he killed the captain of the boat which he was on. He had a trial in the Circuit Court, and was sentenced to the State prison for a term of eight years, as well as I remember. His name was John Taylor, and he was handcuffed to another white man, whose name I afterwards learned was Carter. The other prisoner was a colored man, who was handcuffed to the arm of a seat next to the aisle of the car. The deputy sheriff sat on the same seat that the negro man occupied, and was next to the window. The sheriff sat on the opposite side of the car from the deputy and prisoners. The two white prisoners were seated on a seat in front of the deputy sheriff and the negro man, and that was the position they were in when I passed through the second-class coach, which was the car they were in. After the train left Sweetwater, and I went through the car, I found one of the men who got on at that station seated some distance back from the sheriff, on the same side of the car, and the other one still further back in the car, on the opposite side from the one just spoken of, and back of the deputy sheriff and the prisoners. These men were the two strangers before spoken of. After I had gone through the two coaches that were in the train, I took a seat in the front end of the sleeping car.

The distance between Sweetwater and Philadelphia was seven miles. There was no telegraph office at Philadelphia. I was out on the platform before the train stopped at Philadelphia, and could hear a noise up in front, like a car-load of horses stamping in the car. But I never once thought about any trouble until the train stopped and I heard some one say: "Those prisoners are loose, and have shot the sheriff." As I walked along the side of the train, I saw the sheriff step off the train with a pistol in his left hand, which he was trying to raise up so as to shoot through the window of the coach which he had come out of, but he dropped down on the ground before he succeeded, I ran to the depot agent, who was standing a few steps further on, to tell him who the sheriff was, and ask him to have him taken care of. But before I could do this, I heard some one say, "Get this train away from here, or I will shoot you in a half minute!" Looking around, I saw two or three men standing on the car platform with their pistols pointed towards me. I looked towards the engine, giving a go-ahead signal, and saw the engineer, who had just gotten off his engine to come back to see what the trouble was, I supposed. When I saw him, I halloed, "Go ahead; get away from here!" So he ran and jumped on his engine, and pulled her open. I did not have time to look at my watch to see if I got away inside of the half minute which was given me. But by not being shot, as I was sure the men meant what they said, from their looks, I concluded that not more than half of the time was used in getting away from the station that they had given me.

I stepped on the front end of the coach as we left Philadelphia, not knowing at that time all that had happened; but I remember very well what did happen as soon as I stepped inside the car, for a large man met me and put the muzzle of his pistol within one inch of my breast, and I thought my time had come to pay the last debt I was due. At this moment, John Taylor, the prisoner, jumped by the side of the man that had the pistol pointed at my breast, saying, "Do not hurt that man for he is a friend of mine. He did me a favor once that I never will forget." He also said, "I went on his train when they captured me and took me to Chattanooga a prisoner." Then he said to me, "You shan't be hurt." I never was so glad to hear a remark in my life as the one he made, and I thought that if he just would stand to the remark that I would do him any favor I could. Although I do not know to this day what favor it was that he alluded to me doing for him; but I was glad I did it, whatever it might be that I had done for him.

The man dropped his pistol, and when he did so I could breathe some better. He asked me if I was his friend. I answered that I was a friend to anybody who did right. He then said: "This is a bad thing," and I replied that it was. He said that he hated killing the sheriff, but he had it to do, as he had been deviled with the laws of the d——d State just as long as he was going to be. Then he asked me if I had as much as thirty dollars that I could let him have until he got out of the trouble, and he would pay it back to me then. I told him that I did not have that amount to spare, if I had I would let him have it. He said he did not want the train to stop at Loudon, as they had more enemies there than anywhere else. I answered that I had passengers ticketed to that point, and would have to stop there to let them off. He said if we did stop he would kill me and the d——d engineer also; and a younger man said, "Yes, we will kill the whole d——d crew." I then said I would stop and let them off anywhere they wanted to get off. But the older man said they did not want to get off until they got to Lenoir's Station; that they had some protection there. I said that I would go on the engine and tell the engineer, or he would be sure to stop at Loudon. Then John Taylor said that he would go and see that the train did not stop at Loudon; that he could run an engine as good as anybody. I replied, "All right, John," and he went through the baggage car and on to the engine, the two men following him with pistols in their hands. I was glad when they left the coach. John had shown me his arm where a ball had gone through it. He said he was holding the sheriff to keep him from shooting, and one of the boys hit him while shooting at the sheriff. The deputy sheriff's remains were on the seat that he was occupying when shot. A ball had passed through his head, his blood and brains were spattered on the black prisoner's back, and he (the black man) was standing up in the aisle with one arm handcuffed to the arm of the seat. Carter, the other prisoner, was at liberty, with John Taylor's handcuff hanging to his wrist. All the other passengers had deserted the coach when the shooting commenced.

I was told by some of the passengers who were in the car at the time when the shooting commenced, that the first thing done was to shoot the deputy sheriff and take the keys out of his vest pocket, and unlock the handcuff that was on John Taylor's wrist. It was said by some of the passengers that there was a third man in with the two men who did the shooting. They said this man stood in the aisle with a pistol in each hand, but no one ever knew who the third man was.

After John and his two friends left me, I went into the first-class coach to get some one to write me a telegram, so I could throw it off as we passed Loudon, but found all the passengers as nervous as I was myself. Some of my passengers that were ticketed further on, stayed at Philadelphia. Col. G. J. Foraker and Major Thomas O'Conor were on the train, but neither of them was composed enough to write. So I tried to write the message myself, and finished it just as we passed Loudon, and threw it off. I learned afterwards that it was not found, and I remarked that if it had been found, it could not have been read.

When we arrived at Lenoir Station, John Taylor and the two men who were with him left the engine, got a doctor and made him dress John's wound. After they passed me, I asked the telegraph operator who the two men were with John Taylor. He answered, "Bob and Andy Taylor, John Taylor's brothers." Those men had made the engineer run ten minutes ahead of schedule time to Lenoir's, consequently we had to stay there that length of time, and some of the passengers asked me if I was going to stay there until the men came back and captured the train. I informed them of the time we were ahead, and of a freight train being ahead of us, which we had to pass at the next station. I was told that after the Taylor boys stepped off the engine, that one of them said to the engineer to take his d——d train and go to hades with it, if he wanted to. They kept their pistols in their hands, ready to shoot at any moment.

After we arrived at Knoxville, the coach in which was the remains of the deputy sheriff was set out of the train on to a side-track, and officers of the law took charge of the two prisoners. An inquest was held over the body of the deputy sheriff, and his remains sent back to Chattanooga. The remains of the sheriff were also sent back to Chattanooga from Philadelphia. I was called into the superintendent's office the same evening to make a statement, and, after I had related the facts, he laughed, and remarked that he would take out of my wages and pay the Taylor boys for conducting the train from Philadelphia to Lenoir. This was a day long to be remembered by me, and a day that I wished that I had been most anything else than a train conductor. I would much rather have been a paying passenger on some other train than to have been conductor that day. Horror, sin, and crime still go on down to woe, regardless of the passing time, and just like in years of long ago.

The next day I was walking along the street pavement, and met one of the officers of the road, and he stopped me and asked me to tell him about the whole affair. I did so. He asked me how many pistols were pointed at me when they ordered me to get the train away. I answered it looked to me like there was a dozen, but the boys said there were but four. I said they were the longest and brightest ones I had ever seen. He also asked me if I went over to the engine to collect the Taylor boys' fare from Loudon to Lenoir. I replied that I did not, and that I was truly glad that they passed me over alive and free.

A crowd gathered around us while in conversation, so thick that I could hardly get my breath while talking. I was afterwards asked if I had a pistol, and I would say no, that I never had seen a day in all my life that I had as little use for a pistol as I had that day, for if I had had forty pistols I would have been a fool to have shown one of them. This tragedy was much talked of for a long time afterwards, and is sometimes spoken of at the present day.

I was informed that after John Taylor's wound was dressed, that he and his two brothers mounted horses that were about Lenoir's Station and rode off in a northwestern direction from that place. They afterwards sent the horses back by Mr. Littleton, who was a brother-in-law of the Taylor boys. This man was afterwards accused of aiding in their escape, being arrested and put under a two thousand dollar bond. I learned that Mr. Littleton was killed by one of his cousins (who bore the same name as himself) being caused by a quarrel about the Taylor brothers. This happened some time after the other crime was committed.

A large reward was offered for the Taylor brothers by the State of Tennessee and Hamilton county, but no trace of them could be found after leaving Lenoir's Station. Officers of the law and some citizens were out in search for them soon after the facts were circulated. The affair had created a wonderful excitement throughout the whole country, it being the common conversation. Some said they had gone one way and some would say they had gone another way. In fact, no one seemed to know where they had gone.

Some time after the killing of the sheriffs, and before Mr. Littleton was killed himself, he was on my train one day, and told me that his brothers-in-law, the Taylor brothers, went into the Clinch Mountains after they left Lenoir's Station.[5] This was the same section of country where John Taylor secreted himself for a long time after he had killed the steamboat captain, and before he was arrested.

Mr. Littleton said that the boys stayed on a high point in the mountains where they had a good view for miles around them in every direction. This place, he said, was near a large cliff in the rock, and that every bush from which they had broken a limb or twisted a twig off, where they had stayed, had died after they had left the place. He said they stayed at this place three days and nights without anything to eat. He also said that they had a brother who carried the mail to the Cincinnati train, and that they went to meet him every night for three nights, but on account of their brother being accompanied by some one else, they could not let themselves be known to him. On the third night, however, they found him alone, and notified him of their whereabouts and that they were starving for want of food. So their brother kept them in provisions until Bob and John fell out about the route they would take and Bob went his own way alone, and Andy stayed with John. These two took a canoe and went down the Tennessee and Chattanooga, and through Chattanooga to Lookout Mountain, and remained there for some time. Bob was afterwards found in Missouri, where he had a sister living, and was killed on a train by a sheriff of a county of that State, who had been shadowing him for a short time. This took place just one month after he and Andy had killed the sheriff and deputy sheriff on my train at Philadelphia, Tennessee.

Bob Taylor's remains were shipped back to Chattanooga, and I was there in my room at a hotel asleep that night they arrived there. The noise of a crowd of men whooping and halloing awoke me. I could not imagine what the cause of this was. The next morning I learned that Bob Taylor's remains had arrived in the night, and when taken off the train had been placed on a wagon or dray and pulled by men over town. These men, who were friends of the two sheriffs who were killed by the Taylor boys, after dragging the remains over town carried them to the courthouse.

I went to the courthouse to see the remains of Bob Taylor, and when I got there I found such an immense crowd that it was almost impossible to get through it. But at last I succeeded in getting to see the dead men, and as I turned to make my way out, some asked me if it was Bob Taylor. I answered that I did not know, all that I did know was that it was the remains of the man that wanted to kill me so badly the day on which the sheriffs were killed. When I left Chattanooga I found that Bob Taylor's remains were in my baggage car without any transportation, and I thought to myself that I had seen trouble enough on his account while he was living without being aggravated with his dead body. I wired the facts to the superintendent, and received a message in reply advising me to take the remains on to Loudon and turn them over to the deputy sheriff of Loudon county. I did as I was instructed. I learned afterwards that the remains of Bob Taylor were buried in the paupers' burying ground of Loudon county.

The following is Andy Taylor's statement (which he gave after being captured) of their life after they had committed the murder of the sheriffs: He said that they lived a very hard life while on Lookout Mountain, and at times they ate raw beef. After Bob was killed Andy said that he and John left the mountain, and went to the State of Missouri, where John was taken sick, and lay for some time in an old empty house, where he died, and Andy dug a grave and buried his brother's remains himself. Then Andy left Missouri and went to Kansas, and there procured work on a farm as farmhand. These facts when related were believed by a great many who had known Andy from his boyhood.

The following statement was gathered from the party who brought Andy Taylor back to Chattanooga after he was captured in Kansas: One day while the man who Andy was working for was away from home, Andy, while working about the barn, shot a hole through his hat, in the act of trying to shoot himself, which frightened the farmer's wife very much, and when her husband came home she related the occurrence to him. Andy then told him what had happened in regard to the killing of the sheriff and deputy sheriff of Hamilton county, Tenn. And that there was a large reward for him, and if the farmer would divide the reward with his (Andy's) mother, that he would give himself up to him.

The farmer not knowing whether the statement which Andy made was true or not, wired some of the authorities of Chattanooga in regard to the matter, but when he received an answer to his message stating that the story was true, Andy was gone. And when he was captured he was about one hundred miles from the place where he had been at work on the farm. It was also said that after Andy left the farm that he got on board of a freight train, and tried to shoot the conductor of the train. After Andy Taylor was brought back to Chattanooga a prisoner, he was taken to Loudon on my train, and when I met him on the train he asked me in regard to my health, and asked me not to think hard of him, saying that Bob had got him into the trouble that he was in. I said to him that it was all right, and that I was glad that I was left alive.

Andy was tried for murder in the Circuit Court at Loudon, and sentenced to be hanged. His lawyer applied to the Supreme Court. He was taken to Knoxville and tried; the Supreme Court affirmed the decision of the lower court. It was said that as the sheriff of Loudon county was taking Andy back to Loudon, that he (the sheriff) was standing in the aisle when Andy took a pistol out of a guard's pocket, although both his wrists were handcuffed together, and would have shot the sheriff had not some passenger halloed to him to look out, when he turned around and took the pistol from Andy. Andy said to the sheriff if the pistol had fired when he pulled the trigger that he (the sheriff) would have been in hades a day ahead of himself. Andy Taylor was hung on the following day at Loudon, until he was dead. I suppose that his remains were buried in the same burying ground that his brother's were.

As well as I now remember, it was on the fourteenth day of September, 1882, that Bob and Andy Taylor killed the sheriff and deputy sheriff of Hamilton county and released their brother John. There were many stories told by different parties who were in the car when the shooting commenced. But none of them stayed in the car to witness anything, after the first shot was fired, for they got out any way they could, so it was the quickest. Some went out through the windows, for they told me so afterwards. From the time the train stopped at the station until it was moving away, could not have been more than one moment. If the two sheriffs had had the least thought of such an occurrence, or the deputy had not been killed in an instant, one or both of John Taylor's brothers would have been killed at the time. If John had not held the sheriff, even after one ball had struck him, he would have emptied every chamber of his pistol, for after he was shot four times he walked out of the car, stepped off and tried to raise his pistol to shoot. They were both brave men. I had known them for years. The deputy sheriff was dreaded by all criminals that knew him, on account of the brave and daring acts of his earlier days.

Not long after I had gone through the ordeal just related, and my mind was about relieved of the thought of it, another trouble, unexpected and unthought of jumped on my train. One night while going east, a young man was found on my train beating his way.[6] When discovered, he asked me what the fare was, saying to me: "You do not know where I got on." I said to him that I did not, but told him where I thought that he got on the train. He answered, "Yes." It was where I thought. I asked him where he wanted to go, and he handed me a two-dollar bill and said to the next station. I gave him the change, after deducting his fare from the place he said he got on to the next station ahead. I saw him get off at the station to which he had paid me his fare, and never saw him afterwards. I was surprised to see such a nice looking young man trying to beat his way on a train.

After the train had left the station where the young man had gotten off, and had passed the next station ahead, and had just passed a flag-station further on, a man who was on the train, and who was also an employee of the road, said to me that there was a man on the steps of the coach next to the sleeper beating his way. I took my lantern and went out on the platform of the coach and looked for the man spoken of, but saw no one, and supposing him to be a sleeping-car passenger who had walked out of the coach and had gone back, I thought no more about it.

On my return the next day I learned that the mangled remains of a man had been found at the flag-station. The man was supposed to have been killed by my train the night before. Afterwards the remains were found to be those of the young man who had given me the two-dollar bill to pay his fare when he was found in his hiding-place on my train. On my next trip east, which was about two days afterwards, I learned from some friends along the line of road that I was accused of throwing the young man off the train, and killing him, which news very much surprised me, for this was the first time in my life that I had been accused of murder, or even thinking of committing a murder.

While I knew that I had never thought of such an act, I also knew that this story was not believed by any one who knew me and my disposition, still this worried me no little; and to make the matter worse, I was also told that a party of the young man's friends had threatened my life, and that a warrant had been issued for my arrest. This report reached the officers of the road, and my superintendent gave me a pass to pass as many of my friends as I wanted on the train, to protect my life, a hundred he said, if I wished them. So I ran my train on for some time through the hostile section of country, with a party of my friends well armed, and anxious to meet an enemy at any time.

I was told by an agent at a station on the road that a body of men would come to the station some nights and ask when my train would pass the station; and one night they came firing off their pistols and asked when my train would be along, and he told them the time I would arrive that night, and that I was prepared to meet them and would be glad to do so. Upon hearing this they left the station and did not return any more for the same purpose.

About two weeks had passed after the young man was killed, when I learned from one of the company's attorneys that there was a second inquest being held secretly over the young man's remains. The attorney learned these facts from a young lady, who, in company with another young lady, was on the train the night on which the young man was killed. So the attorney stopped the action until he could get witnesses for the company or myself, as it was believed all this was being done to get damages from the railroad company. When the witnesses were brought the case proceeded.

I learned that the main witness on the opposite side was on the train the night on which the young man was killed, and had been with him, and, as I thought at the time, had beat part of his way that night on the same train. I learned that he was the same one who had gotten up the hostile feelings against me, and told that I went through the car swearing that I would break the man's d——d neck when I went out on the platform to look for him. It was proved by other witnesses who were on the train at the same time, and by some who often rode on my train, that they never heard me use any profane language on the train the night spoken of, or at any other time. The two young ladies spoken of before as being on the train, who were nice young ladies and of the best families of the State, gave the same evidence as the others had given in my favor.

When I went on the stand I gave the facts already related: That when I went to look for the man on the steps of the coach I went to bring him inside, to keep him from getting hurt; and that I never put or tried to put any one off my train until it had stopped still, not even a tramp, if I could avoid it; nor even kicked a tramp, or any one else, to get them off the train when it was standing still, much less throw or try to throw, a man off, who was much stouter than myself, while the train was running at the rate of twenty miles an hour.

The case was given to the jury and I was exonerated, and, with the exception of one or two little occurrences, had no more trouble in regard to the matter. I learned that the young man wanted to get off at the station where he was killed. It was thought that he jumped off the train and struck a stack of lumber that was near the roadside and was knocked under the train; or, in trying to hide by swinging around between the two platforms, had fallen under the cars, as he had been run over by them. In that case I learned how easy an innocent man might be made to suffer for an act or crime that he was not guilty of nor responsible for.

Copied from a daily newspaper:

> A Conductor Exonerated—Our readers will remember the accidental killing by a railroad train, a few weeks since, of a young man named Israel Woolsey, near Midway, Greene county. It seems that a wrong impression got abroad in the neighborhood in which the conductor— one of the best-known and most respected conductors on the road— was accused of kicking Woolsey off his train and causing his death. It went to such an extent that there was considerable indignation aroused against the conductor. In order to clear the matter up the conductor obeyed a summons and went to attend an investigation of the matter, a secondary inquest, yesterday; and when the facts were fully developed the accident appeared in its true light, and a verdict was rendered fully exonerating the conductor from any blame whatever in the matter and pronouncing it an accidental death.

In all my railroading I never had but one man killed on or by my train, that I know of, until after I went on the East Tennessee Road to work, and then not until I had been running on the road for some time. But when it did commence I had my full share.

One morning my engineer struck a wagon with his engine at a road-crossing. The wagon had a man in it, driving two mules and one horse that were pulling the wagon. The man was trying to drive across the track when the engine struck them, killing the man, mules and horse, and tearing the wagon all to pieces.

One night a man was lying on the ground with his head on the end of a crosstie on the outside of a rail, and one corner of the pilot of the engine passed over his head and the end of a bolt scratched a streak of his hair out, leaving a red mark on the side of his head. When we found him we first thought him dead, but afterwards saw he was only drunk, and two bottles of whisky were found in his pockets, and another bottle about half full. He was taken to a hotel near by, and afterwards recovered.

At another time a young man who was on board of my train stuck his head out through a window on account of his nose bleeding. He had just stuck his head out when it was struck by a bridge which the train was passing through, and he fell back on the floor of the coach dead. His remains were taken off the train at Knoxville and prepared for burial, and shipped back to the station where he had boarded the train, which was near where his relatives lived.

A negro woman was struck one night about dark by the engine that was pulling my train. She was walking along on the track in front of the engine, with a bucket of buttermilk in one hand. She was struck by the engine and knocked off the track, dying in a few minutes.

At another time a man was walking on the track in the rain, after dark, with an umbrella over him, and was struck by the engine that was pulling my train. He was picked up and taken back to a station and left in the waiting-room in care of the agent. He lived only a few minutes afterwards.

I had to witness another sickening sight. I met a train one night, and the engineer of this train told me to look out at a certain place along the road, where he had run over something, and said he was afraid it was a woman, as he had found some long hair on the pilot of his engine, but he did not stop to see what it was that he had run over. When I got near the place where I was told to look out I put a man on the front of the engine to keep a lookout, so we would not run over it again, should it be a man or woman. I also took the agent from the nearest depot with me. When we found the object it proved to be a woman, with her head cut off and her body mangled. The agent whom I had taken along, in case it should be a human body, stayed and aroused the nearest citizens and had an inquest held, and the mangled pieces were picked up and buried by the roadside. I had to make out a written statement of the facts, instead of the man who ought to have done so. The place where this happened soon became haunted, or at least that was the rumor among some of the boys on the road. Some of them saw a ghost once in awhile on moonlight nights. One said he saw a woman one night standing by the roadside dressed in white, and that she had no head. It was said that he just ran for life through the sleepers and coaches, scared nearly to death.

I had this same brakeman one night, and knowing how superstitious he was, I thought I would have a little fun at his expense. So when we stopped at a water tank, and he came walking alongside of the train, I said to him, that one of the officers of the road wanted the distance measured from the corner of the rock fence to where the woman was killed. And I said to him, "When we get by and stop, you can step off the distance." He asked why I could not stop before we got to the place, and he could then have the light from the headlight. I replied, "Oh yes, we can do that." He then dropped his head a little, looking down awhile at the ground, then raised his head and said, "Well, captain, if you or the officers of the road want that ground stepped you can step it, for I'll be d——d if I'll ever step it."

One night the engineer stopped and I went out to find out the cause, and he said that he had run over something, and he thought it was a man. I saw something lying lengthwise under the train, but thought it was a crosstie that had been placed on the track. But it proved to be a dead man, and he had been dead so long that he was as cold as clay. By that we knew that our train did not kill him. This happened on the edge of a town that we were just leaving.

The ground was covered with snow one day when a man attempted to run across the track in front of the engine, but he was saved the trouble of running by being struck and knocked across the track by the engine. He was not dangerously hurt. At another time a negro man was struck by an engine and knocked off of a trestle, but on account of the trestle not being very high he was not very badly injured.

One day a boy was trying to drive a cow off the track, just in front of the train. The engine knocked the cow off, and the cow knocked the boy down. As I thought the boy was badly hurt, I had him picked up and carried to a house that was near by. The boy was laid on the porch floor. He had not spoken a word since the cow had struck him. He had on no coat, and there was a hole torn in one of his shirt sleeves, and one of the passengers, who had gone over to the house with us, undertook to tear this hole larger, so as to see if his arm was hurt, and the boy said, "Quit that, confound you, you are tearing my shirt." Upon hearing this, I said, "Let's go, that boy is all right."

Just to show the reader the disposition of some men, I will relate a circumstance that once occurred: After leaving a terminal station one night, the porter of a sleeping car that was attached to the train, came to me and said there was a passenger in the sleeping car who wanted me to let him off at a way station. The porter had forgotten the name of the station the passenger wanted to get off at. The passenger had told the porter that if I could not let him off, for the porter to awake him. I told the porter, if it was not a regular stopping place for the train, that I would not let him off without an order to do so, and for him to go back and awake the passenger, and tell him what I had said, and if he would let me know the station where he wished to get off, I would wire the superintendent and get permission to let him off, if it was not a regular stop for the train. So that was the last I heard of it, until I had left the station, which was the last stop until we arrived at Knoxville. As the passenger's ticket was to that point, I thought by not hearing from him any more that he had decided to go on to the destination of his ticket.

But just before the station was reached where he wanted to get off, I learned from him, when he had gotten up from his berth, the name of the place where he wanted to stop. He said that his father, who lived there, was expected to die. I said to him that I would have asked for a permit to stop, and even waited at the place we last stopped at and have wired from there, if he had come to me there. I also said to him that I had told the porter to awake him when he came to me just after I had left the terminal station. I asked him why he did not get an order to have the train stop for him. He replied that as it was not a regular stop for that train he was going to ask to have it stopped for him, but an official of some other road had told him it was not worth while, as any conductor would stop and let him off under the circumstances. I informed him of some trouble that had come up heretofore on account of the same thing, and of the restrictions of the road, and while I would like to accommodate him, was sorry I could not do so, especially under the circumstances. I did not feel like taking the responsibility on myself, so I did not stop.

I was told by the same sleeping-car conductor that was on the night of this occurrence, that a brother of the passenger spoken of was going to have me discharged from the road's service. This man's brother was a man I had known for many years. I had made his acquaintance when we were in Augusta, Ga., with the East Tennessee rolling stock. I had always thought him a perfect gentleman. I had done favors for him in former days, consequently I was surprised when I learned of the steps he had taken to have me discharged.

Papers were sent me which he had sent to the officials of the road. He had the sleeping-car conductor's statement, which was basely false, as to what he had said to me in regard to letting the passenger off. He was in his berth when I took the train and never saw me or spoke a word to me that night, nor until after daylight, when I was near the end of my run. A statement was attached to the paper sworn to by the porter of the sleeper, which said that I had told the porter that I would let the passenger off when he first spoke to me in regard to the matter, and that was why he did not awake the passenger, which was as black a lie as the negro was himself. There was also a statement from the passenger himself, who said that when he came to me I talked to him in an insulting manner, and made light of him, laughing at him while he was talking to me, which was proved to the contrary by a passenger who had a seat by my side when the conversation took place between us. I also learned that the brother who made the report, wrote a letter himself, in which he bemeaned me ridiculously, but this letter was not shown me with the other papers.

After the papers had taken the rounds, I was called into the superintendent's office in order to give the facts in regard to the matter, and after I had done so, I was sustained in regard to the action I had taken in the case. This was another case wherein my superintendent stood square for me. The report and papers were all sent to the general manager of the road and then to the superintendent's office.

There were six passenger crews on the main line running the day and night passenger trains, which was a day train each way, and one each way of nights. Six crews had been running them for a number of years, but after so long one crew was taken off, and five conductors had to do the work that six had been doing, and without any increase in wages, and with a shorter lay-over. After air brakes were put on the passenger cars one brakeman was taken off of the night trains, which left only one train hand on each night train, and this still put more work on the conductors that run those trains.[7]

Air whistles were also put on the engines, and an air hose and valves fixed on the coaches and engines, so as to give signals to the engineer, and took the place of the old bell-cord, and also the gong in the cab of the engines. A great improvement was also made in the way of lights in coaches. All these improvements, besides many others in connection with engines, coaches, and sleeping cars, and improvements in various other ways, were made while I was on the East Tennessee, Virginia and Georgia Railroad.

A general superintendent was appointed, and some time after his appointment conductors on the main line had their wages raised to one hundred and ten dollars per month; and I am sure if a conductor did his duty that he earned every dollar of it, for in those days a conductor got no additional pay if he was laid out on his run. I remember one time when I was laid out a day and night on account of a connection from another road, losing a whole round trip and the time, when I was ready for duty at any time.[8]

At another time my engine left the rail and turned over to one side so that she could not be put back without the help of the wrecking car. My engineer went to bed and slept the remainder of the night, and was paid for over time, while I worked hard the remainder of the night. It was in the early part of the night when I commenced working, and the sun was up before I could get the track fixed so as to get another engine and the train over it, for it was a very cold night, and it was almost impossible to get men to work. I went on and made my trip, but received no extra pay when pay-day came.

At another time the road was blocked in a cut by a freight wreck, and my engineer slept on his engine, while I worked all night at the wreck in order to clear the track so I could pass. The engineer got pay for his sleep, while I got nothing for my work.

One day I was flagged down on account of the roadbed being washed out from under a piece of the track, and I went three and a half miles on a dump car, with four men to push it, in order to get to a telegraph office to report the facts to the superintendent. As we went back I had the dump car loaded with crossties, and the section boss and myself, with the help of his men, put up pens with these crossties, in this way fixing the track so I could cross over with the engine and train. While at work doing this, I had to wade through water knee deep, for there had been a heavy rainfall. When I arrived at Knoxville a train had been sent west from that place on the schedule on which I had started my trip. So I lost a day by that transaction, when I was not responsible for the occurrence; and at many other times not mentioned here it was the same case.

I lived to learn that such work as I had done was not appreciated, for if I had a mistake it was seldom overlooked, and a suspension decided on, a thing which had only happened to me three times in all my railroading until I went on the East Tennessee, Virginia and Georgia Railroad.

It was while I was on the Western and Atlantic Railroad that those three suspensions occurred, one of which the cause has already been explained, and the cause of the other two was that the train I was running at the time mentioned was taken off on account of freight being light. But they were put back on the road in a month afterwards. In latter days, on the same road, I remember at one time freight was very slack and when it came my turn with the other boys, I was told by one of the officers of the road that it had come my turn, and for me to go home and stay three weeks and that I should be paid the same as if I had been at work, on account of my going out when called, and doubling the road when business was good. This was one part of railroading which I liked, but a part that seldom came.

The first spring after I went to work on the East Tennessee, Virginia and Georgia Railroad freight fell off, and freight conductors had to take their turns laying off, and I took my week off also, but did not get pay this time for my week's lay-off. I did not mind this, however, as I was the first conductor who had been given employment on the road for several years, for they had promoted their conductors, so of course, I was willing to take my turn with the other boys.

Just after the facts transpired which I have been relating, things went on well for a long time with me, and I was well satisfied, until my troubles commenced again, and when they did take hold it seemed as if they never would let go any more.

While I had some accidents that I was not blamed for, I had some that I was suspended for, at different times and for different lengths of time; once for a mistake I made in regard to a sleeping-car being cut off at the wrong depot, when I did not know the destination of it, or even know that such a line of sleepers had been put on the road. The sleeping-car had been coupled to the rear of my train, and the yardmaster that had it done did not know the destination; said he just had orders to put it on my train, and the porter of the car did not know where the car was going and the car had no conductor. Afterwards an order was put on the bulletin board, and my attention was called to it, and I remarked that it ought to have been put up a week ago; and I learned that the superintendent had ordered such an order in regard to the new sleeping-car line some time before the sleeper was put on my train and the master of trains had failed to do so, and I never did learn whether I was stopped off ten days for the mistake or the remark I made.

There is no doubt but what I could gave gotten out of some of my misfortunes by telling a lie once in awhile, but away back in my childhood, about as far back as I can recollect, my mother gave me the worst thrashing a boy ever had for telling a lie, and I have not forgotten it yet, and if I ever have told one since it was unintentionally, or as a joke, or in telling a story. I may at times vary a little from the truth, but not in my railroad or business transactions. The time I have spoken of one passenger crew being taken off, was done not long after a general superintendent or manager had been appointed, and he did not remain on the road long, and if any one was sorry when he left the road I never knew it.

The next general superintendent who came on the road, was the one who raised passenger conductors' wages to one hundred and ten dollars per month, and was quite a different man in many respects to the former one, not only in knowing how to treat men, but in experience in railroading, and also a good man to work for and was liked by all his employees, for I have often heard many of them speak well of him and none a word against him. At the present day he is the assistant general superintendent of two or three divisions of the Southern Railway.

On one occasion, there was a train or a connection to be made at one end of the road where a train was taken from another road and run through, and there was no engine or crew to take the train at that time from the connecting road, which was due the morning afterwards. An engine, engineer, fireman, and myself and crew were started out on an extra run one afternoon to get the connection spoken of. We got along all right, meeting all trains without any trouble. A local freight was ahead of us, and we stopped at a telegraph station and asked the telegraph operator in regard to this train; he said it was on time, which would have put it at the end of its run over two hours ahead of us. But when we reached a station, which was within twenty-five miles of our destination, just after dark and raining, we struck the caboose of the freight train, standing at the station, over two hours late. No one was killed, but some few who were in the caboose claimed to be hurt; one man who claimed to have been hurt in the caboose, I was told afterwards, was not in the caboose at all; at the time the caboose was struck he was standing some distance away talking to another man, and was not touched by anything. But he wanted damages, and I learned that he got it.

The conductor of the freight had no flagman out. He came to the engine and said: "Who in the devil is this, and what are you doing here?"

The engineer replied to him: "Just wait till I get this flambeau lighted and I golly you will see who it is."

The rules of the road at that time, when an accident happened at a station, held the crew of the approaching train responsible for the accident. Yet it did not relieve a delayed train at a station from having a flagman out to protect itself. There was no rule to notify regular trains on the line that an extra was out on the road. While I think it would be a safe one, when a train in the same direction is ahead of another, yet it would be of little use if all conductors would carry out a rule and send back a flagman as the rules require. Well, as soon as the track was clear we went to our destination.

I did not think that I would have to bear any of the blame, at the same time I thought that I ought to have said some word to my engineer that I had thought of saying to him before we reached the station where the accident occurred; I was sorry that I did not do so. The engineer and conductor were held equally responsible for the violation of any rule in regard to the running of trains. Just those words might have cleared me. This was what I thought of telling my engineer: "To approach the station slowly and look out for the local freight." But knowing his disposition and temper, I did not tell him, thinking he might tell me that he knew his business. After an investigation my engineer and myself were suspended for ninety days, the longest suspension I ever heard of. No blame was attached to any one else.

What to do at this time I did not know, as there was no other work that I could do, and I had no income for a support outside of my wages.

I thought it next to a discharge, and the longest ninety days that I had ever passed through. Had this happened during my younger days, it would have been my last trip over the East Tennessee, Virginia and Georgia Railway. But on account of my large family, and not knowing where I could get work, I had with a sad heart to bear it.

Some time after I went back on the road, I was going east one night, and had orders to take on a private car at a station where a road branched off from the main line. When arrived at the station I saw a freight-train standing on the track of this road. Supposing it to be going out on the track it was standing on, I paid no attention to it at the time, but went on and backed in on a side-track to get out the private car which I had orders to take from that station. When the rear of my train got near the private car, my engine and part of my train was left on the main track. About the time we had coupled to the private car, I heard an engine exhausting and looking in the direction from which the sound came, I saw it was coming on the main track. I ran to the main track with my lantern and gave the engineer a signal to stop, and hallooed to him; he paid no attention to me, but came on and struck one side of a part of my train, breaking two sets of steps off the coaches. No one was hurt by this accident. This train proved to be the one which I had seen standing on the track of the branch road. They had backed out and pulled right after us, when the rules required a freight-train to remain at a station ten minutes after a passenger-train had left the station; my train was but a short distance past the depot, and was not near outside the switches, and a longer distance to the station limit-board. In this case the freight engineer was discharged, and also my flagman and the freight conductor, and myself were suspended for thirty days each.

So it is a safe plan to always take the safe side and run no risks, even if the rules of a road do not cover the case. It often saves life and property, as well as being called into an office and being suspended or discharged. I have saved accidents by doing things that the rules did not require me to do; and I had some accidents that if I had carried out the rules of the road, I would not have had them. Sometimes men get careless and take chances on some very important matters. There is no such a thing as being too particular in regard to running trains as the rules of roads require them to be run.

I was stopped off ten days once for turning two or three tickets and one pass into the auditor's office that I had failed to cancel, and while it looks strange that a conductor would fail to cancel a ticket, when he has a punch in one hand and a ticket in the other, they are liable at times to do so, for many unexpected things at times happen when trains are out on the road. For at times I have been lifting tickets from passengers, and have a ticket just taken from a passenger, when some excitement would get up on the train, or the train would make a sudden stop at an unusual place, I was apt to drop punch and tickets into my pocket, without cancelling the ticket, and run to see what was the matter, and forget the occurrence, whatever it might be, when I would go to put my tickets in shape for the auditor's office. I have also been so worn out while making a report of some trips, on which I had much crowded trains, that if I had undertaken to cancel tickets as I lifted them, I could not have possibly gotten through my train between the stopping-places.

At other times, when I would have excursion parties on my train I have had to have the help of the baggageman and flagman, and at times the sleeping-car conductor, in order to lift the tickets before a stop was made. And when I would have time, I would straighten my tickets, canceling five and six in a punch, and in this way one ticket might not be straightened out good, and so miss being cancelled; and being in a hurry to do something else which I had to do, some of the tickets might be turned into the auditor's office uncanceled in this way.

Well, I had become perfectly familiar with suspensions, but never got to like them, as it had cost me so much to make their acquaintance.

At one time there came very near being a strike on the road, on account of an engineer being discharged from the road's service. When I heard this talked of, I talked to some of the engineers and advised them not to go into such a thing, for I had heard merchants and business men say that if they did strike they would not sympathize with them. I said to them that if it was a matter of low wages it would be different; and that the most of the engineers had good homes, situated so that they could be at home a good part of their time; and their wages were as good as any road was paying their engineers; that a strike would throw them out of work, as well as a good many other men, and they could not get as good runs and wages on any other road.

I also said that the engineers struck once before I came on the road, and nearly all of them lost their places. While the trains were only stopped for a few days, and then ran on the same as ever, and the striking men had to go and hunt work wherever they could find any work to do, for some of them came on the road that I was on at the time, and were glad to get an engine to run even over as bad a road as that was, and some of them were good men. So just before the strike was to take place, the engineers had a meeting, and a vote was taken on the matter, and the strike was lost; and there was no strike, by a wise action of the engineers.

In all my railroad life I have never known of a strike that did any one any good. Not even those men that are called scabs, for their jobs were only for a short while, and their places were soon filled with good men again. It is like dipping a bucket of water out of a river, which makes a little wave, then the place is filled, and the river runs on just the same. So it is ever; when a noted or great man dies, or gets killed, his place is soon filled by another, and the world goes on just the same as before.

At another time business began to fall off, and the road was not doing much, either in freight or passenger business, and the employees' wages were reduced and other expenses cut down. A contract was agreed upon to put the wages back for a certain length of time. When the time for the cut had expired the wages were put back for one or two months, and then reduced again. Engineers and conductors were reduced ten per cent as before. Some of the men, as well as myself, were willing to accept the cut, as we knew the road was not doing the business which it had done before. Some others were dissatisfied; and a lawsuit was brought about; I never did understand just how or why, but the same employees lost the case. So conductors had to run at reduced wages, which was ninety-nine dollars per month.

Notwithstanding the bad track and dangerous bridges and trestles which I had run over, and the length of time I had run on railroads, I never had many bad accidents in the way of wrecks. The first wreck I ever had in which any one was killed, was at Reader's side-track, the same station spoken of where the young man was in some way killed accidentally. A freight-train had side-tracked, in order to let the train that I was on pass, and had failed to set the switch back to the main track. As it was just after dark, my engineer failed to notice this in time to stop before his engine struck the rear end of the freight-train, and the engineer, fireman, and an ex-engineer, who was on the train at the time, were all three killed outright.

While I was on the road a through-train was put on, and arrangements made to run the train through from Washington, D.C., to Memphis, Tenn., and a sleeping-car was attached, which was run from New York to New Orleans; I was put on one of these trains. They were nice little trains when first put on. Two conductors were all that was put on to run them from Bristol to Chattanooga, a distance of two hundred and forty-two miles. We had to run this distance every day, but had the nights to rest, which made it a very good run. The roadway had been improved, until it had as good track and bridges as any Southern road, or better. The schedule was fast, and very few stops were made on this run. When I was put on this run it cheered me up considerably, for I had become very low-spirited on account of my suspension, and so much sickness in my family, and heavy doctor's bills to pay. I had saved up but little, while I had hoped that some day in my old age to be able to quit railroading, and go home and make a living there.

This train was a vestibule train, and I thought it would not be so dangerous when passing from one car to another. I also believed that the officials of the road had appreciated my services on the road more than I had thought beforehand, and I felt more grateful to them and tried hard to do my duty and please them. A dining-car was attached to this train, and later on the express and mail was put on it, and then for awhile an observation car was attached to it. When this car was taken off another coach was put on and more stops were made. This made it a hard run for only two conductors. Well, I only asked for work when I first went on the East Tennessee, Virginia and Georgia Railway, and before I left the road they gave me all I could do when I was at work.

While we were in Augusta with the rolling stock of the old East Tennessee and Georgia Railroad that was run out of East Tennessee, I heard some of the officials of the old East Tennessee and Georgia Railroad talk and laugh about how they worked their men when they were operating the road, and I think it is still kept up to the present day, but there is no better road than the old East Tennessee, Virginia and Georgia Railway to pay their employees what they promise to pay them.

After the Southern Railway Company purchased the East Tennessee, Virginia and Georgia Railway there was a connection made at Morristown with the train I was on, and we handled another sleeping-car between Morristown and Chattanooga. The Southern Railway Company raised the wages of conductors on the main line one dollar per month, making their wages one hundred dollars per month, but they also raised their work. More reports were required. Some of these had to be made out on the train. So I had all the work that I could possibly do.

It was on a bright Sunday afternoon in October, 1894, when I left Bristol, and was taking up tickets in the second-class car, when the engine that was pulling the train leaped the rail on account of a bolt-head being placed on the rail, on the bearing side of a curve, by some unknown person. The engine ran into a cut that was just ahead of her. When she left the rail she turned over on her side, the mail and baggage-cars running over her. The mail-car turned over on the bank, on one side, and one end of the baggage-car ran up on the bank on the other side of the cut. The second-class car, which I was in, ran upon the top of the engine and turned over on the side; the other coach turned lengthwise across the road with one end upon the bank; the other cars stood in a line with the track, all but two being on the ground, as the track was torn up.

This accident occurred so suddenly that I hardly knew what had happened. I was thrown down in the aisle at the time of the shock. The first thing that I remember, after I had gotten up, I was asking what had happened, and some one said they did not know. Then I saw some one crawling out through a window. By this time the car was half full of smoke, which, with the heat, stifled me so I could hardly get my breath. I tried to get my foot upon the arm of a seat in order to reach a window, when I found that one of my knees was hurt, so I gave up hope of getting out, and thought I would be burned up. I looked around for help, but could see no one. The next thing I remember is of having gotten my head through a window and was crawling out of the car. Whether I raised my good leg and put my foot on the seat, or some one helped me up, I do not know. A man said afterwards that he lifted me up to the window, and then got out himself. He said he was the last one getting out of the car. I heard men crying for help, when I first got my head through the window and I called to some men to run to the rescue. One end of the car that I was in was on fire when I got out. After I got out on the top side of the car that I was in two gentlemen met me and helped me along on the top of another coach, and then to the ground.

After I learned that the engineer, fireman, postal clerks, baggageman, and express messenger had been gotten out, I took in the situation at once, and realized at once that there was no chance to check the fire, so I had the trainmen that were in the Pullman service to take all out of the Pullman cars that they could get out, and also the seats and cushions out of one coach. But the heat of the fire was so great, and the fire spread so rapidly, that there was but little saved, if anything. Very little express or baggage was saved, and all the mail, except a few packages, was burned. I got help enough to push one sleeper back out of the way of the fire, and could have saved one other if the front wheels had been on the rails, but they were dropped down on the ground.

I could have saved this and two or three others if I had had an engine soon enough to have pulled them back, but when one came it was too late. The train consisted of a postal-car, baggage and express-car combined, and three coaches, one dining-car, and two sleepers, and all except one sleeper were burned.

My flagman went back when the accident first happened, and I sent a man on a horse with a message, and told him to make all the speed he could and send physicians at once. I thought they never would get there, although the distance was three and a quarter miles back to Bristol. I also sent for the yard engine. There was no one killed outright, but several were injured, some seriously. The engineer was the most dangerously hurt, and died a few days afterwards. He was a good man, a splendid engineer, and one of my favorites. When the engine did come, the physicians came and the wounded were taken back to Bristol and cared for. None of the others died.

It was the most wonderful wreck I ever saw, and created a great deal of excitement from one end of the road to the other. Hacks and other vehicles came from Bristol loaded with people, and at times one could scarcely get through the crowd.

It was enough to make one quit running on a railroad, and I thought for awhile I would do so; and I wish now that I had done so, for it would have been best for me. But, like all railroad men, I thought that I could not make a living any other way, and after my sprained knee got better I went to running again on the same run which I had been on for two years or more, as I did not think that I could afford to lose the time to rest. As I said before, the work on the train increased, and there was no hope of a third crew being put on the run, which would have made it better for the ones on the run, and it would have given three crews all the work that ought to have been required of them. I ran on this run about eight months longer, when I was given another run.

Had the little vestibule-train stayed like it was when first put on I would have been all right, for I wanted nothing better than it was at that time. I suppose I was changed from this run on account of the work being so voluminous, and my feebleness. The run I took was a night run, and it paid me the same wages that I was getting on the run that I had been on before; and had it not been an all-night run it would have been a good train to run, for the work on it was comparatively nothing to the work I had been doing on the train I had left.

I had been on my new run a little over a week when one morning I arrived at the end of my run. I boarded a street-railway car for the hotel I was stopping at. The car seldom stopped still for one to get off as it was in about one block of the end of the line, and generally I was the only passenger on board when they would get so near the end of the track, and at one time I was carried to the end of the track and walked back because they did not stop or slack speed, so I thought it safe to get off. So the morning I speak of I saw the motorman was watching me when we were passing the hotel, but I kept my seat until we were near the proper place for them to stop for me to get off. I went out on the platform of the car and I saw they were not going to stop still for me and as the car was moving very slowly I stepped off the car with my right foot. I had hold of the hand-hold with my left hand, and the shoe-heel on my left foot caught against something on the bottom step, and the car was given a quick and sudden jerk and jerked the step from under my left foot and my hand loose also, and I was tripped up as quick as lightning, throwing me on my back, or rather right side, parallel with the track, breaking the top of my thigh bone. I have been a cripple ever since and have not been able to work, and do not know that I ever will be, but do hope I will.

When a man runs on railroads over a half of his lifetime he is fit for nothing else, for he knows nothing else—and at times he don't know that.

Part Two

General Observations

Chapter Twelve

Railroads and Employees

How fast time passes by! Yes, so fast that we do not see or realize it until we stop and look back and think it over. Then years seem almost as if they had been days of the same number; at least it seems so to me. For just a little while ago I was a little white-haired boy and did not know what a railroad was when they were first talked of, or of what use they could be; but now, when my hair is almost white again with age and sorrow, I, by experience, have learned that steam and railroads, as well as electricity, are the most valuable inventions that have ever been utilized by man.

Railroads, as well as many other things, give capitalists a chance to invest their money, and by their investments the poor and the laboring man find employment. Were it not for capitalists, O laboring man, where would you be? Probably fighting your battle through life with the ground against the grass and weeds, and more than likely some playing their parts on somebody else's land.

Look back at men on horse-back, or in the old stage-coach, traveling slowly to different destinations—congressional members to Washington, merchants to New York—out on the roads for weeks, those roads leading over mountains, and many rough places. By this same way the United States mail was carried from one place to another.

Time was of little consideration in those days; it was worth but little in comparison to what it is to-day. When railroads were beginning to be built, and it was said that fifteen or twenty miles could be made in one hour, it was hardly believed by many. The building of railroads awakened the nations, and they found that they had slept a long time, and that time was worth more than they had dreamed of. Yes, a day at some time, and to some men, was worth hundreds of dollars, after they had slept so long.

When I first went to running on a railroad fifteen or twenty miles per hour was counted good time for a passenger-train, and freight-trains ten or twelve miles per hour. Afterwards twenty-five miles per hour was counted very fast time for a passenger-train to make. The speed of trains was increased as the tracks were improved.

I have run freight-trains when the limit was seventeen miles per hour; and under no circumstances were we allowed to run any faster than that. But in later years I have been on freight-trains that in some places would run at the rate of thirty or thirty-five miles per hour, though this was a great deal faster than the schedule time. I have also been on passenger-trains that were run sixty miles per hour, but this was faster than schedule time. The schedule time at the present day, through the South, is about thirty-five or forty miles per hour for passenger-trains, but faster time than this is made when trains fall behind. The time is not far off when passenger-trains will be scheduled to run sixty miles or more per hour through the Southern States.

I remember when coaches were lighted with a liquid called fluid, which was used in a small lamp or cup, fastened to the sides of the cars. Those lamps made very poor lights. The lights were afterwards improved by a coach candle being used; these were also placed on the sides of some of the coaches, and some other coaches had them overhead. Afterwards the lights were improved still more by oil lamps placed in coaches overhead. The conductor still had to carry his lantern on his arm while going through his train at night.

The next improvement on coach lights was gasoline. When this came into use a conductor could set his lamp in the baggage-car on the end of a coach, and go through his train and read the destination of his tickets without any trouble. The next lights used in some coaches and sleeping-cars was gas, which was an improvement on gasoline; and ere long, if not already in use, electric lights will be used in lighting sleeping-cars and passenger-coaches.

While so many changes have been made in various other things, from early days to the present time, there has been the grandest change, with some exceptions, in regard to the employees of railroads in improvement of morals, charity, and conduct. While the most of them were once looked upon as the most reckless and wicked men on earth, by some people, there were some good and moral men among them in those days; still there were others who were of a reckless character, which gave all railroad men a name alike, where they were not personally known. At the present day there is as much difference in railroad employees and the employees of former days as there is in the old-fashioned tallow candle and the electric light.

In my early railroad days I was looked upon by some of the boys as not being much of a railroad man because I would not go around with them and play cards, pool and billiards, and drink beer and whiskey. While I knew I was not much of a railroad man, I thought if it took all that to make one, that I never would be much of a railroader, and so it turned out. I was once asked what I did to pass off the time when I was out on the road. The man who asked the question said that he never saw me out with the boys playing at games. I replied that I had never in my life played a game of cards, pool or billiards, and that I passed off my lay-over time taking my rest, so as to be refreshed for my next trip. He said that he could not see how I could be a railroad man.

Engineers and conductors are generally self-made men, not so much as regards wealth, but by working themselves up from a lower to a higher position and from low to high wages. Most of the engineers nowadays commenced firing an engine on the road. Some others commenced wiping engines in a round-house, and worked themselves up to first-class engineers. I have known some few, but very few, sent out to running on a road from the machine shops. The majority of conductors in this section of country commenced braking on a freight-train, or as flagman or baggage-master, and worked themselves up to freight conductor, and on up to passenger conductor; but few seldom got any further up.

By the good behavior of the men, or by the restrictions of the rules of the officials of railroads, or by kind Providence, there is no class of men where better men can be found than among railroad men—even baggagemen, flagmen, and firemen. I have worked under twenty-seven different superintendents, besides general superintendents, receivers, general managers, presidents, and vice-presidents, and I have learned that the better men were treated the better men they would be.

Sometimes men's good conduct, and confining themselves to the rules of the officials of the road, causes good treatment. Good wages make men more attentive to business. But of late years, when the wages of employees of railroads are increased, the work also is generally increased or a shorter lay-over allowed. A long lay-over is a thing that employees ought to have, for a railroad employee that runs on a road ought to have some little time to look after his own business matters, for he cannot well afford to stop off and lose the time very often, unless he has some other income outside of his wages. Again, when a man has sufficient rest he feels more like going out when his time comes to go. I have seen the time in former days when I was glad when my turn came to go out on the road, for I had become tired of rest, as the lay-over was so long that was given the men, after they had made a trip over the road.

When I went on the East Tennessee, Virginia and Georgia Railroad to work, the men had a very good lay-over, notwithstanding the freight and passenger business were both good. If freight conductors ran a day train, they had the nights to rest in; and those who ran a night train had the days to rest in, and also Sundays, the management of the road not allowing freight-trains to run on the Sabbath day. Passenger conductors also had a good rest after making a round trip. The run was one hundred and thirty-one miles, and a day or night to lay over; and then two hundred and forty-two miles, and a day or night to lay over; and then one hundred and eleven miles, and a day and night to lay off. One time when a passenger-train was made a mixed-train there was no train run over the road Sundays at all except the night passenger-train. If this was the case to-day throughout the United States it would appear more of a God-fearing nation. If the sound of iron wheels and rails could not be heard rattling along the road it would appear more like a Sabbath day and a day of rest. But life is too short, they say, and the wandering dollar must be found while it is day. The mails must be delivered, the money sent by express must be sent at once, the news must be read the day on which it is printed, the traveler must make his destination by night or he will lose a good investment—time flies too fast, we cannot wait.

I think it a good thing for railroad employees to have good orders to protect themselves, and to be beneficial to one another, in the bounds of reason. But no hot-headed striker.

Many years ago I talked of such organizations, and afterwards joined the Old Reliable Conductors' Order, and paid out some two hundred dollars or more.[1] The treasury was robbed, and my assessments were stopped being sent to me, or at least I was told so by the corresponding member of the division that I belonged to, for I went to him time and again to pay the assessments, as I wanted to keep it up. When I learned that this order was still kept up, I wanted to join again, but on account of my age could not do so. I felt like this was not treating me right, as it was not my fault in its not being kept up. Some three or four years after I went on the East Tennessee, Virginia and Georgia Railroad, one of the men, a yardmaster at the time, wanted me to get up a lodge of a different kind, and I agreed to do so, and we soon had enough names to have a lodge at Knoxville. The officers of the road were kind enough to issue passes for some of the members of the order to come from Nashville and organize a lodge, and after the passes were given me to send to the

Nashville members, the very first man who spoke to me in regard to the matter backed out, and that broke it up. It was a long time afterwards before a lodge was organized at Knoxville. Some time after the lodge was organized at that place, I became a member of the O.R.C. I liked the order very much, but could not attend the body as often as I would have liked to on account of the run I was on. At one time I became a little dissatisfied with the order on account of a lawsuit that was brought up, and for awhile I thought I would withdraw from the order, but afterwards became perfectly satisfied to remain, as my brethren were so kind to me, and I became more familiar with the order, and found it to be of more importance than I had thought of. In two cases my brethren paid my dues for me, so as to keep my membership, once when I had sickness in my family and the death of a son; and at another time after I was crippled. I have decided it is as good, if not the best organization of employees, as there is in the United States. If the Order of Railway Conductors and the Brotherhood of Locomotive Engineers were consolidated it would outnumber in members more than any other order I know of. If the Order of Railway Conductors keeps improving as it has for the last few years, it will in the near future be one of the grandest orders ever organized by railroad employees, while the Brotherhood of Locomotive Engineers are hard to beat. If railroad employees, or employees of any other corporation, have any grievances they will find it to their interest to compromise, if possible to do so, without a strike. And in case a strike is decided upon, the best plan is to strike out and get a job somewhere else, if they can; that was my plan in my younger days, when I became dissatisfied. I found it the best plan to have another job somewhere else, if one could do so, before he started out on a strike. Those who have gone through what I have, and partly on account of strikes, will say that I am right, if there have been any who have done so.

While I know that sometimes employees are imposed upon, and also some of the railroads are, and, of course, a man's work seems to be not so laborious as at others. When business on a road slacks off, he does not have so much work to do. Even an engineer himself does not have so many cars to handle with his engine. When a road's earnings are not sufficient to pay its expenses, we cannot expect the company to go back and use the money that has been made beforehand. In a case of that kind, the company, so far as their interest is concerned, had best let the road stop being operated and save the wear of the rolling stock and machinery. Sometimes when the officials of a road say the business is falling off and the road is not paying expenses, it is not believed by some employees. But it does seem to me that any employee of the transportation department could see when business was good and when it was light. I have worked for some officials that I would have hated very bad to have disbelieved anything they would have told me.

While it is true that very few employees ever get wealthy, or even money enough ahead so as to quit a road, at least I have known but few to do so; and those few, I suppose, inherited the larger part of their wealth. It is a very hard matter for one to save but little when he has no income outside of his wages, or at least I have found it so in my own case. Yet it is thought by some people that all passenger conductors are rich, or ought to be, if they have been on a road any length of time, as they are supposed to "knock down," as it was called in former days; but now stealing, which is the proper name. Some of the same class of men that believe or talk such talk, would act as they think conductors do if they had a chance. And a man that would board a train, and by falsehood or any other way try to get a free ride, when he is not entitled to it, is as big a thief as any conductor that ever stole a nickel from a railroad company. A man who thinks that there are no honest railroad conductors, would himself steal the thread from the eye of a needle. For there are as honest conductors as can be found among any other class of men on the face of the earth. It is a hard thing to do, to make a thief out of an honest man, and a great deal harder to make an honest man out of a thief.

I had run a train for some time before I ever heard tell of "knocking down," and I cannot see why the public opinion has formed such an idea in regard to conductors, unless it was on account of so many cash fares being collected by conductors in the early days of railroads, and before the ticket system was inaugurated and perfected, and a conductor had a chance to "knock down," if he was disposed to do so when the temptation was so great. Another cause may have given currency to this idea from the fact that some conductors have fine dwelling houses, and fine spans of horses, as some few whom I have known had, and would take in the town after having made a round trip. If conductors had have stolen what some people think some of them have, they would have been as rich as ever Jay Gould was. But if those who think this of conductors as a class will visit their homes, they will find out that the majority of them are nothing but common men when at home, although they may cut a grand appearance while out on the road.

At the present day, if a conductor was disposed to do as the old saying goes, "give the company half of his cash collections," and wanted to buy a farm with his share, it would take him a year or more to get enough to buy one acre of good ground anywhere in the country. In other words, what he would get in a year would not pay a detective or spotter's wages for one month. I have known passengers, when they were at a station ready to take a train, not to get on on account of not having a ticket because they would have had to pay one more cent a mile on the train if they had gotten on without a ticket. About all the cash fare collected by conductors is when a passenger decides to go on beyond the destination of his ticket. I heard a conductor say once that when he was making a run he was worried almost to death all the time for fear he would get his money mixed with the company's money and that he would keep some of the company's money by mistake.

A man said to me one day while on my train that he wished that he could make his living as easy as I did mine. I said to him if he did not make it easier than I did, he must have a very hard way to make a living, adding that I supposed he was a farmer. He answered that he was. I then said to him: "You make your living much easier than I make mine, for you work when you please and rest when you feel like it; get your night's sleep and Sundays to go to church or to rest; eat your meals regularly, and while you sleep you have something growing which is an income to you. But when I stop all my income stops. I sleep and eat when I get the chance to do so; get up at any time in the night and go out and run all night at times, and sometimes work all night or all day, as the case may be, at a wreck, regardless of cold, rain, or snow." He answered, "Well, you are right. I had not thought of that. I thought you just had to ride along on the train."

If I now had what I was beat out of on the Alabama and Chattanooga Railroad, which is now the Alabama Great Southern Railway, with the interest, it would be a blessing to me at the present day, amounting to about ten hundred and sixty some odd dollars, which I had earned at hard work. If there is not a law to protect employees of the operation of a new-built road, there ought to be one passed. While it would do me no good now, it might benefit some others. On some roads, when a conductor has been a faithful servant for many years and begins declining, he is given an easy position at the same wages that he was getting for running a train; and on other roads when his best days are passed and he becomes old and feeble, he is turned loose to live or die, like a worn-out government horse, and another picked up to fill his place; or else he is thrown in a scrap-pile, like an old driving-wheel by the side of the round-house, with the tire worn out.

I have had a great many brakemen, baggagemen and flagmen in my railroad days. For some roads allowed conductors to hire their own men, and as a general thing conductors had better men then than when they were employed by the officials; for the man hired by the conductor would be more apt to please his conductor, as he knew the conductor could discharge him at any time, without going to any of the officials, while the man hired by the officials does not care so much, as he can go to the office and be placed with some other conductor. But I have had some of as good men, whom the officials employed and put on my train as any I ever had. I have had many a man to run his first trip on a railroad with me.

A great many of the men I have had run with me worked themselves up to freight-train conductors, and some to passenger-train conductors, and made good conductors generally; but some of them afterwards let Robertson or Lincoln county or Bourbon get the best of them, which caused them to lose their places on the roads where they were at work, while the others are running trains as conductors at the present day.[2]

One evening I wanted my engine turned around, and my two brakemen refused to help turn her, and as they were somewhat under the influence of whiskey when leaving time came I would not let them go out with me. I wired the superintendent what I had done, and I did all the work myself until I met a train with two men on it, who were sent to me to take the other's places. This took place in time of the war, and I saw one of my discharged men afterwards in camps with other soldiers, and as I passed by he held up one foot without shoe or sock, so I could see it, and said to me: "If I had taken your advice, I would not have been in this fix now."

Another incident which happened in time of war. One morning while I was taking the number of cars in the train which I was going out on, the yardmaster said to me: "I want you to take this young man on your train as brakeman. He is a very nice young man, and his father does not want him to go into the army."

I said, "All right," as I knew some of his relatives, who were well-to-do, and his parents were wealthy also. The young man said all I had to do was to tell him what I wanted done, that he was not afraid of work. I told him what his duty was, and let him ride in my caboose with me and attend to the caboose with me and attend to the caboose brake, while I had my other man on top of the train.

So I let him stay in the caboose until late in the evening for fear he might get hurt, as he was a new hand. I had been letting my men take turn about. In the evening he said he wanted to go out on top, and I told him all right, but cautioned him to be careful, He said he wanted to learn all about a train. In those days we had a great many hot boxes, and they gave me a lot of trouble.[3] I had my new man throwing wood in the tender at wood stations, as coal had never been thought of in those days as fuel for engines in that section. And I also had my new man packing hot boxes. At one time while at work at one, as I was in a hurry, I said to him: "Get away, and I will stick my hands in the bucket, if you can't get the grease out with the paddle." But instead of moving, so as to give me the chance, he stuck hands and gloves down into the grease bucket, and we were soon away from the place. He made as good a brakeman as I ever had, on his first trip, but when we had made a round trip, and the train was put away, and all our work done for that trip, he came to me and asked me if our work was done for the evening. I answered that it was. He then said to me: "Well, captain, if I was to railroad, I would sooner run with you than any man I know of; but before I will follow railroading, I will be d——d if I don't go into the war first, if I get killed." I told him that I was sorry, for I knew he would make me a good man. But that was his first and last trip.

After I went on another road where I was running a mixed-train, and doing local work, one morning my two brakemen went to take their breakfast at a weigh station on the road, and stayed away so long that I had all my work done that I had to do at the station, and I sent them word to come on or I would leave them. And they sent word back to me that they would be there as soon as they drank the bottle of whiskey which they had. I sent them word back that they would have plenty of time to get another bottle and drink it. So I left them, and did the braking, and loading and unloading freight myself for thirty-two miles to a station where the trains lay over nights. I arrived there early in the afternoon. The superintendent had asked me to take a young man on with me the first vacancy I had on my train. So I hired a man the same evening, and as the superintendent lived at that place, I sent him word to send the young man down the next morning. The next morning the young man came to me, and I was surprised when he said that he had orders from the superintendent to report to me, for he had on a cloth suit, a high beaver hat, boiled shirt, and a silk necktie.

I said: "Are you the man whom the superintendent spoke to me about, a few days ago?" He said he was. I then said to him: "You cannot do the work that a brakeman is required to do." He was a stout man. He asked why. I answered: "You will spoil your hat and clothes." He asked: "What do you want me to do?" I answered: "Go around to the place where the engine stands, and help shovel a tender full of coal." He went, and when he returned from shoveling coal, his face and shirt bosom had changed wonderfully. But he made a good man, and after he had run brakeman for some time I gave him my baggage-car. Afterwards I got him in with the express company as messenger. He run that for some time. But afterwards [he] left the express company, and run as train conductor. He was inclined to be a little wild, and I learned that he became more so after he left me.

I had a brakeman while I was running through Alabama; he was a very stout man, and a good brakeman. But he would drink a little too much whiskey at times, and sometimes while on duty if it was offered him by a passenger on the train. He would do anything for me that he could. I called him Georgia, because he was from that State, as well as myself. If I wanted a man put off of the train, he was ready for the job, and he liked it very much. He would stand on the coach platform by his brake-wheel while the train was moving.

While I was taking up tickets one day, just after leaving a station, I found a passenger who had been drinking and was somewhat intoxicated. He had no ticket, and swore that he would not pay any fare. He said that he had shipped a carload of mules over the road and had sold them on a credit, and was entitled to return free of charge. I asked him if he had any papers to that effect, and he answered no, and he did not want any. I worried awhile with him, and then motioned to my Georgia brakeman. The stockman was a middle-sized man. My brakeman came inside of the coach and asked me if I wanted him put off. I said yes. I had already pulled the bellcord. When the train came to a full stop the brakeman took the stockman by the arm and said to him: "Come on!" But the man pulled back like a mule, and my man picked him up in his arms as though he was but a little child, and walked out with him and stood him down on the ground, and he was left standing on the roadside. This created quite a laugh among the passengers, and some of them said my brakeman was the best man they had ever seen for that business, and that I ought keep him for that purpose.

I once had an Irishman braking for me. He was a young man, and never ran on a train before. He ran with me one trip—his first, I think it was. I sent him to the engine, where we had stopped at the regular stopping-place, to tell the engineer to stop at Keewanee, which was the next station ahead and a flag-station. I also said to him to tell the engineer that I had a lady passenger to get off there. When we approached the station spoken of, I noticed that the engineer was not going to stop. I pulled the bell-cord and stopped him and helped the lady off. It was in the night, and we ran a little past the platform. This fretted me a little, as I had sent him word to stop. So the next stop we made I went to the engine and asked the engineer why he did not stop the train at the proper place, when I had sent him word to do so and also that I had a lady passenger to get off. He said that I did not; if I did so, that he did not get any such word. So I got after my Irishman about it, and he said that he did tell the engineer what I told him to tell him. The next stop I told the engineer what the Irishman said, and the engineer said: "Oh, yes; he did come and tell me that you said for me to stop letting the water off; that I was scalding the passengers back there.

A superintendent that I was working for once asked me to take a young man on my train as baggage-master. The young man was a relative of the superintendent's. I said all right; that the first vacancy I had I would do so. About the same time the general superintendent asked me to take a friend of his on my train as a baggage-master. Also the general manager asked me to take a man on that he wanted to make a conductor of. This all came about the same time, and I told the general manager of the other applications that had been made, and it was decided on for me to take the general manager's man first. He ran awhile with me, and I gave him all the instructions I could in regard to conducting, as I had instructions to do. When I was asked about his ability in regard to making a train conductor, I said that I thought that if he would let whiskey alone he would make a pretty good conductor, but that I would be afraid to risk him on that account. But they gave him a freight-train anyway, and about the second trip that he was making he ran about forty-eight miles on another train's time, in the opposite direction from the way he was going, right facing the other train, when, according to the rules of the road, he had no right to pass the meeting point for the two trains without an order to do so. But he was drunk. There would have been a collision with the two trains had not the train that had a right to the track run off the rail and been delayed. The drunken conductor said that according to his almanac he had all the rights he wanted to the track, and he refused to put his train on a side-track at that place, and backed it back to the regular meeting-point. He was not started out any more in charge of a train. He called the schedule his almanac. He was of good family, and would have made a good conductor if he had let whiskey alone. I have known many other men who have been ruined by the same habit.

After this man of whom I have been speaking was given a train, I took the general superintendent's friend on in his place. He did not last but a few trips, for he was in a fuss nearly all the time with some passengers about the baggage. He would check saddles or anything else that one wanted him to, and then would not deliver them when the duplicate check was presented, without some bother. He told me himself that he only wanted the job so as to get over the road without paying his fare, as he was an agent for a flouring-mill, and wanted to sell flour along the road. I said to him that if that was the case the company had better give him a pass, if they wanted to do him a favor; and as he did not attend to the business of the road to suit me, I would notify the superintendent of the facts. He answered all right. So I did, and the superintendent said for me to discharge him, for he had just bothered him so much that he put him on the train to get rid of him. So I let him go.

The next man I took on was the superintendent's relative. I was on a night train, and my new man would lay down on a train-box in the baggage-car and sleep all night, and my brakemen and I would have to receive and deliver the baggage and railroad mail. If I woke him up he would be asleep again before we reached another station. One night the weather was cold and the fire had gone out of the stove, which woke him up. He asked me to have one of the brakemen to make him a fire in the stove. I told him if he waited for that he could freeze to death, and if either of my men made him a fire that I would stop the train and put the one off who did so. After I had put up with him about as long as I could, I told the superintendent that his kinsman would never make a railroad man, and informed him how inattentive he was to his business. So he was sent back home to take his sleep and rest.

I knew a conductor who run on the same road that I was on years ago. This conductor was allowed only one brakeman, as he was running a through freight-train. It was said that those two men, who were in the habit of getting drunk, made a bargain after they were put on this through freight, to take it day about getting drunk. C was to get drunk one day and B the next, and they got along very well for a time until at last they both got drunk on the same day. They got to their destination all right, but were discharged from the road's service. Each one of these men claimed that it was his day to get drunk. C asked B why it was that he got drunk on his day, and said, "you know we were to take it day about." And B answered: "Yes, I know we were, but you got drunk on my day."

A story was told on a conductor while the State of Georgia was running a part of the Alabama and Chattanooga Railroad. I was told this story by one of the conductor's brakemen, who used to brake on my train in former days. The brakeman said that he had lighted his signal lamp, which had a red globe, and had set it on the rear platform of the rear coach in the train. This was just before it had got dark enough to put the lamp up in its proper place, and just before the schedule time to leave a terminal station. The brakeman said that he was standing on the ground just opposite the platform when he saw the conductor step out of the coach, and knowing that he never had run a train before and did not know anything about running a train, he thought he would have a little fun. So when the conductor stepped on the platform he said: "Look there, captain, that lamp is red-hot;" and the conductor said: "Well, d——n it, kick it off," at the same time he kicked it of himself, and broke it all to pieces. It was said afterwards that the same conductor made a requisition for red oil, as he was out of red oil.

While the road was under the same management spoken of, an old conductor who was on the road at that time told me that one of the officials put a man on the road with him, and he told the man that he must call the names of the stations in the coaches in order to let the passengers know, so as to get off at the stations their tickets called for. The brakeman said that he did not know the names of the stations. The conductor said the next stop is Rising Fawn. When the train arrived at the station and before it stopped still the brakeman stuck his head in at the car door and halloed out in a loud tone, "Rise and Fall," and a passenger ran out of the car, jumped off and fell down, and when he got up he cursed and swore that the station had the most appropriate name of any that he ever heard of.

I had a brakeman on my train one time and he did not know the names of the stations on the line of road. he had run with me on a different road, which was the first railroading that he had ever done. He was a good man. I gave him a card with the names of the stations on it, so as he could learn them, and the first trip (this was on the second road which he run with me), and the first station at which we arrived after leaving the terminal station he made a mistake in calling the name. The proper name of the station was Coosada, and he called it Coosedadedo, which created quite a laugh among the passengers who knew the proper name of the station.

Chapter Thirteen

Passenger Trains and Conductors

Not even the officials of railroads know what a conductor of a passenger-train has to contend with, unless it is some that have run on a passenger-train themselves as conductors. It is a nice business for one to follow, if he cannot get something better to do, that is, when he has a run that is not so long as they are run at the present day, and the proper time given him to rest, and when coaches are not crowded so that passengers have to stand up in the aisles of the coaches.

I suppose I have handled all classes of people that ever traveled through the Southern States, and perhaps all kinds that God ever created, and some whom I have doubted whether he had anything to do with their being created. I will relate some facts which transpired on my train during the part of my life on railroads.

Once I had three men board my train who wanted me to pass them over the road. They said that they were out of money and wanted to get home. I stopped the train and had them to get off. Afterwards I learned that they had lost their money playing cards at the station where they boarded my train. And many other similar cases I have had to deal with, and often some of the men in these cases were well perfumed with red eye, or rye whiskey. I have had some men board my train half drunk, and a bottle of whiskey in their pocket, and say that they had no money and wanted to be passed free, and then when they found that they were going to be put off the train they would pay their fare. I have at times asked such men why they did not keep the money which they spent for whiskey, and they would then have had enough to pay their railroad fare. I have also heard men remark that they had rather spend money for whiskey than to pay their fare on a railroad train. I state those facts to show how free and foolish some men spend their money, and how badly they hate to pay it out to a railroad company.

I put off a nicely dressed and lady-looking middle-aged woman, who claimed to be traveling on charitable business, and who seemed in very much of a hurry to make her destination, and wanted to be passed on that account. I left her standing on the depot platform cursing me on account of not being passed over the road. At this same station I once put a man off my train who claimed to be deaf and dumb, and carried his little slate and pencil to write what he wished to say. He wrote upon this slate the station which he wanted to be passed to (as he had no money), handing me the slate at the same time, and put his finger first to his ear and then to his mouth, shaking his head as though he could neither hear nor talk. I wrote on his slate that he would have to get off at the next stopping-place. When the train stopped he stepped off, and as the train moved off he said, "You can go to hades with your train."

I have seen a great many women, as well as men, who would try to get out of paying their railroad fare, or a part of it, and have known some of them to declare that they had given up all the money they had, and afterwards find out that they had more, and get their full fare by telling them that they would have to get off the train. Once an old lady and a young one got on my train, and the old one gave me, as she said, all the money she had, to pay for both of their fares. I told her how much the amount of money she had given me lacked of paying their fare to the station that she said they were going to. She said that she had given me the last cent she had. I told her that I would let them go as far as the money she had given me would pay their fare. She replied that she was going to see her daughter who was lying at the point of death, and that I surely had Christianity enough about me to take them on. When I arrived at the station that the amount of money given me paid their fare to, I said, "This is the place you will have to get off at." The old lady said to me, "You surely are not going to put us off here." I replied, "I am, unless you give me money enough to pay your fare on." And she handed me a five-dollar bill, which she said belonged to another lady, but was sent by her to a friend of the lady's. I told her it made no difference how she came by it, just so she paid her fare.

I have found it a very hard question to decide, when a lady-like woman, or one who was an object of pity, boarded my train and told a sad story, what to do. It looked bad to put them off the train. Yet it must be done, unless other passengers would take pity on them and pay their fare for them, and I have seen them do so many a time. Sometimes I have let some go on to their destination under such circumstances. I could not ask for transportation for them, and would report the facts to my superintendents when I would get to the end of my run, and they would sustain me in the action I had taken in the matter. Once I went to a superintendent to report myself for something which I had done, and did not know whether I would be sustained in the action or not, but I was when I reported the facts. He remarked that I always reported myself, and nobody else, and I told him that I only knew what I did myself.

In one case of the kind, last spoken of, I saw a white-looking object run under, or between the cars, just as the train was moving away from a station. I was running a mixed-train at that time, and it was about dark one evening, so I could not tell what the object was which I had seen. I sent one of my trainmen over the top of the box-cars that were in my train to see if he could find anybody in between the box-cars.

He soon came back badly frightened, and said he saw a woman between two cars, sitting on the drawheads. I had the train stopped at once and found a pale and feeble, but respectable-looking, woman in the position spoken of. I asked her what she took such a risk of losing her life as that of her present position was. She said that she had accompanied her sister, who was going West, that far, and intended to walk back home, as she had no money, and was taken too sick to do so. I made her go back in a coach and let her go back to the station where she said she lived, which was a distance of ten miles. I told her then of the danger there was in such acts as she had taken, and she said she would not try it again. When I reported the facts, the action was approved of by the officials reported to.

At a station where I had a connection from another train, a well-dressed lady changed from the connecting train to my train, and she told such a sad story about the loss of her money and her troubles that the passengers on board the train made up money and paid her fare to her said destination. Some time afterwards she boarded my train a second time, and her way was paid the same as before. A third time she boarded my train and did not have half money enough to pay her fare to the point she wanted to go, and she could get no help from the passengers as before. I had her alight from the train when she had ridden as far as the money she had given me paid her way. After she had alighted from the train she said to me that I was the hardest-hearted conductor she had ever traveled with. She had said many tender-hearted words to me, so as to get me to let her go on without paying any more, but I had met her before on my train, and I was not bothered with her any more.

I went through my train one night and collected tickets from all my passengers, as I thought, and afterwards, while passing through the ladies' coach, I found a large boy seated by a lady who had already given me her ticket but had not given me any for the boy, for I had not seen him. As I passed through taking up tickets, I saw a large bulk of some kind covered over very nicely, but I supposed it was a large provision basket, or some kind of musical instrument, and I had found a living one. I claimed a half fare ticket more than I had received from the lady. But she said the child was only ten years old, and asked me why I did not collect the fare as I went through lifting tickets. I answered: "Because you had him covered up and hidden from me." She shelled out a half fare for the music box.

Another case of this kind took place on my train, when a lady had a nine-year old child covered over and stuck in between her and the side of the coach. She said she had no money, and told me herself the child's age was nine years. She was ticketed and her baggage checked to a summer resort in North Carolina. She became very much offended at me for wanting a half fare for the child, but finally said she would give me the checks to hold her trunks until she redeemed them. I had explained to her the rules in regard to collecting fares on children, and she appeared in a better humor, but afterwards refused to give up her checks and said she would get the money from a friend at the place where she had to change trains, but she failed to do so. I told the baggage agent at the changing point to collect the amount. She had talked to me so insultingly that I did not intend to be beat if I could avoid it. So when she arrived at her destination she found that she could not get her baggage until she paid the amount of money I had claimed for the child.

She reported me to the general ticket and passenger agent, and the papers were sent to me. She had stated in her report that she had already paid me the child's fare and I had kept it, and now wanted to collect it again for the company. Well, it was a very insulting letter. I have no idea that she ever once thought of me seeing it. I explained the facts as they had occurred, and I learned afterwards that she got her trunks as soon as the amount of money was paid that they were held for and not before.

At another time I got into a similar case. A lady with a party of children and a nurse got on my train. The lady had tickets for her party with the exception of one half fare ticket. I collected a half fare for a child who she said was over eight years old, and there were no unpleasant words passed between us in regard to the matter. I had counted the number in the party and found that I was lacking a half fare ticket. She went to the office of the general passenger agent and said I had collected a half fare on a child that was barely old enough to walk. I received a letter from the passenger agent in regard to the matter. he asked me in the letter if I was collecting half fares on children that were not old enough to get out of their mother's laps. This made me mad, and I thought I never would ask another passenger for a ticket for a child, old or young, as long as I run a train. But when I explained the matter, and the lady found out her mistake, as she said she thought her nurse was entitled to free passage, it was all satisfactory, and my action approved of.

And again I found a man and wife and a girl, who, the man informed me when I asked her age, was going on eleven years old. I asked him why he did not purchase a ticket for her, and he said that he had traveled thousands of miles with her and had never paid a cent's fare for her, but this was an old and familiar story. I said to him that he would have to pay me a half fare for her. It was in the night and I had my lantern, as this was away back when candles were used for coach lights. Well, he talked very insulting and paid me, and remarked that it was the first time that he had ever paid the girl's fare. I said to him that he could not say this any more and tell the truth. He said that the money was for my own pocket, and the company would never see it. I raised my lamp with the intention of smashing it to pieces in his face, when a better thought struck me. I was in the ladies' coach and I knew of a conductor on a connecting road who had been discharged a short time before for a similar offense. I concluded to fight it out with my tongue. So I told him that he had done all that he had to do with it, he had paid the fare and it was none of his business whether I kept it or gave it to the company, and that a dishonest man thought all other men like himself. He wanted my name and said he would report me. I gave it to him on a slip of paper and told him that he would do me a favor by reporting the facts. So I saved my lamp and probably a thrashing, and when daytime came he came to me and made all necessary apologies, which I accepted.

I had a man put off of my train one day who was full of "Johnnie, how came you so?"[1] He refused to get off at the station that his ticket called for and claimed that it was farther on that he had paid for a ticket to. He swore that he would not pay any more. So I had my brakeman help him off, and he fell on his all-fours when the man let him loose. But after the train left he raised himself up and took from his pocket a long pistol and fired it off in the direction the train was going, and scared my brakemen so that they ran through the coaches for dear life. He could not have hit any one on the train with a Winchester rifle on account of the distance between them.

I found two men on a platform between two coaches. They had been drinking freely and refused to pay any fare. So I made them get off at a flag station. It was one evening about dusk. Just as the train moved off one of the men fired off a pistol at me and the ball struck the corner of the coach just above the step that I had just been standing on and from which I had stepped on to the platform of the coach.

Among all the tramps which I have found on my trains were four I found one day all in one closet in a second-class car, and all four of them were large, stout-looking men. One had a wooden leg; another had but one arm, and one looked as if his face had been badly scalded in time past. They said that they were old railroad men and wanted free transportation. I gave it to them, as they had no money, to the first station from there they had got on. Some time afterwards I found the same four men seated in the second-class coach. The first one that I asked for his ticket pointed to the wooden-legged man, saying that he would pay for all four. So I asked the one who had been pointed out to me for their tickets or fare. I soon found out that he wanted to pay for all four with his tongue as he had the most lip. I pulled the bell cord and put them off before I got out of the yard.

Once there were three very nice-looking gentlemen boarded my train and asked me to pass them as far as the end of my run, and said they were railroad men. I asked them why they did not get passes, as they had got on at the place where all the offices of the officials were, and they said they had asked for passes but were refused. I said: "If you are railroad men and the officials of the road would not give you passes you cannot expect me to pass you." I collected their fare. Just before we got to the end of my run they said to me: "Well, captain, we would like to see you up about Cincinnati some time. If you will come up, your board nor railroad fare shall not cost you a cent." I knew that they said this to make me feel bad and not because they meant to do as they said.

I thanked them and said it was very kind of them, and added, "Gentlemen, if you ever see me north of the Ohio river I will be handcuffed or chained." I said this to play even with them for I had good friends and relatives north of the Ohio river as well as south of it.

When I had time to do so, I always looked around my train where stops were made, as it was an old railroad rule, and have often found things wrong about some of the cars on account of their disability. At one time while at a water tank taking water, I found that a spring had been lost out from underneath one end of the baggage-car. I blocked it up and took it to a side-track, and notified the section boss to go over his section and look for the spring. When the spring was found it was found at a blacksmith's shop and half of it worked up into some other use.

I once found a pair of trucks disabled under a second-class car and it was in the night, and the train was crowded with passengers so that I had not room for them if I set the coach out of the train. So I had the engineer to run very slow to the next station ahead, where I found two idle coaches, which I took on, setting the disabled car out; and the passengers I had in this coach, with the ones who were not seated in the first-class coach, filled both of the coaches which I had taken on.

At times going round my train, as I have spoken of, I have found as many as four or five boys at a time, under sleepers and coaches. I drove some of them out one time, saying that I would not ride under there for a thousand dollars a mile. They said that they would ride under there for nothing if I would let them; but I told them that it was too cheap and I could not afford to let them ride underneath the cars at that price.

I once lifted a ticket from an old lady passenger who was on my train, and on the same train I had a lot of raftsmen, which was a common thing in those days, whenever there was a good river tide sufficient for them to raft their logs down the river. At the time of which I speak, I had two or three extra coaches full of them, besides a lot in my regular coaches. They were generally a pretty rough set of men. After I had gone through the train collecting tickets, I was going back through the train, and as I stepped inside the coach I heard the old lady that I have spoken of say: "There is no conductor on this train." I do not know whether she meant for me to hear what she said or not. I don't think she cared if I did. I went to where she was seated, and asked her how she found out that there was no conductor on the train. She said if there was, he did not attend to his business. I asked her what the trouble was; and she said there were some men in the car drinking whiskey and using profane language, which she thought was very unbecoming in the presence of ladies, and asked me why I did not move them out of the car they were in. I said, "All the cars I have in the train are full." She asked why I did not have more cars. I answered, "I have all that was given me and about all the engine can handle." "What road is this?" she asked. I gave her the name of the road; and she exclaimed, "Oh, my! do not have Virginia in it, that is my old State, and I do not want any such a road as this is called after it." I asked her to point out the men to me that she had reference to, and I would put them off the train if they misbehaved any more. She pointed them out and I went to them, and they denied the charges made against them. One of them said that he did take a bottle of brandy out of his pocket to smell of, but did not taste a drop of it.

I went back to the lady and said to her, "If they misbehave any more, let me know, if I do not happen to see them." From the destination of these men's tickets I knew where they belonged, and I said to the lady that the men she had complained of were from Scott County, Va. I had no more trouble with her that trip. I told the conductor that I connected with at the end of my run, that I had Josiah Allen's wife on board.[2] He said, "Have you?" I said if it was not her, it must be a sister of hers. I had this same old lady every summer, for three or four years, on my train going east one trip and returning west later on. She always had a round-trip ticket, sold in New Orleans and to some point in Virginia.

When she returned, on the trip I have spoken of, on my train, I seldom passed through the coach she was in without being asked some question by her, about the connection she would make, and if the train was on time, and the time of arrival at different places, and the changes she would have to make, and at what time and places. I gave her the information asked for, and she said that she knew that I was mistaken about the first change she would have make, for she did not come that way, and she knew her ticket was to return the same way she had come. There was a branch road from the main line, which branched off at a station where a connection was made with one train from the South, but not the one I was on at the time. She said that she knew that she would have to change at the time spoken of. I said to her that if she knew more about it than I did, that she could get off at the place and lay over all day, and then she could get a train; or she could go on to the end of my run and make close connection. She then asked if her ticket would take her that way. I said it would, for the roads belonged to the same company, as far as the station named on the coupon of the ticket for the road. She said: "Well, I will go on with you, but if it costs me a nickel more, or I miss the connection, I will have you discharged." I said, "All right."

A young lady, who seemed to be a friend of the old lady, boarded the train at a way-station, and was going to Nashville. The old lady said for me to see the young lady on the Nashville train, when we arrived at the terminal station. So when we arrived there I helped the ladies off, and the last one that I went back in the coach for, was the young lady, and as one of my men had picked up her hand-baggage, I took her bird-cage. She said: "Do not hurt my birdie." About this time some one struck my elbow, and the bird-cage struck the arm of a seat, and she said: "Oh, my poor birdie." And said to me: "I told you not to hurt my bird!" I then concluded that she must be a near relative of the old lady. When all were off the train, the old lady asked me where the conductor was that she had to go with. I saw him at the time, going in a run towards the rear of the train, and I said; "Yonder he goes." And she said, "Why don't you give me an introduction to him?" I said, "I will if you can catch him."

And the bystanding ladies burst out in loud laughter. Afterwards I did introduce her to the conductor, and asked him to please look after her; and she said if he did not do so, she would have him discharged.

When I got a chance to speak to the conductor privately, I said: "Charlie, that old lady beats all I ever saw before"; and he said, "That's all right, bring all that kind to me, I know how to work them." But the next time I saw Charlie, he swore that if I ever gave him any more of the kind that he would kill me. The last time I ever saw the old lady, she was on a return trip from the East, and when I lifted her ticket she called a conductor's name and asked me if it was not my name. I said it was not. And she said it did not make any difference whether it was or not; and said: "You are the one that is always so kind to me when I travel with you."

In the early days of railroads I have no doubt but what the conductors and engineers that run in those days could tell many things that would be interesting to railroad men of the present day. An old-time passenger conductor told me one time, that when he first went to running a passenger-train, that he thought he would soon get the people all home, and he would be out of a job, and wondered how so many people had got scattered away from home; and when he found out the facts, he said that he was scattering them instead of taking them home.

After I had left a terminal station one night, I found among my passengers, a man fast asleep, and I could not get him awake. So I asked a passenger to help me search his pockets for a ticket, or something to show where he wanted to go. After so long a time his ticket was found, and it read, from Atlanta, Ga., to Bristol, Tenn. Seeing that he was on the right train I let him sleep. A tag was on his valise upon which was written his name, and address, I suppose it was, "Wm. Greesey, Rural Retreat, Va.," and the passengers in the car had a big laugh over this. When I left the train William was still asleep, and I suppose he was awakened at Rural Retreat, when the train arrived at that place.

Once I found a young man on my train, who was bareheaded; when I asked for a ticket, he said that he had stuck it in his hat, and his hat and ticket went out the window. I stopped the train and made him get off, and told him to go back and get his hat. Such as this, as well as many others, was a common occurrence on passenger-trains.

I put a tramp off my train three different times, and myself and crew watched him every time he was put off. The third time we made sure we had kept him off. But about day-break, when we were approaching a terminal station, which was the end of our run, I was standing on a coach platform, and the same tramp ran out of the coach, and as he passed by me, said: "Much obliged to you, captain, I will ride with you again some time." He then jumped off the train, and ran off down the street at full speed. I was told by a passenger who was in the car that the tramp came out of, that he crawled out from under the seat.

A woman from the old country beat her way on my train one day over a hundred miles, by crawling under a long seat in a coach, and packing her luggage around her. And when she was discovered and pulled out from under the seat, she was so stifled that she could hardly get her breath. From what I learned afterwards, I have no doubt but what she beat her way, or a large portion of it, all the way from her starting point in the old country, to the point in America where she was found under the long seat.

One day I put a very well dressed man off my train, who claimed to be a telegraph operator, and claimed to have had a pass, but lost it. I told him he would have to pay his fare, and if he found the pass I would refund the money. He said he had no money, but would pay me when he got to his destination, as he had a job at a certain point on the line of road. I said to him that I did not do business that way, and he would have to get off. And he said if I put him off that he would lose his job, for he had to be there that same evening, or lose it. I said I would rather he would lose his job than for me to lose mine. And when he got off the train he said it was a h—— of a way to treat a man.

While assisting a lady off the train one day, I picked up a very heavy valise that belonged to her, and it was all I could do to straighten up with it. And just as I did get straight, she threw a shawl on the valise and said, "Take that out too." I had a mind to drop the valise down on the floor.

After leaving a station one night and going through the train, I took collections from a passenger who had just got on at the station just left. I afterwards found a well-dressed, lady-looking woman seated in the ladies' coach. I asked her for her ticket, and she said that she had given me a cash fare. I asked her where from, and she named a station some distance back. I told her she was mistaken, for no passenger boarded the train at that point, and that the train did not stop at the station, and that I knew that I had not seen her on the train before that night. She became very much offended, and said that she had no more money, that she had given me all she had. But I knew better, for if a conductor can recollect anything it is his cash collections. When she found that she had to leave the train or pay her fare, she found money enough to pay to her destination. And afterwards a passenger told me that he saw her get on the train where I had said she did, and hide herself in a secluded place until I passed through the car.

A very pretty little bird flew in a coach one day when the train was running through a belt of woods, and one of my brakemen caught it, and a couple of young ladies, who were seated together in the coach, asked for the bird, and it was given to them. While they were petting and making ado over the bird, some young cadets passed along through the aisle, and as they got opposite these ladies one of them said: "I wish I was a bird," and one of the ladies said to him: "If you were, you would be a buzzard."

With all due respect and sympathy for the blind, I can say for a fact, with the exception of the better class, that some of them can beat the world in the way of trying to ride free over the railroads; and it seems that some follow it regularly and expect free passage on account of their misfortune, and at the same time expect the conductor to take the responsibility upon himself of passing them free. While I never saw a blind person that I did not feel sorry for, I never thought that I had any right to pass them free. Yet, when a conductor refuses to do so, some of them are the most abusive people I ever handled on a train. It is pretty much the same thing with some crippled people.

One night on my train a blind man claimed to have lost his ticket. He said he had put it in his Bible when he was arguing Scripture with Brother So-and-So while waiting for the train. I was told that he was a minister. The night was dark and the rain was falling fast, and I knew if I put a blind preacher off the train on such a night what a feeling it would bring up against me, and as like as not an insulting newspaper report would appear the next morning fixed up to suit themselves; so I decided to loan the poor blind man enough money to pay his way to the end of my run, as that was as far as he wanted to go that night, as he said he had paid all the money he had for the last ticket. He asked me where I stopped at and how long. I answered the questions asked. He said he hoped the Lord would bless me, and that he would return the amount of money which I had loaned him the next morning. I had heard of his preaching before I had ever seen him. Since the night spoken of I have never seen him, but afterwards heard of him being at Rockwood playing cards with some gamblers.

I had another blind man on my train one day. After he had rode as far as the money which he had paid me would carry him, I told him he would have to get off the train. He halloed out for some one to give him money. But none was given him, and when he got off the train he said: "Go to hades every d——n one of you!"

Another blind man was on one day who wanted to be passed free. He spoke as if he ought to pass on any road free on account of his affliction and as a deed of charity. I told him the railroads were not built for that purpose, but if he would go to the proper authorities that they might give him a pass over the road. He had five dollars which he said was given to him, and that he was going to keep it to get him something to eat with, and was not going to pay it out for railroad fare. I told him I would stop at the first station that we came to, and he would have to get off the train, as I would not pass him free. When he got off he said that he prayed to God that the train would run off and kill me before I got to my destination. I said to him that the prayers of the wicked availeth nothing.

A station agent said to me that they had put a blind man and his wife on my train one day, and that they had made up money enough to buy two whole tickets and had given them to the blind man and his wife, but did not have money enough to buy a half-ticket for a boy that they had, and for me to let the boy go on. When I left the station and went through the train they claimed that they had lost their tickets, and as the agent had told me that they had tickets, and they said they had no money, and the first stop was where they were going, I took them on to that place. I told the agent about them losing their tickets, and he said that they had been to the passenger and ticket agent's office with them to get the money refunded for them. I reported the facts to one of the general passenger agents, and I learned afterwards that the money was refunded to them.

A Jewish woman got on my train once and gave me a local ticket to the first station that the train stopped at after leaving the station where she got on. I helped her off the train when the stop was made. When I returned on my trip I learned that the same woman had also returned and claimed that she had been put off the train by the conductor; that she had handed him a ticket and he took it and handed it back and said, "The ticket no goot." and put her off his train. She said she showed it to some men after she was put off and they said it was "goot," and that the conductor had no right to put her off. I learned that her husband had been to the office of the legal department and showed a ticket that had been sold and stamped some days before she went on my train and claimed it to be the ticket that his wife had handed the conductor and which he refused to honor, and put her off. The ticket spoken of read to a terminal station. I went to the Jew's house with one of the company's attorneys, and when the woman saw me she said, "Yes, dat de very conductor dat put me off de train." I said to her: "You gave me a ticket to the station you got off at, and you know it as well as I do myself. And you know also that I canceled the ticket which you gave me and put it in my pocket, and I can prove it by other passengers who were on my train at the time; and you gave me no other ticket, neither did I hand you back one; and you did not say a word to me about going any further than the station where you got off."

If ever a suit was brought for damages about this, it was thrown out of court; but that was a plan to get damages from the road, and hundreds of similar cases come up on railroads to beat railroad companies out of money, as some people seem to think it no harm to do so. A man asked me once if I could see a little scar on his cheek, and I said I could, and I do not recollect now how many thousand dollars he said that he got out of a railroad company for that little scar.

Some of the traveling men get aboard of trains wide awake, while some go to sleep as soon as they take a seat, and a conductor sometimes has a hard time to get them awake in order to get their tickets. Some will have their mileage torn off to a certain station and then not get off when they get there, and when asked again for a ticket they say, "You have my ticket," or "I gave you my mileage;" and some want a conductor to wait until they decide where they want to get off. Anything to worry a conductor or beat a railroad.

But the Jews beat them all when one of them travels as a salesman. The cheapest ticket which can be purchased is his choice, and the scalper's ticket is mostly used by them and as many trips taken on one as can be planned. I once heard a Jew telling how he had beat railroads by getting a ticket on which stop-overs were allowed. The rules in those days on some roads in regard to stop-overs were to cancel the coupons for the road on which it was used, and write on the back of the ticket with a pencil where the ticket had been used to, and it was then handed back to the passenger. This Jew said that he would rub out the pencil mark and buy another ticket back, and then use his old ticket again on the same road. So it is not everything that beats the Jews.

I have seen the day, when the train was crowded, that a gentleman would get up and give a lady his seat rather than see her stand up, but at the present day this is seldom done.

I know that a railroad company has to have strict rules in regard to the traveling public; and it is well they should have them, for they have people of all classes and character to contend with. But it is impossible to make rules to suit all cases that come up, therefore conductors are compelled to use their own judgment in some cases. For instance, I once gave a gentleman a stop-over on a limited ticket, which was not allowed according to the rules that I was governed by. The reason why I did this was that he was accompanied by his wife, who was going to some springs for the benefit of her health, and the gentleman wished to go with her to her destination and then return and use his ticket to its destination, and as they had to take a branch road to do so, she wanted a stop-over on his ticket. I explained the rules in regard to the matter to him, and he said he did not ask for a limited ticket when he bought it, and that he also had a pass over another route, but preferred the route that he had come, as he could avoid a stage line by taking this route. He could also see his wife safely to her destination, and if he could not go over this route without paying out more money for his passage, that he would never travel over the line again. So I gave him the stop-over and reported the facts, which were approved.

In some other cases when people wanted favors that were not allowed by the rules of the road and found they could not have their own way, they cursed the road and all connected with it, except the conductor, as that was a roundabout way some had of cursing the conductor. They swore they never would ride over the line or ship another pound of freight over it, as they had shipped thousands of pounds over it before. In such cases as these I would say, "That will be all right. If you don't, some one else will."

Chapter Fourteen

Old Stories and Other Things
Connected with Railroads

In a former chapter I have already spoken of the Order of Railway Conductors, and as I wish to say more, I will now do so; as they have done a great deal of good and they will do more. They have already arranged to build a college for the benefit of the children of the members. I hope the day will soon come when they can be able to have churches built at the most suitable places throughout the United States, regardless of denominations, just so they worship the true God and believe in the Lord Jesus Christ, so as to induce railroad employees to attend church, not but that there are plenty of good churches for them to go to, but it would be an inducement, and it would also be beneficial to the railroad companies, and when a committee is looking after such matters they ought to be allowed full time.

In consideration of my age, my brethren in the lodge where I keep my membership, have been very kind to me in all my troubles and misfortunes, and I hope to live to see a day when I can reward them for what they have done for me.

Just to show how a dishonest member stands with the order, I will relate a circumstance that occurred on my train between a member and myself, not long after I had joined the order. He at one time had been yardmaster in one of the company's yards that I at the time was working for; he boarded my train, and I knowing that he did have a pass a short time before while he was yardmaster, that read between two certain stations, I called on him for the pass, and he said he had left it in his other coat pocket, and I told him that he would have to pay his fare, and he said he did not have the money with him to do so; and there was another conductor, who was also a member of the order, on board, and he told me that he knew the ex-yardmaster had a pass, and I, thinking the ex-yardmaster to be an honest man, and by his telling me he would show me the pass my next trip, I let him go to his destination. My superintendent was on the train also, and a short time after my arrival at the end of my run I was called into his office in regard to the matter, and after I had stated the facts, I came very near being discharged, as the superintendent knew that the ex-yardmaster had been given but one pass and the limit of that one, he said, he knew had expired. So sure enough, when the pass was taken up and compared with the pass-book in the office, the pass proved to have been changed to read, "and on line of road," and also the limit extended to a longer length of time, and the handwriting imitated that of the one that issued the pass, and on that account, as well as some other dishonest actions, the ex-yardmaster was expelled from the order.

I will now relate a fact that occurred one night after I had passed a station where there had been a circus show performance in the early part of the night. My engineer was flagged down by a man who was standing in the middle of the track, with a pine torch in his hand. I went out to learn the cause of the unusual stop. The engineer had stopped his engine near the end of a trestle, the trestle was about twenty or twenty-five feet high, and I saw men running as though they wanted to get on the train and I tried to stop them, for fear they might fall through the trestle, but one man fell through in spite of all I could do. When the others saw him disappear so suddenly, they stopped, and one of the men stepped to the embankment and said: "Andy, are you hurt?" and receiving no answer he said: "Yes, boys, Andy is dead. Come ahead and get on the train." I went around the steep embankment, and went up the ravine to where Andy was lying. I found him speechless, but not dead, and had him taken up and put on the train. The men all appeared to have been drinking, and said they were going home from the show, when they found lying near the track the remains of a young man, who was supposed to have been killed by some passing train, or by some train that he was trying to beat his way on. A bonfire had been built and the men seemed to be very much frightened, and they were afraid to go any further and had stopped there to await some train, so they could flag it down and get on board of it.

I left the remains of the man lying as they were found and a citizen to watch them, that had come to the place to see what the matter was, as the law forbids moving such bodies until an inquest is held over them. But I took the party of frighted men on to a station about seven miles further on, where they said they lived and said the parents of the young man who had been killed lived near the same station. When I arrived at the station spoken of, I had the station agent called up and asked him to get up enough of his townsmen to hold an inquest over the remains of the young man and notify his parents, and take them on the first train that was going in the right direction, and have the remains cared for, and he said he would do so. And Andy was able to get off the train without any assistance when the train stopped at the station, and was not hurt, but no doubt would have been seriously hurt, if not killed, had it not have been for the red liquor he had been drinking.

Sometimes a conductor blames his engineer when time is being lost, and again, the engineer blames his conductor when he cannot make schedule time. Allowances ought to be made, for sometimes one has more work to do than at other times; and when an engine has a regular train of seven or eight cars, and at times two or three extra cars put on, she ought not to be expected to make as good time as with her regular train. Allowances ought to be made when the rail is wet or frosty. Moreover, it is not right for conductors and engineers to fret and find fault with each other, or to blame one or the other for delays or mishaps which often occur on railroads, for often a conductor is hindered at stations by some unavoidable cause, of which the engineer knows nothing, and makes many unnecessary remarks, when if he knew the circumstances he would not have a word to say; and it is the same way by the conductor in regard to the engineer. Sometimes an engineer runs past a station from some cause, probably at times by the air brakes not working all right, and the train has to back so as to do the work. In the days of hand brakes, such was the conductors' and brakemen's fault; well, of course, it is that much time lost, and maybe no one ought to have any blame attached. When one has old or crippled people to get on or off his train there is no hurrying them and one has to give them time to do so, and, in fact, I have known some such cases that trying to hurry them made the matter worse.

I once had an old lady on my train, when the train stopped at the station where her ticket called for and she went to get off, she would not let any one assist her, and would say: "Just let me alone and let me have time and I can get off myself," and she would wobble along the aisle of the coach, holding to the arms of the seats and to the hand railing of the platform, and would not let any one touch her and kept the train standing at least four or five minutes just on her account. Many similar cases I often have met with.

I was always by passenger-trains like I was by freight-trains when I ran them. I thought they were put on the road to do the work and make the schedule time if one could do so, and I always tried to do so, as I thought it best for the company I was working for, and I think now that I have done as much such work and went through as many hardships as any conductor ever did in the same length of time. And as long as I have railroaded I never had a journal to burn or twist off.

I at one time ran on a road where they ran but two freight-trains, one each way a day, Sundays excepted, and I ran one of them, and while I was on that run I was often told by agents along the road that they had freight to ship the day before I passed and had tried to get it off then and could not, as the conductor said he was behind time and that the conductor could take it the next day, for he had to make the schedule time.

Once when I was running a passenger-train a party of colored preachers had taken possession of my first-class coach, and as it was in a section of country where the white people did not believe in negro equality, and I myself bitterly opposed to it, I asked them politely to please take seats in the other coach as they had taken seats in my ladies' car, and they at once refused to do so. I then told them that I would set the coach on a side-track with them in it before I would take it and them in it, as I had ladies outside awaiting for them to take seats in the second-class car, and I went out to make arrangements to set the coach out. After jabbering among themselves they went in the second-class car and I had no more trouble with them. If it had happened at the present day it would have been the cause of a big damage law-suit. And on another road and in a different State, a party of negroes with their families had taken possession of the coach that I had used the day before for a first-class car, but it so happened that I had two first-class coaches in my train, and as it was at a terminal station and some time before time for the train to leave, no other passengers had taken seats in the car but them, and I used the coach the negroes had taken charge of for a second-class and smoking car and the other coach for a first-class coach, and my colored passengers made great complaint about the accommodations they had, and I told them it was their own fault for I asked them to go in the other coach when they first went to get on the train and they refused to do so, and therefore they could blame no one but themselves. They wanted to change into the other coach I had taken for a first-class coach, and I would not let them do so.

It was while I was on the South and North Road, and while I was moving the freight cars between Calera and Montgomery, that I have already spoken of in a former chapter, I had a new brakeman and we had a great many hot boxes, and I had the new man often carrying buckets of water to cool them down with, after I went back on my nice little passenger run. One day when the engineer stopped at a water tank

to take in a tender of water and I stepped off of the train and was standing on the ground, when my new brakeman passed me in a run with a
water bucket in his hand and dipped up a bucket of water from a pond
that was near the roadside. I asked him what he was going to do with it
and he said: "Look how that thing is smoking on the side of the engine.
It is as hot as fire." I looked towards the engine and saw the steam and
smoke coming out of one of the cylinders, and he would have thrown
the water on the cylinder, had I not have said to him that if he did so
the engineer would knock him down with a stick of wood.

I had a gentleman passenger while I was on the same run just spoken
of, when the train stopped at a station, he was out looking around and
in my way at every station. When I went to get on the train I said to
him a time or two that he had best stay on the train or he would get
left, and he would laugh at me and say, if I got on he would also. We
stopped at a wood rack to take on a tender of wood; a saw-mill was
located not far from the wood yard, and the ground around was covered
with saw-logs. My passenger friend and myself both got off the train.
He went hopping from one log to another, and I went to help throw
wood in the tender. I said to my friend that he had best get aboard the
train, that we would be ready to leave by the time he got on the train,
and he said to me that he would look out for himself. So we filled the
tender with wood, and I said: "All aboard," and told the engineer to go
ahead, and as the train passed me I jumped on it, and my friend was left
hopping over saw-logs, trying to get back on the train. It was early one
morning. I sent a note back to the conductor of the next train following
to pick up my passenger that I had left, and that I had his ticket. I
learned afterwards from the conductor that the man was very mad on
account of not getting his breakfast. So that was one time, and the first
time, he was not in my way when I wanted to get on the train that
morning.

A story was told on an engineer once, who had stopped his engine on
the end of a very high trestle, and a peach tree had grown up under the
trestle. The engineer, forgetting that his engine was standing on a trestle, stepped off with his oil-can in his hand, to oil his engine, and went
down off of the trestle through the top of the peach tree and to the
ground beneath. The fireman asked him if he was hurt, and he said,
with an oath, "Do you expect a man to fall a hundred feet and through
a tree-top and then not be hurt?"

A story once was told by some of the boys that ran on the road that I
was on at the time, as having occurred on my train. I had a new man on
my train, and they said I told him that I would announce the name of
stations in the front end of the coaches and that he must do the same in

the rear end of them, and when we were approaching Sweetwater, a way-station on the road, I in the front end of the coach called out, "Sweetwater," and my brakeman, who was in the rear end of the same coach, said in a loud voice, "It is the same at this end."

A thing did occur once at the same station I have just spoken of. Just as we were approaching the station, a passenger on the train went to a water-cooler to get a drink of water, and while he was in the act of lifting up the glass of water, a brakeman passing through the coach, called out, "Sweetwater," and the passenger quickly turned around and said: "Is not this drinking water?" as though he had done something wrong, and it caused quite a laugh among the other passengers. I was an eye-witness to the fact.

In my early days on railroads the employees were, with some exceptions, a class of men that would use profane language, and it's kept up to the present day by some. I was on a road once when some of the boys gave me a nickname, calling me "Parson," and it became familiar among the boys along the line of road, and I was called Parson by some of them oftener than by my right name. I suppose I was called Parson because I did not use so much profane language as some of them did. I would at times, when fretted, say "Ding it," or "Confound it," and that was about my worst cuss words those days.

My train broke loose one day when I had a Dutchman for my engineer, and I told him I should have to chain the cars together, and not to move his engine until I gave him a signal to do so. I was in between the cars working with the chain, and before I got it fixed he pulled out go ahead, without any signal. As it happened, I got out from between the cars without being hurt, but scared almost to death. When I got him stopped and went to his engine and threatened to knock him off of the engine, and would have done so but the superintendent of the road was on the engine and prevented me from doing so. I gave him an old Georgia blessing, went back and fixed my chain, and said to my Dutchman to go ahead, and if he could get me to the end of our run safe and alive I would feel very thankful. The next day I was laying over at the end of my run, and on the street I met the Dutchman, and I was told by another engineer who was with him at the time I met him, that after I passed them the Dutchman asked him what that conductor's name was that they call Parson, and the engineer said that it was Parson Bell, and the Dutchman said, "Yes, and he is no more fit for a parson than hades."

A conductor that I connected with at times, told me a story on his porter. He said the porter forgot the name of a way-station, and went through a coach saying, "Now-wow," and a passenger asked him what was the name of the station he called out, and the porter said to him: "You heard what I said, and if you don't get off in a half minute you will be carried on."

I was told by a conductor, whom I once employed on my train as a brakeman, the first railroading he ever done, and afterwards he became a passenger conductor after he had taken a trip out West at one time, he said he was on a train one day while he was out West and a young countryman boarded the train he was on and took a seat. As the conductor of the train approached the young man to lift his ticket, the conductor put his hand in his hip pocket to get his punch out, so as to cancel the ticket. The young man saw the move the conductor was making, and he jumped up and said to the conductor, "Mister, for God sake don't shoot, I have no ticket, but I have got the money," handing the money to the conductor, asking him if it would do in place of a ticket. Of course it did, and he would have been the last man that a conductor would have shot, as they generally like to turn in big cash collections.

I once knew a young man who was well-to-do, but, like many others have done, he must go to Texas, and being rather a wild character he soon disposed of his wealth and left Texas for his native State. After he returned, I met him, and he said, when he left Little Rock, Ark., he only had two dollars in money, and he had a partner who was traveling with him that did not have a cent; they left Little Rock on a train for Memphis and passed on transportation that a man had for himself and a gang of laborers whom he had gathered up for the purpose of building some new railroads, and they gave the man who held the transportation their names, or some name, and traveled on the transportation as far as the man went in the direction they were going. When the train arrived at the station where the man and his gang of men left the train, and while the passengers were out at supper that wanted any, the two young men found two other young men seated in the second-class car with a hat check apiece in their hats. After finding out where the young men were going to, and by telling them that if they would go back in the other coach and take seats, that the conductor would know them, and remember lifting their tickets, they got the two young men persuaded to sell the hat check to them for a dollar apiece, and they went back in another coach. So when the conductor came through the second-class car, he saw the two men occupying the seat that the other two had occupied before they sold out their checks, and also their ride, for then the conductor went into the coach where they were and found the two young men without tickets or checks, he stopped his train and put them both off, and the other two went on to Memphis. I suppose my friend managed some other way to get back to his native State from Memphis.

I have had passengers on my trains who would try to beat their way with a hat check, and I have detected it by their check being a different color from the one I was using at the time, and sometimes by the punch, which was different from mine. I have no doubt sometimes been beaten by such.

I have known some to steal checks out of others' hats and try to pass on them, and some others to give the one that had been given them to some friend, so as to keep his friend from paying his fare, just anything to beat a conductor or a railroad, and many that one would think above suspicion. Many of them think it a smart trick and no sin. Some, after purchasing a ticket, try to hold it and beat a conductor.

I have had some few who would hand me their ticket after I had overlooked them when I had a crowded train.

I was told once about a man who was a member of a church, and one that held family prayers every night when he was at home, and one day he was telling my informant about beating a conductor, or the railroad company, out of a ride on a train of over a hundred miles, and he was asked if he thought it a just act, and he said, "Yes," and said while he would not cheat his neighbors out of a cent, it was no harm to beat a railroad company. He was told that it was as great a sin as it was to cheat any other man out of the same amount, and afterwards he said, so I learned, that he considered the matter, and being convinced of the fact that it was wrong, he afterwards gave the conductor the amount of money for his ride that he had beaten him out of. So one ought not to blame a railroad company for having strict rules in regard to the traveling public.

Many years ago a story was told that a man got on a passenger-train one very dark and rainy night and refused to pay his fare, and he had no ticket. He managed to talk to the conductor until the train had run about two miles from the station where he had got on, when the conductor pulled the bell-cord and stopped the train and the non-paying passenger got off, and thanked the conductor very much for his kindness, and said to the conductor: "I live on the hill right up there where you see the light, and it beats walking two miles in the rain a dark night like this." I had a similar case one time, only it was in daytime and a bright, sunshiny day, when a man had no ticket and said he had no money, and I stopped the train and put him off, and he said, "Much obliged. I own this farm and live in that white house back there we just passed," and I thought if he had told the truth that he got it like he tried to get his ride.

In the early days of the Georgia Railroad a story was told that a countryman boarded a passenger-train on that road and gave the conductor fifty cents, saying that he never rode on one before, and he had heard so much talk about the railroad and trains that he wanted to ride the fifty cents' worth out with him; and after the train had run about twenty miles and had stopped at a station, the conductor said to the fifty-cents man that he had ridden his fifty cents' worth out, he got off the train and said he had to walk back to the place he got on, and after being told by the conductor that it was about twenty miles, he said he had no idea that he was half that far from home, and he lit out on foot to go back home.

Just a short time back, I have had old men and women, as well as young men and women, to get on my train, and sometimes would say: "This is the first time I ever was on a train, and you must take care of me and not let the train run off and kill me," and sometimes ask me when they would get on the coach platform which room they must go in, and sometimes ask which box they must take a seat in. An old lady refused to give me her ticket once; said it was the first time she had ever been on a train and that she had bought her ticket, if the little piece of pasteboard or paper she had was what I called a ticket, and paid the money for it, and said she was not going to give it up to no one, and I had to get a passenger to explain to her and tell her that she would have to give it up or be put off the train, before I could get her to give it up.

I took up a ticket once from a passenger who said he bought it eighteen or nineteen years before I lifted it. He said he moved to Texas soon after he bought it and had never used it; it was sold when local tickets had no limit that was sold by the road that issued it; and the last I heard of the ticket it was laid away in the auditor's office as a keep-sake.

I had a man who was a foreigner, and had not been in America long to ask me which side of the train he would have to get on to go to California. I told him it would make no difference which side he got on so he got on the right train and one going in the right direction. I was by him like the ferryman was by the man that had no money and wanted the ferryman to set him across the river. The ferryman told him if he had no money it did not make a d——d bit of difference which side of the river he was on, and by experience I have found it to be a true saying, for one had as well be on one side of the Ohio river as the other, when they are out of money.

I was at Hot Springs, Ark., once, and it was one place where I was glad to meet with any one that I had ever met with before. The first morning after I arrived at the Springs I met up with a well-dressed gentleman, or at least apparently one. My new acquaintance said he had rheumatism, and he had one foot bound up with cloths. He was very inquisitive, and I not thinking of such a looking man as he being a scoundrel, answered his questions. After he found where I was from and what my occupation was and that it was my first trip to Hot Springs, he remembered of having met me before. I also knew several persons that he did. After a very long consideration he invited me to go with him up to where he was stopping; but after our conversation I had somewhat changed my mind in regard to him, as I had met all kinds of characters before I went to Hot Springs and could generally tell what they were after being with them and hearing them talk awhile. So I did not at first accept his invitation, and left him. It was but a short while until we met again, and he said that a conductor was stopping at the place he stopped at, who run on the Louisville and Nashville Railroad, and his name was Joe Harris, who he said was a jolly fellow; and as I once knew a conductor on the Nashville, Chattanooga and St. Louis Railway by that name and who had left the road and gone West somewhere, I at last decided to go with the man I had met, in order to see if Joe Harris was my old acquaintance, at the same time I had but little faith in my man's story; and as he said the distance was only two blocks, I went to see if Joe was there and to find out for sure what he was so anxious for me to go with him for. I soon found out, for we had not gone more than two blocks when we came to a flight of steps that run from the pavement up to a second floor of a building, when he said he stopped up there. "We will have to go up the steps," and said, "Oh! this rheumatism is so bad I can hardly get up the steps." I knew then I was into a trap, and I ought to have turned back then; but thought that it might be Harris was there, and I went on. When we stepped in the room at the top of the steps, I saw from the furniture it contained that it was a gamblers' den. My friend asked for Joe at once, and it was said by a man that sat at a table in the room, that Joe had just stepped out. There were two tables in the room and a man sat at each one, and the tables were supplied with gambling equipments. My acquaintance appeared to be very green in the games; but after asking me to take a game, I informed him that I played no games. He soon won ten dollars, and went to the other table and took another chance, and wanted me to make a guess for him. I said to him, "If you wanted any guessing done you could do it yourself," and I walked out. It was all done in less than five minutes after we went in the room, and I have no idea that Joe Harris ever came back.

In all my life I never had any use for a rascal or a dishonest man; but regardless of where a man comes from, or his religion or politics, so he is an honest man, he is a man I like to deal and associate with; and if a man is a gentleman in principle and does unto others as he would like to have them do unto him, if he is not a Christian he is almost one; but a two-faced man is the most hypocritical thing on earth, for we never can tell whether he is a friend or a foe. I always had as little use for such men as I had for a pug dog or a boy that smoked cigarettes. A man may travel in different sections of country, but never learn the ways and the rights and wrongs of some people like one that has handled all classes in different States and from other States and countries. I have found a great many men, as well as some women, who had but little control over their tongues, and while I hated a dispute or a wrangle with any man, I dreaded women much worse, and if possible to do so, let them have their own say so. I made it a rule to never have any unpleasant conversation with either man or woman if I could avoid it, for the tongue often hurt one's self more than it does good to them, or harm to them that one is trying to harm. If we were to use our tongues to help each other along instead of harming each other, we would not use them so much and do more good.

A conductor who handles passengers becomes familiar with the ways of the human family and can generally tell the sheep from the goats, unless a goat is covered with a sheep-skin, and then it is a very hard matter to decide the question unless the goat happens to drop his sheep-skin off; then it is a very easy matter to decide.

Of all classes of men conductors and engineers ought to be the most sober and moral of any, and more especially the engineers, as they have so much at stake—the lives and property they have in their hands, and besides their own lives, and one that will get drunk while he has charge of an engine that is pulling a passenger-train, cares nothing for his own life nor the lives of them that are on the train that is coupled to his engine, and it is a surprising thing to me that a man will get drunk, and so drunk that he does not know what he is doing, while on duty; and it does look to me like that if one has no respect for himself that he ought to have some for his parents, or family, or company he is at work for; and if he is compelled to get drunk once in awhile to try to drown his troubles, which only adds to his sorrows, let him stop off and take his spree; he then would not endanger any one but himself, and would be more likely to hold his position. When I knew it I never would let a drunk engineer handle an engine that pulled my train, but no doubt they have done so unbeknowing to me; and if I were an engineer I would not haul a drunken conductor, or if I did, it would be off the train, while I would do most anything I could to befriend a man under any other circumstances.

I had an engineer one night to start out of a terminal station with me and he was so drunk that he did not know whether it was day or night; but I did not know it until we had got out about twelve miles on the road, and he stalled while going down a heavy grade. I went to his engine to see what the matter was, and I found him drunk, and he was a man that I did not know ever drank a drop of whiskey; so I took him off the engine and made the fireman run the engine, as it was the best thing I could do, and knowing him to be an old fireman and a good man to handle an engine; and I put one of my trainmen to fire the engine and went on all right and made my connection.

I have found it very troublesome just after leaving terminal stations and going my first round through a train taking up collections and answering questions asked by passengers, for some can ask so many, and ask the same question over so many times, that one cannot help being worried when he has a train packed full of passengers, and has so much to do, and that has to be done in a certain length of time, when, if passengers would just wait until one could get through the train the first time, a conductor would have more time and give a better explanation, which I always took a pleasure in when a passenger would do so, and any way, I always did the best I could under any kind of circumstances.

I have found some cases where, if the passengers had looked at the destination of their tickets, or have read the printed contract on them, it would have saved them, as well as the conductor, some trouble. I have no doubt but what some superintendents have to do things at times that they hate to have to do in regard to the employees, as it often comes from higher authority; but, any way, we ought to be glad that railroads have, and are still being, built, and railroad men ought to try to run them successfully for the railroad companies as well as for themselves, and make the best of this life they can. As we have but a short stay here in this world, try to prepare for a better one after death.

While I was running on the road, one night I had on my train six or eight prisoners and two guards. They were government prisoners, and from the State of Georgia; they were seated two on a seat, along on one side of the aisle, and two handcuffed together, and a chain fastened from the two front ones back to the two rear ones—two old-like men; the two guards sat on the opposite side of the car from the prisoners; the car they were in was a second-class coach, and an old negro woman had a seat in the same car they were in; we were running through Upper East Tennessee, when we stopped at a water-tank to take water, and it was after midnight, and while we were at the tank, the two old men got loose from the chain somehow, and, I suppose walked out of the car, and while the guard was asleep, or at least supposed to be. After we had run some distance after leaving the water-tank, one of the men who had charge of the prisoners came to me to stop and back the train, so as he could catch them. I asked him where they got off at, and he said they jumped out a window just a little ways back. I said if they did so, there was no use to go back for them, as they were dead, if they jumped off where he said they did and the train running at the rate of speed it was at that time. I proposed to stop the train and let him off, but told him I would not back the train; so he did not want to get off. He asked every one that was in the car if they saw them get off, and all said they did not; even the old negro woman said, when she was asked in regard to them, "Knaw, bless de good massa, I did not see de mens go out; I walk down the aisle, and I see de mens setten dar, and I walk back and, bless de Lord, dey was not dar." So, from that night to the present time, I have never heard from the two old Georgians; but I suppose they got back home all right.

The fact I have just related reminds me of a circumstance that happened on my train while I was on the old Alabama and Chattanooga road, and in its early days, and it took place near York Station. Leaving Meridian one morning, I had on my train, outside of other passengers, two men that claimed to be stock-men, and one of them carried a whip in his hand like stock traders do sometimes. I also had a minister of the gospel on board, who was a very nice-looking gentleman, and after leaving a water-tank that was near a canebrake and not far from York, the preacher came to me and wanted me to back the train to the water-tank. I asked him for what, and he said that two men had stolen, as well as I now remember it was, four or five hundred dollars from him and had left the train at the water-tank while the train was standing there. I said to him that I could not go back without flagging, and it would be of no use any way, for the men could not be found if they went in the canebrake, and if they had not done so, by the time he could find them he would not know them. They were all three in the second-class car when the circumstance occurred. The preacher said he would not have cared so much had it been his own money, but it belonged to the church, or was money that was given him to help build a church, and a passenger who was in the same car they were, told me that the two men were three-card-monte men, and that the preacher thought that they gave him such a good show to win that he bet on their game and put the money up, and he cried when he lost it and said he thought he would win and have that much more to help the church along. It goes to prove that when a sheep associates with goats, even if they do set out their salt for the sheep to lick, the goat will give him a hunch in the side with his horn and afterwards bleat and run off so as to show the sheep that they have got the best of him.

So I guess the preacher learned that it were best for the sheep and goats not to mix, unless they be black sheep.

Chapter Fifteen

Right and Wrong

"What time is it?" is a question often asked by the railroad men as well as the traveling public, and when we find out the exact time, we find that we have slept almost too late. Let the conductor and engineer take out their watches and compare time and see if they have the correct and standard time, and if they have time to make the meeting-point with the west-bound train, or if they have time to make preparations for their last trip, and the safe schedule picked out to run on, or if our evening sun is too low down, that we are too late and have not time, and it would be best for the traveling public to open the lids of the Old Guide, that by some is so seldom looked at, and look out the best road and schedule and safest train before they step on board to make their last journey. And be sure that the Conductor is the same One that gave His earthly life to save them that believed in Him. And when our time is up and the go-ahead signal is given, if we are not on board of the right train we are left and will have to take the broad-gauge, for we all have to go in some future day, whether we have our baggage packed and checked or not.

So when the time comes to go, we are not in so much of a hurry. We do not ask for the fast train, and say: "Tell the engineer to make faster speed, as the connection must be made"; and the engineer prefers a slow speed, it gives him a better showing to look out for switches, and bad places in the track. And the conductor would love to have more time at way stations along the line of road. He would not mind so much helping an old lady on and off the train, or an old crippled man, and he would have more time to shake hands with his old friends at stations along the line, and talk over old, old times.

A slow train is preferred by each of us in making our journey towards eternity, for we are in no hurry. In fact, we had rather go by private conveyance, and we will then get there sooner than we wish, and sometimes sooner than we expect. But when the time comes, and crooked railroads are made straight and the road-bed is made smooth, all will come down to a level grade and cross over our last river financially the same and get our equal rights wherever our lots may be cast, whether in Heaven or in Hell.

Notes

INTRODUCTION

1. Bureau of the Census, *U. S. Census, Whitfield County, Georgia, 1860;* Bureau of the Census, *U. S. Census, Cobb County, Georgia, 1870;* Bureau of the Census, *U. S. Census, Dade County, Georgia, 1880.*

2. U. S. Department of Commerce, *Historical Statistics of the United States, Colonial Times to 1957* (Washington, D.C., 1961), p. 92.

3. Walter Licht, *Working for the Railroad: The Organization of Work in the Nineteenth Century* (Princeton, 1961), pp. 81, 96.

4. Calculated from Albert Fishlow, *American Railroads and the Transformation of the Ante-Bellum Economy* (Cambridge, 1965), p. 397.

5. J. D. B. De Bow, *Statistical View of the United States . . . Being a Compendium of the Seventh Census* (Washington, 1854), p. 189.

6. Robert C. Black III, *The Railroads of the Confederacy* (Chapel Hill, 1952), is still the best overview of Southern railroads during the Civil War.

7. James Houstoun Johnston, *Western and Atlantic Railroad of the State of Georgia* (Atlanta, 1931), p. 62.

8. Anonymous, *The History of Tennessee* (Nashville, 1887), pp. 863-64; H. V. and H. W. Poor, *Poor's Manual, 1889* (New York, 1889), p. 652; John F. Stover, *The Railroads of the South 1865-1900: A Study in Finance and Control* (Chapel Hill, 1955), pp. 89-92.

9. Stover, *Railroads of the South*, pp. 93, 217-18.

10. Stover, *Railroads of the South*, pp. 103, 114-16, 128, 199-201, 245-46, 258-59; Poor and Poor, *Poor's Manual, 1889*, p. 665; George H. Burgess and Miles C. Kennedy, *Centennial History of the Pennsylvania Railroad Company, 1846-1946* (Philadelphia, 1949), pp. 296-97; James A. Ward, *J. Edgar Thomson: Master of the Pennsylvania* (Westport, 1980), pp. 150-51.

11. James A. Ward, *Railroads and the Character of America, 1820-1877* (Knoxville, 1986), pp. 128-30.

12. Edward L. Ayres, *The Promise of the New South: Life After Reconstruction* (New York, 1992), p. 143.

13. Foster Rhea Dulles, *Labor in America: A History* (New York, 1966), pp. 164-65.

CHAPTER 1

1. There is a dispute over whether the Charleston & Hamburg or the Baltimore & Ohio was the first operating railway in the United States. They were both started in 1828, but it is generally conceded that the South Carolina road was first. For years it was the longest railroad in the country under one management.

2. The Georgia Railroad reached Social Circle sometime in 1842.

3. J. Edgar Thomson, chief engineer of the Georgia Railroad, renamed Marthasville because it was allegedly too long to write on telegrams. To symbolize joining Marthasville with the Atlantic Ocean by rail he coined Atlanta, the feminine of Atlantic.

4. The line to Marietta was completed on 1 September 1845. The light engine Bell refers to may have made the run a few days earlier to test the roadbed.

5. The black men were probably slaves leased from planters along the right of way.

6. Stringers were squared heart-of-pine timbers laid perpendicular to the ties and topped with thin wrought- and cast-iron flange rails. It was the lightest of construction methods and prone to failure.

7. The first train passed through Tunnel Hill tunnel on 9 May 1850.

8. A date for this meeting has not been found, but it was late in the 1840s. The first W&A train to enter Chattanooga arrived on 1 December 1849, before the tunnel was completed. The locomotive and cars were hauled by oxen over Tunnel Hill.

CHAPTER 2

1. Pre-Civil War trains lacked centralized braking systems; each car and the locomotive had to be braked individually. At the engineer's signal with his whistle, Bell ran across the tops of the freight cars and "turned down" their brake wheels until the train stopped. The metal hand brake wheels could be brutally cold on winter nights. Brakemen had dangerous jobs and occasionally fell from the car tops.

2. Four national candidates ran for president in the election of 1860: Abraham Lincoln, Republican; John C. Breckinridge, Southern Democrat; Stephen A. Douglas, Northern Democrat; and John Bell, Constitutional Union party. There were two Democratic candidates that year, and Bell voted for the Southerner. Lincoln carried only three counties in the slave states.

3. Side meat was salt pork and bacon, cuts from the sides of the hog.

4. Trains did not yet receive their orders from the stationmasters along the route. They were scheduled for meets, and if they fell behind their appointed times, their conductors were responsible for figuring out where other trains sharing their track were and for pulling into passing sidings to avoid collisions. With several trains running in both directions on a single-track line, operating under such conditions was nerve-racking and dangerous.

5. This was probably in 1863 when General Braxton Bragg moved his troops into Chattanooga to defend Lookout Mountain and Missionary Ridge.

6. Most likely, this event took place sometime in 1862. Bragg was forced out of central Tennessee on 3 January 1863.

7. Stegall's Station was not listed on any contemporary W&A timetable. It may have been a private siding or simply a flag stop, a place trains stopped only when a flag was displayed.

8. Trains were scheduled for one hour and forty-two minutes running time between Atlanta and Big Shanty in peacetime.

9. East Tennessee and North Georgia were hotbeds of Union sentiment. The mountainous region had few slaves and was ill-suited for extensive cotton cultivation. The war along the W&A and the ETV&G railroads was particularly nasty.

10. The General, a 4-4-0 with sixty-inch drivers, was built by Rogers Ketchum & Grosvenor in Paterson, New Jersey and shipped to the W&A on 14 December 1855. On 12 April 1862 a party of Yankees in civilian dress, led by James J. Andrews, captured the locomotive and its train at Big Shanty and headed north up the W&A. The train's crew, led by its conductor, gave chase for two miles on foot and then commandeered another engine and pursued the spies up to Graysville, where the Yankees, out of fuel, fled into the woods. Most were eventually captured and hanged in Chattanooga.

11. A "wye" is the conventional method for turning a train around. It is shaped like a Y with a longer bar across its top.

CHAPTER 3

1. General Ambrose E. Burnside was a Yankee, whereas General Benjamin E. Cheatham and General James Longstreet were Confederates like Bell.

2. General Alfred J. Vaughan was an engineer who fought for the Confederacy.

3. Information on this locomotive is lacking because Bell failed to give its original name.

4. Turntables were used to turn locomotives around so they could hook on to what had been the rear of the train for its return trip.

5. The Cumberland was probably built by the Baldwin Locomotive Works in Philadelphia and shipped to the Nashville & Chattanooga on 9 December 1852. Baldwin's records indicate it was constructed for a 4'8" gauge, but the N&C, like most Southern railroads, used a 5' gauge. The engine was a standard 4-4-0, or eight-wheeler.

6. The Mission Ridge tunnel was the bore through Missionary Ridge in Chattanooga. It is still used by steam excursions on trains operated by the Tennessee Valley Railroad museum. General William Tecumseh Sherman was with the Union forces that wrested Missionary Ridge from the Confederates on 25 November 1863.

7. Probably General Marcus J. Wright.

8. The Cherokee was built by Baldwin and shipped to the W&A in 1855. It, too, was a 4-4-0 and replaced an earlier 4-2-0 Baldwin product of the same name that had been built in 1844. Baldwin and Rogers each built engines named Alleghany before the war, but both were for Northern roads, one to 6' gauge for the Erie Railroad and the other to 4'8" gauge for the Philadelphia & Reading. The P&R locomotive could have been converted to 5' gauge or this Alleghany may have been a renamed locomotive. The Hiawassee, however, was built by Baldwin in 1844 for the Central Railroad & Banking Company in Georgia. It was a light engine with a 4-2-0 wheel arrangement. No matter what the size, the South could ill afford to lose any motive power during the war.

CHAPTER 4

1. Bell and his party were working their way northeastwards out of Knoxville; Greenville was 74 railroad miles from Knoxville and Bristol was 130.

CHAPTER 5

1. Confederates were running the Union blockade out of Wilmington to Nassau, capital of the Bahamas.

2. Joseph Brown was governor of Georgia during the Civil War and a notorious supporter of states' rights. He gave the Confederate government in Richmond fits because he consistently withheld from it food and military supplies for Georgia's defense.

3. General George Stoneman, a Union officer, was responsible for the raid.

4. Bell refers to the tree from which the Palmetto State derived its nickname.

CHAPTER 6

1. General Robert E. Lee surrendered to General Ulysses S. Grant at Appomattox Courthouse on 9 April 1865.

2. The Crutchfield House stood where the Read House now stands at the corner of Broad Street and Martin Luther King Boulevard.

3. Rufus B. Bullock won the election, took office in 1868, and cleaned out W&A employees, replacing them with his deserving supporters. Bell was one of the trainmen who lost his job.

4. This was Bell's first meeting with John C. Stanton, discussed in the introduction.

5. This refers to Confederate General Leonidas Polk, who was an Episcopal bishop before he took up the sword.

CHAPTER 7

1. Attala, Alabama was 87.2 rail miles southwest of Chattanooga.

2. Bell was probably referring to York, Alabama, located on the Alabama-Mississippi state line, 268.3 railroad miles from Chattanooga.

3. Bell was working his way eastward, and at Livingston he had progressed nine miles from York.

4. This was a short passenger run for Bell, only thirty-seven miles.

5. The South was under "Radical Reconstruction" during this period, and Alabama was occupied by Federal troops. The Freedmen's Savings Bank was a part of the Freedmen's Bureau.

6. General Nathan Bedford Forrest was reputed to have ordered the slaughter of several hundred African-American soldiers who had surrendered at Fort Pillow, Tennessee, on 12 April 1864. Like many ex-Confederates, Forrest became interested in railways after the war.

7. The A&C opened for business over its entire route in 1871. At least twenty-four miles of the road was laid with rails that Sherman's forces had torn up and bent out of shape in his march through Georgia in 1864.

CHAPTER 8

1. A lever car was a hand car propelled by pumping a handle (or lever) up and down. Maintenance-of-way workers used them out on the road.

CHAPTER 9

1. Calera was only about twenty-five miles south-southeast of Birmingham.

2. Drawback tickets were a competitive ploy that required passengers to pay the published price for tickets; the ticket agent or conductor would return an under-the-table amount to them so that they actually rode for a reduced fare.

CHAPTER 10

1. What Bell called the "draw-head" was technically known as the *draw bar head*. On link-and-pin couplers, it was that metal part of the assembly on the outside of the pin that rubbed against the similar piece on the next coupled car. When the piece broke, the train was split into two sections.

2. A "burned engine" occurred when the engineer and the fireman allowed the water level in the boiler to fall below the boiler flues and destroy them.

3. "Pay down" meant putting money on the table, or down, to pay for food rather than putting it on a bill.

4. This was probably in the summer of 1878 when yellow fever epidemics spread all across the South.

5. "Stopped off" meant the engineer was suspended without pay.

6. The editor has found no evidence for this, but it has the ring of authenticity. Stanton doggedly pursued his claims in Alabama for years, and the state may have bought him off. If so, it would have been much later, about 1877. Bell appears to have been referring to the state's taking over the A&C in 1871.

CHAPTER 11

1. A "mixed train" had both passenger and freight cars. They were usually "locals" and stopped at every station. An "accommodation train" was a special run to accommodate someone important—railroad officers, wealthy shippers, or even church groups.

2. The yellow fever epidemic ravaged Chattanooga from 20 July through 15 November 1878 and took 366 lives. Life in the town came to a halt as it was quarantined. All business stopped, and inhabitants fled to higher elevations.

3. The Southern Railway took over the ETV&G and other Southern roads in October 1894.

4. Southern railroads changed their gauge from 5' to 4'8 1/2",

standard gauge, on 31 May and 1 June 1886.

5. The Clinch Mountains are located in upper East Tennessee near Norris Lake.

6. "Beating his way" was beating the conductor out of his fare, riding for free.

7. George Westinghouse patented his air brake in 1869 and tested it on the Pennsylvania Railroad. Despite further improvements to the invention, the industry was slow to accept it because of the costs involved in converting every car. It was not until March 1893, when Congress passed the Railroad Safety Appliance Act that required air brakes and knuckle couplers, that air brakes were reluctantly adopted everywhere. Railroads in the South were slower to change to the new brakes than the large trunk lines in the North that pulled heavier trains that were more difficult to stop.

8. Trainmen were "laid out" most frequently when they reached their destination away from home and found that for some reason the train they were scheduled to bring back had already departed or was canceled. It could, however, also happen at home. In either case it would cost the worker a trip for which he lost pay.

CHAPTER 12

1. The Old Reliable Conductors' Order was a forerunner of the Order of Railway Conductors. They shared the same initials, perhaps by design.

2. Robertson and Lincoln counties in Tennessee were major whiskey-producing areas in the state in the nineteenth century.

3. Hot boxes, caused by excessive friction at axle ends when lubricants dried out or foreign matter fell into the journal boxes, were a constant danger on early railroads.

CHAPTER 13

1. "Johnnie, how came you so" probably derived from a sentimental poem popular in the mid nineteenth century. It is obvious that the unseen speaker of the line was a child's mother. In this case, Bell uses the phrase to indicate a drunk on his train.

2. "Josiah Allen's wife" was Marietta Holley's pen name. Holley (1836–1926) was a popular humor writer in the late nineteenth century, and many of her writings were used by suffragettes and temperance advocates for their causes. Holley hailed from Jefferson County, New York, far from Bell's usual precincts.

Index

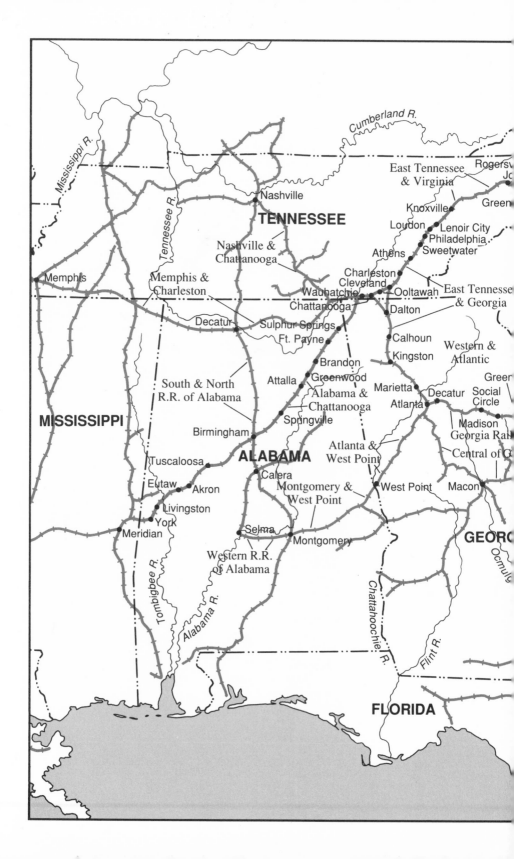